WIN THEM OVER

Efrem Mallach

Published by Folrose Press,

P.O. Box 56354

London SE1 7XZ, United Kingdom

www.folrose.com

FOLR🌹SE
P R E S S

Printed in the UK

Published simultaneously in the United States of America

ISBN 978-0-906378-04-5

Efrem Mallach
Research Director, Kea Company

WIN
THEM
OVER

A guide to corporate analyst/ consultant relations

This book is dedicated, with affection and appreciation, to the analysts and consultants who helped make it possible and whose insight continues to enrich the information technology industry.

Introduction

Welcome to the third edition of what is best described as the "AR bible:" a complete and practical guide to the discipline most commonly called analyst relations (AR) but increasingly morphing to Influencer Relations (IfR) as AR professionals leverage their existing skills and programs to reach out to bloggers, sourcing advisors, consultants, academics, etc.

AR has evolved from the day when only a handful of very large ICT firms had institutionalized a function to handle consultants and analysts relations. We're now in a time where most vendors realize the impact of analysts and try to influence them. As usual in a maturing profession, best practices have emerged and the overall level has risen, notwithstanding the influx of new practitioners.

At the same time, two factors caused a radical shift in the analyst world. The first was increased access to vendor executives, in part thanks to successful AR programs. This has removed some of the information asymmetry that was the sole *raison d'être* and business model for some analysts. The second and probably most important factor is two characteristics of the internet: the information glut—with its corollary, noise—and self-authoring capabilities. When all it takes is 15 minutes to set up a blog, barriers to entry to being an analyst have all but vanished and the definition of an analyst itself is challenged. Information travels faster now, and channels such as Twitter don't leave much time for analysis.

Boundaries are blurring...

As a result, the analyst and consultant landscape has morphed into a palette of influencers, going all the way from dynamic, multi-facetted influencers, bloggers, sourcing consultants, independent analysts, etc., all the way to a few concentrated mega-firms.

AR is slowly but surely evolving into Influencer Relations to cater to this diverse and elusive audience while leveraging social media tools. Those tools can be the subject of another book, but I urge not putting tools before purpose: much if not the entire book is also applicable to different types of influencers, including analysts who blog and bloggers who analyze.

The basics are still there: it's a people business, and today more than ever you need to cover the basics of AR. A is for "Know Your Analyst:" what drives him/her and how you should make your company relevant to her/his agenda. R is for "Relationship Matters," because influencer' relations can't be just transactional –they are strategic in nature.

So dig in. There's no better book to read and read again whether you are new to AR or stepping back to reflect on your AR program and plans. It is copiously illustrated with a wealth of examples that only Efrem Mallach with his unique experience as an academic and as an AR consultant in the field could provide. It is also a very practical book, with templates and worksheets, so that you can get off the mark quicker.

Finally, consider joining the Institute of Industry Analyst Relations (IIAR): a community of AR professionals whose aim is to network, share best practices and foster a constructive dialogue with IT analyst firms. You'll find more information at www.analystrelations.org.

Ludovic Leforestier, IIAR co-founder and board member

Preface

When I wrote the first edition of this book in the 1980s few vendors were aware of analysts and consultants. Fewer had any idea of how to deal with them, or even why they should. As for knowing how: most programs were a shot in the dark.

Fortunately, that has changed. In 2013, every IT vendor knows about analysts, consultants and advisors of all types. Many of them have active analyst relations programs. Several specialized consultancies, even a few analyst firms, will advise vendors how to run a program and train their staff to do it. Despite all that, vendors continue to make many of the same mistakes they made a generation ago.

A lot more has also changed in the time since this book was first published. Ludovic Leforestier mentioned the impact of the Internet in his introduction (for which I am most grateful). Multi-binder consultant reference manuals, with thick envelopes of updates arriving monthly to be inserted page by page, have gone the way of the dodo bird. Neither an analyst nor an AR professional of a decade ago would have imagined Twitter. Yet the basics—understand why you care about analysts and other advisors, understand their value to the industry and to your company, find out what they need, and try to meet those needs—hasn't changed. Nor has the importance of personal factors such as candor, honesty, and a genuine relationship. Those are the foundations on which good analyst or consultant relations must be based. Those will still be the foundations a generation from now. That is the message I have tried to convey in these pages.

No book such as this is entirely the product of one person, even if just one person's name appears on the title page. Among those I must thank are Duncan Chapple, for ongoing encouragement over the years; Ludovic Leforestier (again) for more of the same, Bram Weerts of Kea Company for his support, my wife Carla for her patience when I'd say "just one more page," but especially the analysts and consultants who took the time to tell me how vendors should treat them and why. This book is dedicated to them, in grateful appreciation for their help. I hope I conveyed their messages accurately.

This dialogue with analysts, consultants, and other types of influencers, as well as with analyst and consultant relations professionals of all types, has not just been a contributing factor to this book. It has been one of the most rewarding parts of my professional life over the last two decades. I look forward to continuing it with those who read this book. Please feel free to get in touch with me at efrem.mallach@keacompany.com to join it yourself.

Efrem G. Mallach
New Bedford, Mass., U.S.A.
August 2013

Table of Contents

1 | Who are analysts and consultants?

This chapter will answer:

1. Who are analysts and consultants? Why do they matter to your firm?
2. Why do your customers and prospects use analysts and consultants?
3. What are the different types of analysts and consultants?

This book will help you improve your firm's standing with analysts and consultants. Since we can't discuss anything without knowing what it is, we'll start by defining them. If you already know what they are, please at least skim Section 1.5. We'll refer to its concepts, especially business models, again and again later.

1.1. What are influencers (analysts and consultants/advisors)?

A note on terminology: Words in the area of this book are not standardized. The idea of an analyst is fairly well agreed on, but people who advise users directly for their specific needs can be called advisors or consultants. In specific areas, such as advice on services sourcing, the term advisor is more common. We use both terms here.

When people need a catch-all word for both groups, they often use influencer. Unfortunately, influencers can also include journalists, professional peers, and everyone else who influences purchasers, so we'll use it only where context makes its meaning clear. We'll often use a phrase such as analysts/consultants.

If you're used to different terminology, that doesn't mean it's wrong!

You surely have a general idea of what external influencers, including analysts and consultants in any field, are. Formal definitions contain these elements:

- They have expertise in a specific area.
- They're not on the organization's payroll. Their work ends when they finish what they agreed to do. If they come back, it's to do something else.
- They operate outside the organizational hierarchy. They can't say "do this" or "do that." Their influence is indirect.

How do these apply to those who recommend technology products and services?

- The advisor has expertise in the product or service in question.
- Advisors may be paid by the job; by time unit, such as hour or day; analysts by subscription for a predefined set of services; or other ways—but not by a paycheck.
- The purchaser of these services is the one who must live with the decision. The person or company whose advice helped make it moves on.

Firms that *use* information technology to support their business have one set of reasons to engage analysts and consultants. Those who *provide* IT products or services have a different set. The investment community has a third. Those reasons include:

1.1.1. Why end users of information technology engage analysts and consultants

- To keep up with industry and technology trends.
- For counsel on using IT, strategically and tactically.
- To develop a short list of potential suppliers for a specific need.
- To select one provider from the short list.
- For expertise. Small firms can't justify an expert's salary when expertise is needed only rarely. Large ones may need more staff for workload peaks.
- To confirm internal decisions: sometimes just to facilitate sign-off, more often for genuine review in case any significant factors were overlooked.
- For objectivity. A good analyst or consultant knows the strengths and weaknesses of many providers[1]. An organization's employees may want to keep on using products and services they know, or to maintain a relationship. Even if they don't, management may fear that they could.
- For influence with providers. Using an external advisor can reduce some salespeople's temptation to "put one over" on non-technical prospects.
- For influence over internal staff. Employees may accept an outside opinion when they'd reject the same opinion, equally well justified, from a colleague or manager.

All these affect sales of IT products and services. User perceptions of industry trends influence the technologies in which they invest. An organization's strategic direction with respect to IT determines the products and services it will need. Thus, orienting analysts and consultants to a provider's way of thinking will move users in its direction over time.

1.1.2. Why information technology suppliers engage analysts and consultants

Suppliers of IT products and services have different needs. They use analysts:

- To provide and analyze industry data, such as market size, market shares, and trends. (Some advisory firms specialize in this.)
- To reflect user opinions, needs, and trends. Most analyst (research) firms spend a lot of time meeting with users. Users are more candid with them than they are with providers.
- To contain issues. If analysts and consultants understand the reasons for a problem and a firm's corrective actions, they'll "cut it some slack" and help minimize its impact on prospects. If they don't have the background, they see only the problem. Absent an explanation, they must invent one. Theirs will be less helpful than yours would.

    This shows why trying to hide problems is a bad idea. *Every* organization has them. Analysts and consultants *will* learn about them. It's their job. They do it well. You can't keep

---

[1] We often use *provider* rather than *vendor* to include services providers, cloud storage providers, and so on as well as firms that sell more tangible products such as hardware and software.

them from doing that. All you can control is who they find out from, when, and how: From you, as you provide explanations and describe corrective actions, or from a competitor or disgruntled customer? Then they may blame your firm for letting them, through ignorance, look foolish to their clients.

- Providers may hide problems in hopes of a sale that—were a problem known—wouldn't be made. This happens once in a while, but counting on it is like betting against the house in a casino. You may win sometimes, but in the long run you're sure to lose. Being open about a problem seldom hurts as much as one fears. It's usually the better course of action—not just in theory, but in the real world of sales won or lost.

- To influence prospects and customers. Providers engage analysts and consultants to explain, with more credibility and in user terms, why a technology fits a user's situation or why a products are well made. (The user must know who's footing the bill. An ethical analyst or consultant will never hide the fact that he or she is paid by a provider.)

  Providers also use analysts and consultants for this purpose after the fact. If an objective, independent report is positive about the provider or its products, the provider can (with permission) reprint it, quote it in sales collateral, and use it in other ways.

- To advise on product strategy and development. Analysts understand your firm's technology, markets, and prospective users. They are invariably delighted to be asked their opinion on these subjects and will share their thoughts with the vendor who asks. (Part of their delight comes from the revenue that goes with answering, but they still like this work and tend to be good at it.)

- To assess the competition. Most analysts who follow a technology know the products of all major providers and many innovations introduced by start-ups. They can put those products' capabilities in the context of user needs. This gives them a unique ability to evaluate the competition objectively.

- To assist with product positioning, launching and messages. Analysts have seen dozens of major announcements, hundreds of minor ones. They've seen how users and the press react to them. If a firm shows them its announcement plans, they can predict the reactions it can expect. If its management doesn't like those reactions, they can suggest how to get better ones. (Management can also look for analysts who will say nicer things, but that won't change the reactions an announcement gets once it's made. Don't shoot the messenger.)

Since the ways in which providers use analysts differ so much from the ways IT users use them, some research firms specialize in one type of client or the other. Others serve both. This can be useful when a provider needs user feedback. Analysts with user clients may have a better handle on what users are thinking than those who serve primarily providers. For other types of advice, provider-facing analysts can often do a better job.

A provider's analyst relations group seldom needs of any of these services itself. However, it's an important link to those who do. People in analyst/consultant relations must be aware of these opportunities to use these services and work closely with other groups, such as product planning or competitive analysis, who can use them. Doing this also raises the strategic visibility of the analyst relations function in the organization.

1.1.3 Why the financial community engages advisors

Investment firms ultimately want to predict the price of a company's stock. To do that, they must understand its sales trends and trends of its markets. They must also know enough about its technology to feel confident that it will work (or be alert that it won't) and to understand the factors that drive its profitability. Thus, they use analysts to:

- Provide and analyze industry data, such as market sizing and demand
- Anticipate trends before they happen
- Predict winners and losers
- Understand the technology better than they could on their own
- Capitalize on analysts' reputation. "We think this market is growing 30 percent per year" in a stock recommendation carries less weight than "Research by Expert Company ABC shows that this market is growing 30 percent per year."

These reasons overlap the reasons that IT providers use analysts. Therefore, analysts that investment firms use tend to be among those that providers also use.

1.2. The value of analysts and consultants to providers

Analysts can be of value to providers in several specific ways:

1.2.1. Direct impact on sales

Analysts' influence on sales is the role that usually comes to mind first. It comes from:

- Writing reports that sales prospects read.
- Speaking at conferences those prospects attend.
- Answering questions that prospects have after reading reports or hearing speeches.
- Advisory engagements. The line between analysts and advisors (consultants) is blurred here. Analyst firms look to consulting to boost revenues, to connect with their clients and to see how their general recommendations play out in specific situations.

Analysts and consultants influence about half of a typical high-tech provider's sales. Influence depends on:

- Size of the sale. Small purchases are more likely to be made without outside advice. Use of all types of external advisors goes up with the size of a procurement.
- Maturity of the market and technology. Mature markets and technologies are usually well understood by an organization's staff. When one changes rapidly, they may not have time to keep up with it. Rapid change therefore calls for advice from people who follow a field closely. Also, in a mature market, most users already have a satisfactory incumbent provider. That lessens the need for external advice.
- Complexity of the technology. This also affects the ability of user staff to keep up with it and understand the selection issues.

- Use of a provider's other products. Many firms will stay with a satisfactory supplier even if a procurement doesn't replace something directly.

- Impact of the product or service on the prospect's business. "You bet your company" decisions are reviewed to avoid disasters. When the scope is more limited the risk is smaller. So is the need to spend money to avoid it.

These items determine what fraction of a provider's sales are influenced by analyst recommendations. This, in turn, justifies much analyst relations spending.

1.2.2. Indirect impact on sales

Analysts affect sales indirectly through speaking, being quoted in the press, and influencing consultants who rely on their reports. The value of making an impression on an analyst is therefore more than that analyst's influence on his or her own clients.

Analysts can shape a market without saying anything about providers. Suppose there are blue and green widgets. An analyst could say "green widgets are better." If your company makes green widgets, this can help even if the analyst doesn't mention its name. If you make blue ones, it can hurt. This is one reason why it's important to work with analysts who have little sales impact and are also not likely to be engaged for advice.

1.2.3. Strategic advisory value

It is common to value analysts and consultants solely for customer influence. That's a mistake. It's particularly common among PR agencies who are used to working with the press, a one-way communication channel. They may feel the same way about other publics, including analysts, without being aware of it.

Analysts earn client respect because they understand an industry, the providers, their products/services and how those products/services are used. This understanding can benefit products/services suppliers as well.

Using analyst advice is essential to strategic analyst relations. As well as providing the benefit of the advice, it improves the relationship and the analyst's attitude toward the provider. However, analysts are quick to detect an engagement offered solely as a sop. Unless an engagement has value for a provider, using what an analyst knows in a meaningful way, it wastes a provider's money. "Look what they paid me to do, as if they think I don't know why" is a common analyst refrain.

The AR Compass model, developed by Ludovic Leforestier, shows this. The compass points reflect four aspects of analyst value: **S**trategy, **O**pinion leadership, **S**ales, and **M**arketing. All four flow from a firm's business objectives and help accomplish those objectives.

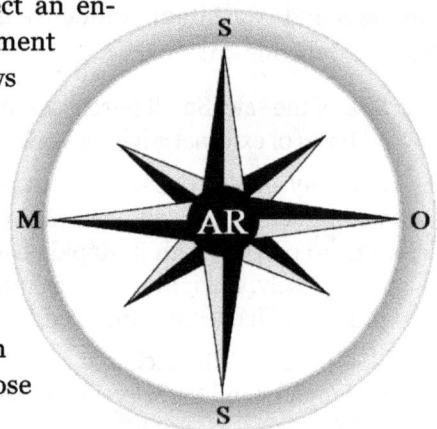

Leforestier suggests assigning each compass point a value that reflects its importance in the organization's analyst relations priorities. This is an excellent way to encourage management to take a position on what matters to it, and to help the analyst relations team focus on what its management cares about.

The basic idea of analyst relations is to maximize the value of these aspects. The rest is fleshing out details.

1.3. The varied world of influencers

Rural voters in Alabama[2] don't respond to the same appeals as do suburbanites on the Connecticut shore. Politicians know this. Candidates try to appeal to a limited constituency: a town, a legislative district. This makes it easier to understand voters and identify issues that concern them. Candidates who run for nationwide office, or for statewide office in a large state, have the resources and experience to deal with multiple constituencies. History shows that they don't always do it successfully.

Information technology influencers are as varied as voters. One program can't support them all. Fortunately, most firms don't have to support them all. Smaller firms can focus on a subset. Firms with broad product lines, worldwide markets and multi-billion-dollar sales have the resources to deal with multiple constituencies, but they must do so with a clear understanding of their multiple targets. In either case a provider must define the types of advisors that its program or programs are trying to reach. Failure to define targets accurately will, at best, waste money. At worst it can hurt, as if a political candidate spoke to farm workers about the need to cut corporate taxes.

The next few sections describe different types of influencers. They vary in the role they play in the industry, the type of clients they appeal to, in the size and type of their firm, in their orientation to their work, and in their leadership role in forming opinions.

Each section that follows deals with a different dimension of the influencer world. Before reading on, ask yourself: Who usually makes the final decision to select your firm's product or service? As you read about each dimension, ask another question: Along this dimension, what types of influencers does this decision maker listen to, directly or via subordinates? These answers determine who your firm must reach to improve its sales. Once you know that, you can decide how to reach them.

1.4. Types of advisors and their roles

1.4.1. Consultants

The first influencers were consultants[3]. These meet with clients, discuss needs, study products or services their clients might need, and make recommendations. The products

---

[2] The US example is just to be concrete. Readers in other countries can use local examples.
[3] Some contract programmers call themselves *consultants* because they feel it enhances their status

or services they might advise on run the gamut from individual purchases, through services such as outsourcing up to complete systems. Consultants who advise on selection are expensive, often charging $250 or more per hour. A lower rate usually reflects:

1. A new consultant or one whose expertise is limited to a specific area. Good answers to "How much RAM do I need for applications X, Y and Z under Windows 8?" can be had for under $100 per hour.

2. The consultant expects additional work on development or systems integration, and prices the entire job at an average rate. Advising rates are high because engagements are short. If a client commits to ongoing work, a lower rate is fair.

3. The consultant doesn't depend on this work for a living. Perhaps he's a college professor who takes on a consulting "gig" from time to time, or she's a network security manager and does this in evenings or on weekends. Such people may charge less than the going rate. Full-time consultants resent being undercut by these "hobbyists" and urge them to raise their rates, but acknowledge that there isn't much they can do beyond emphasizing that they can work on a project full-time and can talk to the client freely during working hours.

Prospective buyers don't just receive advice through direct advisors. Some can't afford them, some don't want to pay $5,000 for advice on a $500 purchase, and some want multiple opinions. These buyers use *indirect* advisors instead, or in addition. Their lower cost per user brings each into contact with more potential customers than any direct advisor can reach.

Indirect advisors fall into the following major categories:

1.4.2. Industry analysts

The average person has heard of consultants, but not industry analysts. One reason is that consumers are exposed to consultants in fields such as wedding planning and pollution control, but few consumer fields support analyst communities.

Industry analysts evaluate an industry segment and report their findings to many clients at a time. An analyst might write a report on "The Future of Fast Ethernet," "Storage Area Networks for Linux Servers," or "Wi-Fi After 802.11ac." They differ from direct advisors (consultants) in that their work reflects a broad range of user needs, not just one client's.

Most analyst (research) firms bundle their offerings into *services*. A service has a focus such as networking, business intelligence, or tablet computers. Each service publishes reports on topics of subscriber interest. For example, a mainframe service could publish a report on IBM System z users' storage-area network upgrade plans. It would be based on in-depth discussions with SAN suppliers and users, would include survey

---

or income. This confusion, over what a consultant really is, is much of the reason that many people prefer to use *advisor*. Contract programmers have expertise and aren't on the payroll, but their contribution is direct, not advisory. We're not concerned with status here. When we say *consultant*, we mean someone who advises.

results and statistics not available elsewhere, would analyze the reasons behind the numbers, and would discuss implications for users and suppliers.

These firms' product-oriented reports focus on evaluation. They describe users' hands-on experience with the products in question, the good and the bad. Users are quoted on strengths and weaknesses of the products they use and of their suppliers. Forthright competitive comparisons, assessments and recommendations are made. Technical specifics, such as the seek time of a disk drive or the number of ports on a router, aren't the main focus. Besides products, analyst reports may also focus on strategies, technology trends, market gainers and losers, or any other aspect of that industry segment.

The three defining characteristics of all external advisors apply to analysts:

- The analyst has expertise in the area. (This varies, as in any profession, but incompetents tend to be weeded out before they cause too much damage.)
- Analyst firms are typically paid for reports, conferences, or services that include a combination of several elements—not for time their staff puts in on a job.
- As with direct advisors, the person or organization who relies on the analyst's advice has to live with the eventual decision.

Analysts who sell general reports are often called in for specific advice for their client's situations. At that point their work moves into consulting. (Some research firms sell subscription services at a low price to acquaint clients with their work, or post analysis on the Web, in the hope of selling profitable consulting work later on.) A service subscription may include some consulting hours, also called *inquiry hours*, for this purpose. Some firms also have staff members whose only job is to consult. The information they need to provide indirect advice (analysis) is similar to what they need to provide direct advice (consulting). This is another reason that both direct and indirect advisors need similar support from providers, and are worth discussing in the same book.

Some research firms sell primarily by subscription. A subscription typically includes a number of reports and the privilege of calling the firm with questions—up to a X hours to answer them, with more available for a fee. A newsletter may be included, often posted on a subscriber-only Web site. Subscribers may receive tickets to conferences where analysts and other experts speak about the computer industry, with additional tickets available for a fee. These conferences are gathering places for industry observers, who share information (not all of it correct!) and opinions. Annual subscription fees are often in five figures. Customers of these firms tend to be IT providers, eager to learn about competitors and meet sales prospects, and large users. Small users can't afford their prices.

Other firms also operate by subscription, but at a lower price point, typically in three or the low four figures. They issue monthly reports in the form of a thick newsletter. These firms may also sponsor conferences, but these are self-supporting via registration fees.

Still others operate as publishing houses, selling individual reports. Authors may be freelancers who are not on the firm's staff. (This isn't always advertised.) They list available reports, typically selling for a few hundred to several thousand dollars, on their Web sites. There may be discounts for multiple reports, but no true subscriptions. These firms don't have annual conferences or other accoutrements of an ongoing service.

Finally, some firms focus on custom services, much like consultants but from a foundation of analyzing products and markets in depth. Their clientèle is mostly providers, not users.

Hybrids are possible, of course. A firm may distribute reports individually and also publish a newsletter. However, the above categories cover the major variations.

Analysts and advisors/consultants differ in their customer base:

- Advisors/consultants serve primarily users. Their impact is direct, immediate and obvious.
- Analysts serve both end users and providers. The mix varies from one analyst firm to another, but to the industry as a whole, both customer segments are important.

Or: Consultants focus on a single user at a time, evaluating many providers, products or technologies for that user. Analysts focus on a single provider, product or technology at a time, evaluating it on behalf of many potential users. This figure illustrates this:

Many alternatives   One product, etc.

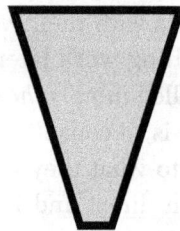

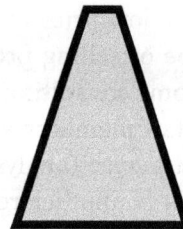

One client   Many potential users
The Consultant   The Analyst

Analyst impact on provider sales is less direct than consultants', but can be stronger because they reach more users and also reach other users' advisors. User clients read a series of reports over a period of time, and as a result develop opinions that affect their decisions. Analysts without user clients are still influential as noted earlier: as opinion leaders, through press quotations, by speaking at conferences that users attend, by writing reports that user-oriented analysts and consultants rely on. Their perspective lets them advise providers on both a strategic and a tactical level.

This leads to an important difference between analyst relations and advisor/consultant relations programs. A provider has many sales prospects, but fewer products or services. It will therefore encounter many direct advisors, but fewer analysts. Advisor support must be broad, hence shallow except when intense activity is called for. Analyst support will focus on identified individuals. A firm with a limited budget can concentrate its analyst support on a handful of key influencers. With consultants, that wouldn't work.

1.4.3. Financial Analysts

Fund managers, equity analysts and other investment professionals try to predict firms' financial fortunes. Part of their futures depend on the quality of their products, so they try to assess products. Sales prospects may sometimes read financial analysts' reports to gauge the long-term viability of a supplier. However, these are seldom a major factor in purchase decisions.

Investment banking and brokerage firms are a significant client base for several research firms, especially those (such as IDC or Gartner's Dataquest) that focus on market sizing. They use market forecasts as an input to their financial analyses: 20 percent of a growing market may imply good future profitability, but the same share of a static or shrinking market might not.

Because financial analysts choose firms to cover primarily for their investment interest, they focus on larger, publicly traded companies. Such companies usually have an investor relations department to keep the financial community informed and enthusiastic. Analyst and/or consultant relations programs may be able to share materials with IR, but working with financial analysts and investors is seldom part of a CR or AR program.

1.4.4. Publications

Publications, including newspapers and magazines, have an advisory role. Virtually everyone who buys information technology products on a regular basis reads at least one trade press publication, in print or online. Many read several, to say nothing of IT columns and opinions in business publications or the business sections of general-interest ones. (Most businesspeople have seen Walter Mossberg's "Personal Technology" column in *The Wall Street Journal*. He is an influencer by any definition.) While working with the press usually falls under a firm's public relations program, the major advisory aspects of the press are covered here for completeness.

Announcement coverage. The factual side of your firm's announcements—press releases, etc.—is part of its PR program. Announcement articles often include quotes from opinion leaders about the new product. You can improve your firm's coverage by prior contact with those likely to be quoted. Lack of contact can damage coverage, since analysts whom reporters call won't know as much as they could and may be offended at not having been pre-briefed. (We'll discuss announcement preparations in depth later.)

Product reviews. Reviews are a major source of information for software, peripheral device and accessory buyers. Magazines that cover such products try to publish a variety of comprehensive, thorough and objective reviews. This is especially true of publications that cover desktop products, since their buyers are often not technically sophisticated and can't justify engaging a consultant for a $199 purchase. Reviews are a major component of every issue of desktop-oriented publications such as *PC* Magazine or *Macworld*. Reviews also exist for products used with larger computers. The weekly *InfoWorld*, which focuses on enterprise computing, has its own testing laboratory to put products through their paces and runs reviews in every issue. So do focused publications in areas such as networking or security.

Prospective purchasers of these products, if they get a publication in hard copy, often save reviews and check them before making a purchase. Others search for them on the Web prior to a purchase decision. A person who doesn't have access to a paper copy can find a review with a few mouse clicks—as can those who do have paper copies, but find it easier to ask their favorite search engine to do the legwork.

Good reviews help sales, especially of a product from a new firm that isn't well-known and can't afford much promotion. A bad review may not sink a product from a firm that can afford to keep it afloat, but will be felt in the sales figures.

Reviewers sign their name to their reviews. They take pride in helping a product with praise where it is warranted, being frank about deficiencies where they exist. They know their credibility depends on giving the bad with the good. Many reviewers develop a following to which their word is gospel.

Articles. Magazines and some newspapers (for instance, *Computerworld* with its "In Depth" section) run thorough articles about product areas. These focus on technology and market trends. Products are described to illuminate these trends. These articles may be written by publication staff, product provider staff, or outside experts.

- Publication staff-written articles take material from magazine or newspaper files, supplemented by quotations from users and providers. You can call or write the editor in charge of your firm's product area. Willingness to make experts available to discuss an area with the press will improve your firm's chances of being featured.

- Articles written by provider employees may stress their employers' products, at times to the point of reading like unpaid advertising. This is as true of technical articles written by engineers as it is of material produced by a firm's marketing department. (Many firms require review of all employee-written articles prior to publication. A PR staffer may spin an article even if its author, a totally objective engineer, didn't.) A good editor will ensure that provider-written articles mention other firms' products as well as those of the author's employer. If the editor is able to suggest your firm's products as candidates for such mention, its chance of coverage will improve.

- Articles by outside experts will discuss products with which the author is familiar, often with assistance from the publication's files. If your firm's materials are in them, its odds of being mentioned improve. You can send publications materials for their files.

- Outside authors are often analysts or consultants. They write articles to enhance their own and their firms' reputations. Supporting those groups will pay off in what they write.

Directories. Articles about a particular product area, such as solid-state storage or firewall software, often include a product chart or provider directory. Users save these directories and refer to them long after the article appears. Material for these usually comes from the publication's files. The publication may conduct a survey to update its files just before it compiles the directory, but it can only survey firms it knows about.

"How come you didn't list us?" letters come in after each directory appears, with the same information as listings. Magazines are happy to publish them. The firms that send them are included in the following year's directory. Unfortunately, additions are never as prominent as articles, people seldom save them, and they're not easy to find in a Web search. After-the-fact updates therefore have little future reference value. Don't let it happen to your firm. Make sure every periodical that covers its area knows about it.

Special-interest Web sites often include directory pages. While they're not exactly advisors, every firm should be in them since writers and analysts use them as information sources. The problem of corrections appearing separately doesn't arise here. Updates go in as soon as the webmaster can get to them and look the same as original information—as one would want, since regular updating is key to successful online content.

1.5. Characteristics of research and consulting firms

Size of the firm

Providing advice on information systems and technology is a multi-billion dollar business, with estimates ranging from $5 to over $10 billion. Analysts and consultants are estimated to leverage $250 billion to a trillion dollars in information technology sales per year. This demonstrates how important advisors and their recommendations are to IT provider sales.

Gartner (with acquisitions such as Dataquest, Datapro, G2 Research and META Group) accounts for the largest portion of analyst industry revenue, about $1.5 billion in 2011. Other major firms include Forrester Research, which acquired Giga Information in early 2003; IDC, AMR (purchased by Gartner at the end of 2009) and Ovum (the largest non-U.S. firm). Moving down from there, some firms are the business names of individuals operating on their own. Business cutbacks in the 2000s forced some research firms to let senior staff go, and quite a few senior META Group analysts left that firm in the wake of its acquisition by Gartner. Many of these people, rather than redirect their professional lives, "hung out their shingle." Since the amount of money they need to bill on their own is less than what they had to generate in the corporate structure, most have been able to survive. Some of these people hope their new firms will grow, some hope to work for a larger firm again, and others are happy as they are.

On the consulting side, over 20,000 firms derive a major portion of their revenue from information systems advisory services. Many more provide management consulting services that include information systems. Most of these firms are small. Numerically, there are probably more one-person consultancies than there are larger ones. In fact, there are many part-of-one-person consultancies, where the advisor holds a full-time job and advises in his or her spare time. At the other extreme some IS consulting firms employ thousands of people, many of whom function regularly in the advisory role on which we are focusing here.

Industry watchers estimate the global market for IT management consulting services to be about $100 billion today. It is growing faster than management consulting services overall. (Not all of this figure represents sourcing advice.) Their sourcing advice is often given with one eye on the possibility of lucrative development work later. The providers they recommend are those their programmers can work with.

The largest information system consulting firm is IBM, including both its Global Services organization and what was previously PricewaterhouseCoopers Consulting. Next comes Accenture, once the information technology consulting arm of accounting firm Arthur Andersen. These are followed by EDS, Capgemini, Deloitte Consulting (almost, but not quite, spun off as Braxton in early 2003) and Computer Sciences Corporation (CSC).

Some consulting firms are part of larger firms that also sell information technology products. IBM is in the above list. Unisys, not far below those six, is another example. Most major hardware and software providers offer some consulting services. These services often involve product recommendations, especially when the client needs something that can operate alongside that provider's products. (For example, SAP's services arm may be called on to recommend a business intelligence package that can use SAP data, or HP may be asked for advice on enterprise software that has been tested on its servers.)

When a captive consulting firm is called on to make a recommendation in an area where its owner has its own products, its people generally make a sincere effort to be objective. After all, they were engaged because the client trusts them, not because it wants an unthinking recommendation. If it needed that, it wouldn't need a consultant at all! The problem is not that they always recommend their corporate owner's products. They don't. The problem is that they think along the same lines as their employer, and don't fully appreciate approaches that diverge too far from its offerings.

For example, suppose a client asks Oracle Services to recommend database management software. (Oracle is just an example. The issue transcends any one firm.) They might not recommend Oracle. However, because Oracle built its business on relational database management, they're virtually certain to pick a relational database. Other types, possibly better for this application, won't be considered. Oracle's consultants can overcome their feelings for Oracle, but not their subconscious bias in favor of its traditional approach.

Unless your firm is a direct competitor of such a "captive" consulting firm's parent, treat it as you would treat any other consulting firm of the same size and scope. Even if your firm competes directly with the parent, try to support its services and consulting arm as well as possible without disclosing proprietary information.

Bias can also exist in firms that don't also sell products. Many consulting firms have strategic alliances with providers. BearingPoint, which would have been right after CSC on the above list of firms, is an example. It has alliances with Cisco Systems, Microsoft, and others. If a network is needed, its first impulse might be to recommend Cisco. The reason is not malice. It is familiarity, which breeds confidence that the partner's products will do the job, plus knowing that the firm's development staff will, if called upon to put the network together, have experience with the hardware to be used.

There was a debate a few years ago as to whether accounting firms should work on clients' information systems. Firms were accused of conflict of interest, lack of independence in auditing IS clients, and undue influence in "cross-selling" IS consulting to audit clients. In denying these, the firms pointed out that influence might get them one contract with an audit client but would never lead to repeat business. This has largely been resolved in favor of separation, in part after scandals rocked the audit field and led to legislation such as the U.S. Sarbanes-Oxley Act.

Several information technology consulting firms have internal technology advisory groups. These groups function much as analysts, but just for consultants in that firm.

Down from the giants are the smaller firms. Many "boutique" consulting firms advise clients on information system strategies. This includes suggesting new applications and IS approaches, ending with selection recommendations. These recommendations are a natural part of these firms' ongoing relationship with their clients. These firms aren't looking for a programming contract, but want to maintain their management connection.

Other firms do primarily system development. Their selection advice tends to recommend products with which their staff is familiar. The question "If the client goes this way, will our programmers be OK with that?" is top-of-mind.

Finally, there are thousands of small IS consulting firms. Most are freelance programmers, individually or in small groups. Some are experienced people who just advise. University professors may do this part-time. It's impossible to target all these individually, but we can deal with them *en masse* as we'll see in the following chapters.

Business model (for research firms)

The major research firm business models are:

MODEL	DESCRIPTION
Scheduled	This applies to firms who analyze and forecast market shares and volumes. They follow a quarterly or annual cycle. They need specific information at certain points during their cycle. Earlier, it's not available. Later, it's too late to be useful.
Planned	These firms plan their research and report publication calendars months in advance. Some publicize it as a selling point. Others keep upcoming topics confidential until it's too late for competitors to copy their ideas.
Event-Driven	These firms report on industry events, analyzing new products and services or discussing strategic positioning. They can't tell you what they'll write about next month, because they don't know what you (or any other provider) will do next month.

Client-Driven	These firms or analysts operate more as consultants. In some cases they're hard to tell from any other consultant. In others, they apply their firm's research to individual clients' needs. Either way, they don't know what they need to know until a client asks them a question.

Large firms may fit two or more of these models. However:

- Their business is usually built on one model, with others added as needed.
- In firms with multiple models, each analyst usually fits one most of the time.

Understanding a research firm's model is important in planning how to work with it.

Professional orientation

Nobody is an expert on everything. TV repair people don't fix cars, and vice versa. Selection (sourcing) advisors can be broadly categorized by a primary focus on business or technology. The figure shows the idea. As one leaves its lower left, rates go up. Business expertise plus technical competence get expensive!

These categories can be divided further. A business-oriented consultant may be an expert on banks, hospitals, retail, or any other sector. A technically oriented one may focus on wireless networks, cloud applications, data mining, a specific product or operating system, or hundreds of other

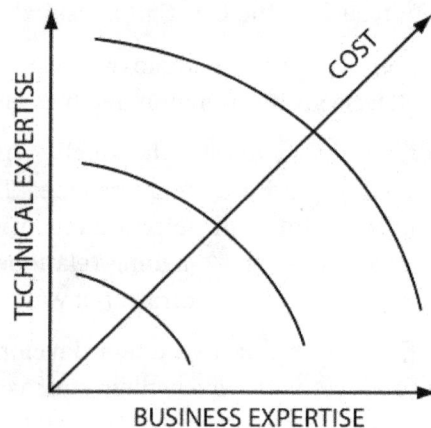

Consultant Expertise Spectrum

options. In smaller firms the specialty defines the organization. Larger firms may not have a single focus, but its individual analysts almost certainly do.

The support analysts or consultants need, and the advice and counsel they can give your employer, depend on their orientation. What you do should match it. Pick executives to put in contact with them, case studies to send them, speakers to invite them to hear, and experts to answer their questions with this in mind. When it comes to advising your firm, choose people whose strengths match its needs. Those whose business lies elsewhere will know it and won't need an explanation of why you don't engage them.

Leader or Follower

Few influencers of any type form opinions purely from personal experience. Most rely at least to some extent on what they read and hear.

A small number of people serve as opinion leaders (*gatekeepers*, in the original sense of the word before it came to mean a roadblock) in every industry. They tend to be well known. Most are analysts. These may be senior people at large firms, heads of small firms, or work as individuals. Their influence isn't from recommendations they make personally. Rather, they influence other influencers through writing (often in their own blog), speaking, and being quoted. In large firms, the teams they lead produce reports that go to many clients.

The remaining 99% of influencers have less impact. The staff of large consulting firms fall into this low-impact category. These firms' overall impact is large only because the firms are large. Their staff's influence is generally limited to their own clients.

Reaching opinion leaders is more productive per person than reaching other advisors. Those who matter to you are few in number and easy to identify. Their contact information is public. You can call, write or e-mail them easily.

Unfortunately, your firm isn't the only one that wants their attention! If it has a novel, effective solution to a need they will sit up and take notice. Publicity "gimmicks" will have little effect: they've seen them all. A product with major deficiencies is best not brought to their attention: the negative publicity will hurt long after the problems have been fixed.

1.6. Specific characteristics of analyst (research) firms

There are many ways to categorize analysts and firms. Before talking to an analyst, ask yourself these questions about that analyst and firm. *Every difference affects the information analysts need, how they need it, when they need it, or some other aspect of what they need.* If you know what they need, you can approach those needs as closely as you can within budget and corporate policy constraints. If you don't, you may waste money and have a negative impact on analyst opinions at the same time.

Even if you can't answer every question, the answers will help you meet analyst needs. Ask: are you dealing with ...

1. ... a futurist (primarily interested in where things will go in the future, and is therefore interested in strategies) or one who is primarily interested in where things are today, and may hence care more about products?

    • A futurist says "Products leapfrog each other. What matters is where a firm is going."

    • A "nowist" says "Anyone can talk futures. All that's real is what's here now." Both are valuable, but they provide different value and have different needs.

2. ... a generalist or a specialist, as a firm? If a specialty doesn't match your firm's products and services, why are you talking to them? (There are reasons. It's important to know yours.) If they specialize, is it by industry, technology, geography or other?

3. ... a generalist or a specialist, as an analyst? Again, if the specialty doesn't match your firm's products and services, be sure you understand the reasons for the contact.

4. ... an analyst who focuses on products and technologies, or one who focuses on markets and financials?

5. ... a conceptual person, or one who deals in concrete realities?

6. ... an analyst (and firm, they may differ) with primarily user or provider clients?

7. ... an analyst who provides primarily standardized services/reports, or whose work is more customized to each of his or her clients?

8. ... an analyst whose work is primarily scheduled in advance, or one who responds to industry events as they occur? (This was discussed earlier, with business models.)

9. ... a negativist who delights in finding flaws, or a "supporter" who believes there is good in every firm, product and service, and will try to find it?

10. ... a large, medium or small firm?

11. ... an analyst who has any known product/provider "hang-ups" or pet questions?

Some of these are related. Large firms are more likely to be generalists, thought their analysts usually specialize. Futurists are likely to be conceptual. Analysts who seek out problems tend to have user clients, while most "cheerleaders" serve primarily providers.

There are thousands of combinations of answers—more than any provider can cope with, more than there are analysts in the world. Fortunately, we don't have to treat each combination separately. Each piece carries a message about what a firm needs, what it will respond to. The overall picture defines how best to approach a person or firm.

In addition to these differences, research and consulting firms have cultures to be aware of when you work with them. For example:

- Among consulting firms, Accenture is known for uniformity. They tend to hire bright people straight out of college or university. They put them through standard training and into offices that resemble each other. They use standard methodologies that their entire staff is familiar with, to provide quality results even with inexperienced staff and protect their clients in case of turnover.

  By contrast, BearingPoint operates almost as a collection of individual fiefdoms. A local office can even create an entrepreneurial practice in a specialized field that the rest of the organization has no interest in, let alone any desire to standardize.

- Among research firms, Gartner is known for a confrontational style. People who aren't familiar with it may take such a confrontation as negative. It's not. Their analysts enjoy the intellectual challenge of the give-and-take. Their hiring process selects for this: Applicants for analyst jobs may be asked to develop a position on an issue, then to defend it to a group of potential future colleagues. They're just as confrontational in internal meetings. They believe that a position that emerges from hard debate will be more robust than one that had a gentler birth, and will be able to stand up to external questioning better if it first survives tough questions within the firm.

  Analysts from some other firms are less aggressive. This doesn't mean either is more competent than the other, doesn't hint at the tone of what either will later write. It's just culture, style. You need to understand a firm's style so as not to get upset by the appearance of negativity that isn't there or lulled into complacency by a friendly meeting that, compared to that analyst's meetings with other providers, wasn't so great.

Finally, two other questions to help get a "handle" on a research firm:

- Do they use a standard analytical framework or structured representation? Gartner's Magic Quadrant is the best known, but is not the only one. Knowing a firm's framework, if it has one, and what goes into it will help you position your company and its products or services for the best possible positioning in that framework.

- What is their revenue breakdown among subscriptions, inquiries, consulting, speaking, databases customers can access, conferences, etc.? Knowing this will help you focus on their major revenue drivers, earning their respect for your business acumen.

The rest of this book will help you figure out how to work with these firms and people in order to maximize the value of working with them to your firm.

2 | How analysts and consultants influence sales

This chapter will cover:

1 How analysts influence your customers
2 Where this influence comes from
3 Why analyst/consultant programs work
4 The IDEAL framework for analyst/consultant relations

While sales influence isn't the only reason for a provider to work with analysts and consultants, it's a big one It is often the main one. Were it not for analysts' sales influence, most providers wouldn't care much about changing their opinions. This chapter looks at how their sales influence works, first recapping parts of Chapter 1 briefly from a slightly different viewpoint.

2.1. Analyst/Consultant Influence

Buyers are flooded with technology information. Product choices become more complex every year. Mistakes become more costly, as high-impact applications such as e-commerce and business intelligence take over from the back office as the dominant uses of IT. The pace of technology is accelerating. Time to market is shortening. Users can't keep up. They turn to analysts for guidance on technologies, providers, markets, and products, and for validation.

Most large organizations therefore use analysts. Research confirms this. Analysts are used in the majority of procurements over $8 million and a substantial fraction of smaller ones. They also influence smaller users indirectly. The trend is up.

Once a user organization (your prospect!) becomes familiar with a research firm's work through its published research, it wants to apply that research to its own situation. That means engaging the firm for consulting. Analysts thus become directly involved in that user's provider selection activities, reviewing contracts and in advising on negotiations.

But analysts influence more than just their own client base with their opinions. Their influence on your customers and prospects is far-reaching. They are allied with financial analysts, members of the press, media and online research content aggregators. Their opinions reach many audiences via direct *and indirect* channels such as:

- Direct contact with customers (inquiry, onsite visits, consulting)
- Published research
- Comments about you and your competitors in the press

- Media engagements (radio, television)
- Presentations at industry events
- Relationships with other industry influencers (financial analysts, press, other experts)

Providers who dismiss analysts for their value must still acknowledge their reach. They convey messages about your company to customers and prospects. *They will send these messages whether or not you try to influence them.* Your company has no choice in this. It *will* happen. Your only choice is whether or not you take action to influence what they say. By communicating effectively with analysts, the right messages will reach your targets and will benefit your sales. By not communicating with them, or by communicating ineffectively, your competitors will gain this benefit.

2.2. The Analyst/Consultant Influence Model

Every purchase has a decision maker, a person who says "we'll buy this" or "we'll buy that" with no fear of being overridden. This person can always be identified.

The decision maker must be sold on the product or service. Even when the bulk of selling time is spent with other people, usually those who make recommendations to this person, it is ultimately necessary to make sure that he or she is convinced as well.

"Selling" a decision maker may not involve telling him or her about your product. Decision makers are often too busy to bother investigating alternatives in detail. Even if they have the time, they may not have the background to assess options. This is especially true in high-tech. A CIO who came up through the ranks decades ago, cutting his or her professional teeth on COBOL transaction processing, may not be able to assess the pros and cons of cloud providers. This is even truer of managers from financial, marketing or manufacturing backgrounds who, as CEO or another senior officer, may be called on for final sign-off on a major purchase.

Given this situation, executives rely on external advisors because:

- An organization may not have competent recommenders. Even where a good MIS staff exists, it may lack expertise in an emerging technology.

  Advisors here may be direct or indirect. Consultants can work at any level, including the decision-maker. Analysts are most often seen at lower levels, since their reports can be more technical than top managers need. (Some, however, are written for a high-level audience.) Reports are also cited to help justify a recommendation.

- Internal advisors may not be familiar with the options. Having used server A with software package B from vendor C for years, they may not recognize that X, Y and Z are better for today. This can be true even if they are objective and open-minded.

  When perspective is needed, consultants can do the job while analysts and other indirect advisors can't. Analysts exert influence in situations like this by (a) helping make internal staff aware of choices, and (b) influencing those consultants.

- Internal staff may have a vested interest in how things are done. Machiavelli noted centuries ago that few people stand to gain from change, however beneficial it seems, while many have a lot to lose. This is still true. An organization's staff fears its expertise may lose value with different products. It also has relationships with incumbent providers. So, management may feel that internal advice would not be objective.

  Here, direct and indirect advisors provide expertise and objectivity. If an analyst report tells an executive that your products shouldn't be used, it will be almost impossible for any amount of selling to offset it.

The first two reasons may lead staff charged with selection to look for advice. The last may lead management to use external advice as a check on their staff.

We can visualize providers, their customers and their advisors (of all types, both analysts and consultants) as the figure at the right.

During the sales process, your firm creates links to the prospect. These include your sales force, Web site, advertising and PR programs, and perhaps others if you use indirect channels such as VARs or stores. In the ideal provider world—the second figure—these are the only way prospects learn about your firm's products and services.

For reasons such as those discussed above, this ideal world seldom exists. Prospects bring in advisors. This creates the link shown in the third figure.

Prospects trust information from advisors more than from providers. *You cannot change this.* The prospect brought in the advisor, and must trust him or her to justify that. (In psychology terms, ignoring paid advice would create *cognitive dissonance.*)

There are several ways to deal with this. Some salespeople try to discredit the advisor to the prospect. *This never works.* It reinforces the prospect's conviction that providers can't be trusted, that subscribing to an advisory service or engaging a consultant was a wise move. It may occasionally get a prospect to change advisors, but it will never remove all advisors—and the new one may be worse than the first. The effort to discredit an advisor will

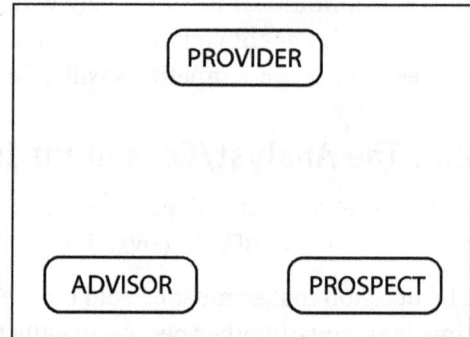

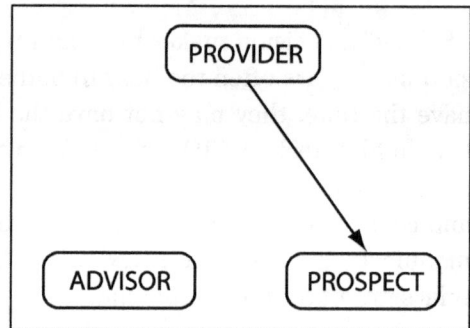

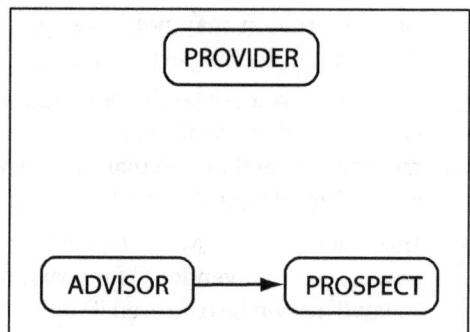

also leave a bad taste in the prospect's mouth about whoever recommended this course of action, even if the recommendation is followed.

The best way to live with advisors is to recognize their value to the prospect and work *with* it, much as a skilled cross-country runner uses hills to advantage. A runner doesn't try not to slow down on hills. All runners slow down on hills. It's about slowing down less than competitors, using the course better. Likewise, the provider who works best with the prospect's advisors has, all else being equal, the best chance of a sale.

Advisors have many information sources. The challenge is to ensure that your firm is among them—ideally, a trusted source that provides much of the advisor's information about it, its products and its services. To make that happen you must create the third link shown here. *This link is your analyst/consultant relations program.*

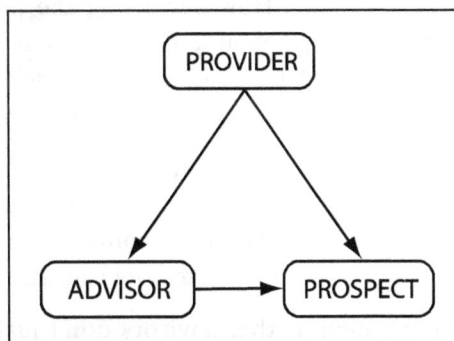

What your firm sells, who makes purchase decisions about that, the reasons advisors are used, and the type of advisors that are used are related. Those factors determine how to reach your prospect's advisors:

- If you sell products to non-technical users, your prospects may not have the skills to evaluate them. Consultants here tend to be business-oriented. They like products that offer better solutions. They will be familiar with a few technical options, but usually not in depth. They may be sensitive to this and try to hide their lack of technical expertise. If your product has unique technical features, your firm must explain them without condescending or to insulting the consultant's intelligence.

  Analysts who follow such products also tend to focus on business benefits. In evaluating customer relationship management software, for example, they will focus more on end-user Web interfaces more than the index structure of their databases. Technology has to be there, but it's secondary. Discussing it is important only to add credibility to your firm's claim that its products meet user needs effectively.

- If your products spearhead a new technology, you'll also encounter situations where the prospect can't evaluate your offering, but in this case consultants will usually be experts in your field. Technical nuances will matter. If your predictive analytics algorithm provides better throughput than competitive ones, explain exactly how.

  Analysts who follow such products may or may not fit the same mold. Some will be experts on technical details. Providing them with access to your firm's R&D staff, or to technical papers that don't skimp on depth, will matter. Others, however, don't care about this. They want to know "what will it do for my client's bottom line?"

- If your products provide a better way to do things, you will find advocates among top management advisors. Internal staff may oppose you: sometimes overtly, sometimes covertly. As Machiavelli said, they have little to gain from change but risk seeing it hurt their value. If top management sees change as beneficial, they will overrule their staff. Such consultants are often senior people in small "boutique" firms.

Analysts in this case are often futurists and visionaries who write and speak on the IT environment of the next decade. These people appeal to decision-makers who don't want to be left behind, who want their organization to be in the vanguard of change.

Because all these advisors affect your sales, you want them to have a positive impression of your firm and its products. This is an important aspect of analyst/consultant relations program value. However, using the information link you have created to analysts and consultants is not simple. The reason is that the messages you send them are not what matters. You care about what they tell their clients, your sales prospects. The messages you send to them are only a means toward this end.

You can't control what advisors tell their clients. You can only control what you tell advisors. This isn't like communicating to a prospect, where you control the messages that he or she receives. (You can't control what a prospect does with them, but that's a separate question. We'll leave it to books on effective selling.)

The problem is that advisors don't just repeat messages they receive. This differs from the press, which has no choice: it can't editorialize about provider messages in news articles. (Opinion columns are another story, as are some European writers due to a stronger "activist press" tradition there, but this is true of news articles in North America.) For example, suppose Dell announces that the sky is now green. A reporter can't say "I don't think so" or even "I'm looking out a window, and I know better."

Journalists can convey opinions by positioning articles in the paper, arranging content within an article, and writing headlines. But if they want to say "the sky is blue," they need another way. Often, they find an expert to say what is needed. The reporter can then write "Analyst Claude Monet, of the sky coloring service of Giverny Research, says 'We feel the sky is blue, and we advise our clients to use blue paint to draw it.' "

For all these reasons, it is important to do what you can to ensure that analysts convey your message to their audiences. However, this is not as simple as sending them your message along the new communication link you have created. The reason: analysts and other advisors don't just parrot what they hear.

Your message is only one of analysts' information sources. They also consider what they know of a technology or service and its uses, experience with your company's credibility, what they hear from your competitors, customers and competitors' customers, what colleagues say, and every other scrap of information they can lay hands on. The result, shown here by a dotted line, is a new message. It includes some

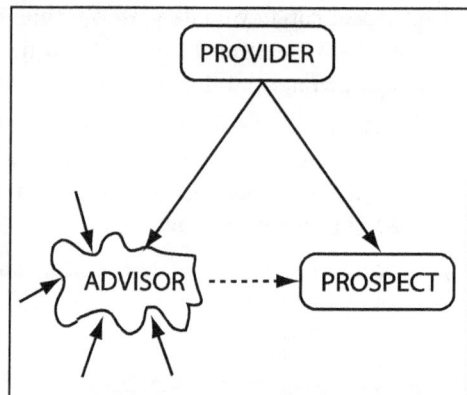

things you told the analyst, some that are related to it, some that are unrelated to it, and perhaps a few that directly contradict it.

Your objective with every analyst/consultant message is to optimize what reaches their clients. Toward this purpose, you must often perform an unnatural act: to say something you'd never say to the press or to customers, perhaps more negative than you'd like them to hear, to lead to a better result after your message goes through the influencer's filter.

For example, suppose Release 5 missed its schedule last year. Your Release 6 announcement wouldn't mention this. After all, if people who read the announcement know this, you don't have to tell them, and if they *don't* know, why tell them?

Acknowledging this to analysts can only help. They know it already. They're unlike sales prospects: prospects seldom pay much attention to your company when they're not potentially interested in buying something, but analysts must stay informed on it. Owning up to something negative in the past increases the credibility of what you say about the future. Analysts won't harp on your earlier problem in what they tell their clients about your next release: it's not important any more. They will, though, probably put a more positive slant on what they say because of your candor.

Another example is what a product does *not* do well. No product or service is all things to all people. You know this. Your prospects know this. Analysts and consultants know this. Yet providers ignore the obvious reality: for everything a product or service does, there is something it does *not* do. They let their audience try to figure out what that is.

What happens? The analyst's job is to provide an objective view of your product or service. This includes the bad with the good. If an analyst must do this with no guidance, the best possible outcome is to get it right. Even then, the analyst will waste energy that could be used to understand your message. More likely, though, he or she will get part of it wrong. In that case, your product or service will be given negative characteristics it doesn't have, which will cost sales; or not given negative characteristics it does have, which will lead to dissatisfied customers when they buy it and to resentful analysts when their clients complain about bad advice. Your firm may be able to survive a few dissatisfied customers. Resentful analysts, however, have long memories. Unless one more sale will avert Chapter 11, the short-term revenue won't be worth it.

This is often lost on people whose experience does not include channels that edit a message before passing it on. It can be hard to convince such people that saying something you wouldn't tell the press or customers, perhaps something negative, can improve the end result. However, it's necessary. This chapter (or a summary) may help.

2.3. Why Have an Analyst/Consultant Relations Program?

For two reasons:

1. To save money.
2. To get better results.

Your firm will save money because it costs less to do any job when it's done by people who know how to do it and are motivated to do it well. This reflects economies of scale (the more of something you do, the less each unit costs) and the learning curve (the more of something you've done, the less the next unit costs).

Your firm will get better results because people who are hired to do a job do it better than people who have it tacked onto their other responsibilities.

2.4. The Analyst/Consultant Relations Idea

Part of what analysts and consultants think about you is objective. You either do or don't have a router with eight ports, an office in India, or the ability to import .xlsx files. Analyst or consultant support cannot affect any of those. If an analyst or consultant mentions anything in this category, the facts will determine what he or she says.

The rest is subjective. Will your firm stay current with technology? Is its strategic direction aligned with industry trends? Is your support up to par? There are no objective measures for any of these, yet they are important to any recommendation.

Your analyst/consultant relations program is not their only source of information on these. Take support. Analysts will ask your customers about your support. That, however, is second-hand information. Their only *direct* information about your support comes from how well you support *them*.

2.5. The IDEAL Framework

Every part of an analyst/consultant relations program fits one of the five **IDEAL** categories:

> **I**dentify
> **D**rive
> **E**xecute
> **A**lign
> **L**everage

Identify refers to *identifying* your analyst/consultant relations targets. As a category of activity, it also includes planning the program: *identifying* what needs to be done.

Drive refers to putting programs in place that will *drive* operational excellence.

Execute is carrying out the program activities, *engaging* with analysts and consultants.

Align means *aligning* what you do with corporate messages and strategies.

Leverage is taking advantage of analyst/consultant relations to bring value to your company, *leveraging* your relationships for strategic benefit. That makes your program a strategic adjunct to business development. That is your goal.

As you read the rest of this book, you'll see how program elements fit this framework.

2.6. A Bit of Perspective

Analyst/consultant relations are not the only factor in sales success. Companies with top-notch products in growing markets can succeed despite poor analyst/consultant relations. Companies with excellent analyst/consultant relations, conversely, can fail if they don't execute in product planning or development. If a company's R&D is behind the times, its products cost more than they should, or its customer support is inadequate, no analyst or consultant relations program can compensate. Management must understand this. Miracles should not be part of the analyst/consultant relations job description.

A new analyst or consultant relations program is also not a quick fix for years of neglect. It won't make a difference overnight. It's like losing weight: ten years' gain won't come off in a week. Chapter 16 discusses how long it takes a program to have impact.

Analyst/consultant relations are, however, part of the picture. If they are done well and continued they can make a good company even more successful, help any company weather hard times, and in borderline situations make the difference between survival and bankruptcy.

By analogy: a boxer with one hand tied behind his back can win if he is sufficiently larger, stronger or more skilled than his opponent. Despite this, boxers don't enter the ring with one hand tied behind their backs. They can't afford to concede any advantage.

So it is with analyst and consultant relations. They are a competitive weapon. No information technology firm can afford to give them up. The rest of this book will show you how to enter the ring with both hands, ready to do battle.

3 | What do analysts and consultants want?

This chapter will cover:

1 Analysts' and consultants' motivations

2 Finding out what analysts want from you

3 A day in an analyst's work life

We must understand the needs and wants of any person or group we want to persuade. We understand this intuitively at a personal level. If I'm attracted to a woman who likes men with tattoos, but I don't have one, I have a few choices. I can get a tattoo, I can get a temporary one in the hope that it won't matter by the time she learns it's not real, or I can keep looking. The right answer varies, but the point is simple: if I don't know of this need, I can waste a lot of time and effort with no useful result.

It's the same with analysts, though our objectives with them are (for purposes of this book) different. We must understand what they want, what motivates them, to work with them as effectively as possible. This chapter is meant to give you that understanding.

3.1. What do analysts and consultants want in general?

Analysts and consultants are (despite what you may hear!) human. They want what we all want: physical security, comfort, affection, respect, and so on. If you chatted with one at a party, you'd probably find that his or her personal goals are much like your own.

Professionally, though, they differ from most employees because *their job carries little security*. When a consulting engagement stops, so does the consultant's income. In the short run a firm provides some protection against immediate loss of pay, but in the long run the rule applies. No contracts? No job.

The same is true of analysts. If demand for their research drops off, so does their income. If they work for large firms they may have a job for a while, but their long-term employment prospects are bleak.

In theory this applies to everyone. Waiters in a restaurant with a poor chef will soon be unemployed. So will engineers in a computer firm with an incompetent sales force, or salespeople in one with an incompetent R&D staff. But in the world of advisors the impact is perceived as reflecting the consultant's or analyst's personal competence, not someone else's. Hence the insecurity.

That being the case, consultants always worry about where the next engagement will come from. It usually comes from recommendations by satisfied clients. (This includes new work with existing clients.) Even if an engagement was found by cold calling, advertising, a broker, or chance, recommendations and references come into play before a contract is signed. Just as your firm depends on the quality of its offering—products, services, support, etc.—for business, a consultant depends on his or her reputation.

Analysts are equally sensitive to their and their firms' reputations. Service subscriptions, which offer more income assurance than anything else they do, are renewed or not renewed annually. Other revenue sources have even shorter time horizons. No compatibility issues, no investment in software, databases or training, deter clients from moving to a competitor.

In some research firms senior analysts also have sales targets, often known by the polite term "business development." They are expected to generate a certain amount of business themselves. If they don't, that aspect of their job performance is considered unsatisfactory. We all know what happens when one's job performance is unsatisfactory.

Advisors want to make recommendations that will enhance their reputations. These can be direct recommendations, in the case of consultants (including analysts doing consulting); or indirect ones, in the usual analyst situation.

A recommendation that will enhance an advisor's reputation, contrary to what one might think, does not necessarily suggest the best product on technical or any other grounds. To an advisor, *a good recommendation is one that a client remains pleased with as far into the future as that client's opinion could affect the advisor's reputation.*

Conversely, bad recommendations are those that a client becomes unhappy with soon enough to remember who made them. These damage reputations and must be avoided. Client unhappiness comes about in three ways:

The client learns of a product or service that would have been better.

People who subscribe to research services and engage consultants are not stupid. They read newspapers, talk to providers, and talk to others in their industry who use many suppliers. If an advisor suggests a product just because it's from the leading vendor, or for any other reason, and it's wrong for the job, clients will eventually find out.

The client is disappointed in the recommended product or service.

The installation doesn't go as smoothly as the client thought it should, the system doesn't work as well as the client thought it should, it's harder to use than the client thought it should be, enhancements don't come along as soon the client thought they would, it breaks down more often than the client thought it would, or ... The common thread here is "... as the client thought it would." There is no objective standard for what clients should expect. What matters is the difference between what happened and what the client expected, reality versus expectation. Advisors must manage client expectations to prevent this sort of problem.

You help analysts and consultants manage their clients' expectations by the way you set their expectations. This will do more than help them. This will also impress them with your understanding of their situation.

Down the road, the client or customer feels abandoned.

If a product or service doesn't live up to client expectations, the client may blame whoever recommended it. Since a provider that goes out of business doesn't live up to expectations, this may deter consultants from recommending products or services from new firms no matter what their technical merits are. Good consultant/analyst relations can do much to alleviate this concern.

As a provider you can show analysts and consultants where your products fit, that you stand behind them, that you'll continue to support and enhance them, and that you'll be around long enough to do it. Doing so will remove analysts' and consultants' major reasons to consider your firm a poor recommendation risk. The result: **more confidence in recommending your firm.** When their confidence in your firm increases but their confidence in your competitors doesn't change, the balance of recommendations will shift in your favor.

Because analysts and consultants need this confidence, *they will recommend a product or service they know will be satisfactory over one they think might possibly be outstanding*. There are times it may be appropriate to position your firm as "might possibly be outstanding," as when you're vying for visibility in a market with an entrenched dominant provider. That will get the attention of analysts who need to cover many providers for a report and want a sampling of innovators as well as the major ones. If you take this approach, remember that it will only get you visibility and perhaps onto some short lists. You must still create confidence in the final stages of provider selection.

The nature of a good or bad recommendation varies with the type of consultant or analyst. Here's what makes a good or bad one for each:

Consultants/Direct Advisors

Consultants have a direct relationship with their clients and recommend a specific product or service to meet a specific need. Their recommendation should be based on enough study of the client's situation to understand the need, and enough familiarity with various ways of meeting it to choose a suitable one.

Given the effort that should go into a recommendation and how much the client probably paid for it, a client will remember its outcome for a long time. Business issues loom larger than technical features unless a specific feature is an "must" to get the job done.

Example: If your hospital software can't transfer patients automatically from an associated clinic, dozens of people will be frustrated for years, will hate the system, and will curse whoever recommended it. If its master patient index occupies 20 percent more disk space than a competitor's, few people will notice and even fewer will care.

In working with a consultant in this type of situation, therefore, it is important to present objective considerations that will help him or her decide if your product or service, properly implemented by the client, will meet the needs. If you or your supporting staff know of any reasons it won't, or of any competitive products that (perhaps because of factors unique to this situation) will meet it better, you continue with the campaign at your peril. Sometimes your firm will make a sale. However, this will only lead to short-term satisfaction. The client will soon learn of its deficiencies. At that point the consultant will blame you for encouraging a sale that you knew, or should have known, was inappropriate. The damage to this consultant's trust in you and your firm will take a long time to repair—if it can ever be. (Trust is discussed in Chapter 8 and, for consultants, in Section 10.3.)

In the long run, an honest "this isn't the best place for our product" is the best thing you can do for your company. Short-term sales goals and career goals—yours and those of the sales rep—can make this difficult to do. Still, the closer you can approach it, the better a job you will do. Bread cast upon the waters *does* return manyfold. In the other direction, chickens *do* come home to roost.

Analysts and specialized newsletters

These people and firms make generic recommendations, not specific ones for an individual situation. Research reports have a lifetime of 12–24 months before readers consider them obsolete, though reports on fast-moving topics may be updated more frequently.

Analysts therefore need to make statements about the usefulness of a product that will stand up for that length of time, or that can be qualified in terms of identifiable future events that could change the recommendation.

To do this they need detailed information:

- Technical information is normally always needed: product specs, capabilities, interfaces, etc. Existing spec sheets normally give enough information to begin a study. More details, which sometimes require talking with R&D staff, may be needed later.

- Strategy information is also important. Research shows that analysts consider this the single most important type of information they can get from a provider.

- Product positioning is always important, especially if a product is new and doesn't fit a well-known market niche. If your firm has multiple products with overlapping capabilities, make sure each is positioned accurately relative to the others.

- Competitive information is helpful. If your competitive analysis seems reasonable analysts will often accept it in lieu of their own, use it as a starting point, or least consider it when they draw their own picture. Your cooperation with research firms as they study your firm's products will help them form an impression of the support your customers are likely to obtain. Analysts will ask your firm's current customers how good its support is, of course. But, as noted in Chapter 2, that's second hand. The only *direct* evidence analysts have of your firm's customer support is how well its supports *them*. Here's what analyst Chris Willard (then at IDC, at Intersect360 Research at this writing) said about one vendor in a survey interview. The message is for all providers, not just the one he mentioned at the time, so we've deleted its name:

... has good people, but [their analyst liaisons] have trouble convincing people in the company to respond to requests. People are always in meetings. This seems to be the corporate culture. I feel that, if they are not calling the industry analysts back, who else aren't they calling back?"

If your firm is small, polite but assertive courting of research firms can pay off in coverage. Research reports and newsletters can't cover every firm in a market segment. Since the leaders they must cover are obvious, they try to add value via a sampling of smaller firms that readers may not be familiar with.

Analysts select smaller firms to cover based on their having something to offer the report's readers: innovative technology, product features or anything else. If your small firm is more accessible to analysts than others in its class, is more willing to speak to them, or just shows more interest in them, your chances of being covered go up.

Analyst firms also often compile directories, author articles for newspapers and magazines, and do other things that don't fit under the heading of "pure analysis." In situations such as these, they work as discussed in the following sections.

Reference services

These services, which can be a product of a research firm or of a specialist in a particular area, don't recommend or evaluate. They describe. They may include competitive comparison charts that organize and summarize facts obtainable from specification sheets, but these are not true evaluations.

 "New clients" to a reference service mean new and renewed subscriptions. Subscribers will renew as long as product descriptions are clear and correct—and as long as the subscriber organization still cares about the topic, which usually means "as long as it's not obsolete." The easier you make it for reference services to describe your product clearly and correctly, the happier they will be with you. They will never recommend your firm's products. That's not what they do. But their feelings will be reflected in the overall tone of what they write.

Directories, including directory supplements to newspaper and magazine articles and directory Web sites

The value of directories to readers are in completeness. Their compilers want to include you. All they ask is information with which to do so. As parents plead when trying to get their children to wash their hands before meals, "Is that so much to ask?"

Directory compilers generally ask you to fill out forms containing the information they will print, organized in the way it will be printed. Filling these forms out can be time-consuming. Worse, their questions are often subject to interpretation (and misinterpretation).

For example, suppose a questionnaire on desktop computers asks for the number of expansion slots. One system may come with a bare minimum of standard features, but six such slots. Another may have just two—but it comes with sound in and out, four USB 3 ports and a high-speed interface, 10-gigabit Ethernet, a DVD burner, accelerated graphics, a digital camera card reader, and both Wi-Fi and Bluetooth standard, so most users won't need any expansion slots at all. Is it fair to simply list "6 expansion slots" for the first system and "2 expansion slots" for the second? To the casual reader this creates the impression that the first system has more expansion capability, but it really doesn't. What should the supplier of the second system put down?

There's no simple answer. The best one can do is to submit the most positive answer that is objectively defensible, to footnote items where that answer really distorts reality, and to accept any remaining problems as the luck of the draw. The second supplier above could probably argue that most people consider some of its capabilities to require expansion slots, so it could count those built-in items as "slots" even if they do not technically allow the user to expand the base configuration.

If you really feel the answers required by a standard questionnaire would mislead readers, and especially if you feel that other vendors' products are affected by this issue as well, you can call the person who compiles the directory. If you show some understanding of their situation and their need to standardize answers, you'll probably find them reasonable. You won't always talk them into changing. That would be too much to ask. But change has happened and could happen again. In the above example the directory editors might decide to include more check-off columns for standard capabilities than they originally planned, so the system with six expansion slots but little else would stand out because of all its blank standard-feature columns.

If directory compilers must edit your material to fit their needs, you have created a chance for things to go wrong. Don't send them a standard media information kit, even if everything they want is in it somewhere. Give them what they want, the way they want it. If they have a form, fill it out. Never provide less than they ask for. (There is seldom a reason to provide more than that, either. It just creates confusion and increases the chances that they will lose something.)

Product reviewers

Assuming you have a good product that meets a legitimate need, most reviewers will write it up fairly. There is little you can do to sway good ones in your favor except to provide the best possible product with the best possible documentation—and of course your firm does that already.

If your firm has the resources to write one, send a Reviewer's Guide to everyone who will review your product to make sure reviewers don't miss the good stuff. It should be written for readers who know the product area and are well acquainted with the current market leader and one or two others in the same general space, but who may not be fully aware of your product and its capabilities (unless it happens to be that market leader).

Reviewers detest receiving letters that say "You wrote up Release 4 of Zippy Web Site Constructor in June; it's October now and it isn't out yet ..." Reviewing, printing, and distributing magazines take time. Even Web sites, where printing and physical distribution aren't factors, still need time for reviewers to do their job; instant publication can't speed that up. Last-minute problems come up. Sometimes they're unavoidable, but try to minimize them. If you have to send reviewers a beta version, do what you can to assure them that it is shipping or shippable. In the long run, a good review two or three months later is better than a questionable one early. This is even more so now than in the past. Few people saved paper magazines and searched them for year-old reviews, but today anyone with a browser can find them in seconds.

Another reason to be careful is that reviewers, once burned, are twice shy. Most publications have a small group of reviewers for each topic area. They return to those people time and again. These people are not likely to forget that your firm misled them once about the product status. Their elephant-like memories may come back to haunt you.

Newspapers

Newspaper articles are written under time pressure. The deadline day for a weekly publication (most trade press is weekly) varies by section: general articles earliest, news as late as Friday morning before the popular Monday publication date. Writers for publications that post daily updates online are under even more time pressure than their print-oriented counterparts—the luxury of spending three days on a story that happened to break on a Tuesday no longer exists.

As you know if you've worked with the press, the quicker you get back to a reporter, the better. They often call multiple sources in the hope that one will provide the needed information or a quotable comment. The fastest replies are printed. The others are thrown away, or at best filed for (unlikely) future use.

Newspaper deadline pressure is passed on to analysts. Reporters call analysts for insight into your firm and its products. They need answers in time for deadlines. If they are covering an announcement, this deadline is probably within a few days of receiving your announcement kit. If an analyst calls you for information they need it even more urgently than the reporter, because analysis based on your answer must get back to the reporter in time to be used in the article. Since major announcements are usually made on Tuesdays or Wednesdays, the analyst's response window for a Friday deadline is tight.

To help analysts deal with this situation, pre-briefing them can help. This gives them a chance to think over what they hear, see if they have any questions, ask those questions, get answers, and develop a position before reporters start to call. The better an analyst can respond to a journalist's question, the better it is for the analyst: it increases the chances of his/her comment being used in the article and the chances of the reporter calling again the next time an expert opinion is needed. It's also better for you, since what an analyst says in response to a question that catches him or her by surprise is not likely to be what you, or your management, would like to hear.

Pre-briefing is important enough that we'll discuss it in detail in Chapter 7, especially Section 7.12 on announcement-related activities.

Magazine articles

Most of the Research Services section above applies, with a small overlay of newspaper-like deadline sensitivity.

3.2. What do analysts want from *you?*

Just as analysts and consultants are not all the same, providers are not all the same. What analysts and consultants need from you is not what they need from your neighbor on De-Anza Boulevard, the M4, or Interstate 495.

The best way to find out what analysts want from your firm is surprisingly simple. *Ask them.* They'll tell you. They're in the business of telling people about companies. They can't abandon this habit when they tell a company about itself. The result is candor. This may be painful but, if you heed the messages, they will help you design a better program than you could on your own.

Ask analysts for feedback at the end of every significant interaction. It also helps to carry out a deeper survey periodically, ideally before you begin your program or make major modifications to it and about once a year thereafter. (Less often lets things slide for too long. More often does not give changes time to take effect and causes analyst resentment.) There are several ways to determine what analysts and consultants think of your firm and want from it. They are covered in the following subsections.

Individual interviews

Individual interviews with members of any group are time-consuming and expensive. Save these for important consultants or analysts, where the impression you create by treating them as individuals is as important as the information you gather. When you meet with people on your "A list" to update them on new developments, a frank "how well do we support you, what else do you need?" exchange should be part of the agenda.

A structured program of individual interviews can give you an overall picture of how the analyst world views your firm. Such a program or survey can often be contracted out to a specialized market research firm that understands the role of consultants and/or analysts, and that of your program in supporting them. Several firms carry out these studies often enough to have developed relationships with many research firms and with key individuals in them. Outsourcing such a study has several advantages:

- **Objectivity.** While consultants will answer specific questions candidly when speaking with you, their opinions subconsciously shift if they know which provider they're talking to. They are often more objective with third parties.

- **Anonymity.** Most analysts will tell you what they think, but there are exceptions. Some comments, particularly negative ones about identified individuals, could damage relationships. A market research firm can maintain a speaker's anonymity for these, enabling you to obtain information that you could not obtain otherwise. This also lets the respondent attribute some comments while keeping others anonymous.

- **Expertise.** You're probably not a market research specialist. It's a profession in its own right. People with experience in such studies get better results in less time.

- **Cost.** Professionals can do these tasks more efficiently than you can, as any expert can carry out a task in less time than a novice. In addition, studies can be carried out on a multi-client basis. That spreads the cost over several providers.

- **Staff load reduction.** It can be easier to spend money on outside firms than to hire staff. Hiring, even if possible, raises the question: what to do with these people between studies? Hiring permanent staff who can wear multiple hats, one of which is market research, may force you to compromise on other capabilities or to pay more than you would like to in order to get a Jack or Jill of all trades. Asking your own staff to carry out a survey takes them off their main job for the duration or forces them to do it as an overload. An outside firm goes away when a study is over, with no further obligation on your part to keep them busy or to pay them while they're not.

Group interviews

Group interviews, or *focus groups,* are a productive way to get at the heart of analysts' and consultants' feelings. You can get several opinions in little more time than you would need to get one opinion via an individual interview.

Disagreements and unanimity will both surface in a focus group. Differences that depend on the type of participant will be clear when all are in the same room. If technical consultants love your documentation but business-oriented ones can't decipher it, you'll find out. If consultants love your support but analysts think it's below par, you'll learn that too.

Mass (e-mail, mail) surveys

Mass surveys include anything you send that people reply to at their convenience (or not). These include paper "snail mail," e-mail, and Web surveys (often with an e-mail invitation to participate).

Such surveys are easy and inexpensive to administer. Disadvantages: response rate is usually low, respondents are those with an ax to grind or nothing better to do at the time, and interviewers can't pursue interesting lines of questioning.

Use mass surveys in conjunction with other mailings to your database to obtain specific comments about specific programs: What topics would be of interest for monthly e-mails or conference calls? Are your announcement kits sufficient? Is your Web site easy to navigate? Is your staff sufficiently responsive to technical questions? Other methods will get better in-depth opinions.

Analysts' research content assessment

You read analyst reports as part of your reality check. Keep reading them. (You can't write Section 4 of your monthly report, discussed in Section 11.4, without knowing what analysts have written about you.) Your job now is to draw up a picture of analyst opinions, as reflected in their reports, and compare it with a the picture of a year ago.

- Coverage level: Compared to other firms in your sector, has the amount of your coverage gone up, gone down or stayed the same?

- Firms covering you: Put those that cover your space into this grid.

- Your objective is to move everyone to the right and to clear the top left corner (used to cover you, don't any more).

- You can replace the two axis values on with a scale from "not at all" to "in depth," but it's usually not worth it.

		Current Coverage	
Previous Coverage	**Yes**	(Used to cover you, no longer do)	(Used to cover you, still do)
	No	(Didn't cover you, still don't)	(Didn't cover you, do now)
		No	Yes

- Attitude. Rate each mention on a five-point scale from *very negative* to *very positive*, with *neutral* in the middle, and each report on a three-point scale from *mention in passing* (doesn't count much) to *all about us* (counts a lot). Has each firm's attitude gotten better or worse over the past year? Try to understand why.

Press quotations...

... also reflect analyst opinions. Read them the same way: what do they say about what the analyst knows? Is she well-informed or not? Does he understand what we're trying to do? Is she positive or negative about us? How has his attitude changed over time?

As with audits and surveys, you can use outside resources to collect and analyze press quotations about your firm. Two advantages are (a) financial savings achieved by sharing the cost of collecting quotations with other users of the service, and (b) specialized analysis expertise that a firm you engage for this purpose should have.

Your PR department or agency may already collect press clippings for your firm. Tabulating and analyzing them isn't difficult. Collecting and analyzing comments on competitors as well is a bigger project. Your PR people are less likely to be collecting those.

Win/loss analysis...

...looks at customer wins and losses to determine the impact analysts have and to assess, over time, how their impact is changing. Here you must learn, from your sales force or (with their permission) directly from the customer or prospect:

- **Which** analysts, if any, did the prospect use before and during provider selection?
- **How important** were analysts in the selection? What were other key influences?
- **How** were the analysts used: developing requirements, suggesting providers to look at, narrowing them to a "short list," making a final choice, helping with negotiations?
- **What vehicles** were used: written reports, telephone inquiries, in-person consulting, or ...? Was it via subscription service, custom engagement, or some of each?
- **What did they say**—for and against your firm, for and against your competitors?
- **What was the dollar impact** of each analyst or firm and of analysts overall?

One win or loss won't tell much, though you may pick up a useful tidbit or two. The picture really emerges as you get more data. You may start to see, say, that Research Firm A shows up mostly when you win, but B is seen more often when you lose. That can help guide your outreach efforts.

As with other measurement tools, you may want to use specialized resources for this.

Anecdotal information from customers, the sales force, and analysts

Win-loss analysis is a structured process that focuses on quantifiable information. Informal discussions with your sales force, customers and analysts round out the picture. An analyst saying "You ought to put your senior architect in front of analysts more, he talks our language" is worth millions in potential future sales. On the other side of the coin, a customer saying "This analyst said your boxes don't work with Cisco routers; I know they do because we have both" lets you correct the problem before it gets more serious.

Nuggets like these are only dug up by talking to people. Make sure you do.

General considerations:

Compensating analysts and consultants for survey time

Analysts and consultants sell their time. If you want to use some for your benefit, expect to pay. Brief discussions as part of a meeting with two-way information exchange, or meetings of up to an hour or so with a firm's management, usually don't require payment. Individual meetings may or may not be billable, but if they're not, expect to find some fraction of your invitees that doesn't have the time. (Offering to meet for a meal where you pick up the tab can help.) Focus groups, which typically last two to four hours, will usually be on a billable basis, or with a standard payment to avoid different compensation levels for what is essentially the same work. Questionnaires aren't paid, though it's common to offer a summary of the results to respondents as a "thank-you."

If you get non-billable feedback, it's a nice touch to offer a token of appreciation. A book, chosen for the respondent's professional or personal interests, is an excellent choice for in-person interviews. A summary of the results is always appropriate for them, too.

Identifying your firm in a survey

Any survey can be done in your firm's name or anonymously. Anonymous surveys may bring out more concerns. An effective method with individual interviews or focus groups is to start a meeting without identifying your firm, to get general feelings about it and several competitors. This is easy to do if a market research firm is conducting the interview or focus group for you. Then, you or that firm tell participants who is sponsoring the study. Ask directly about your firm for the remainder of the session to get details within the context that has been established.

Some people will be reluctant to participate in a study if they don't know who it's for. A promise to tell them partway through the session, with assurance that it's a major firm (if it is) in the field they follow (it should be) often brings them around. (If its sponsor is a client of the analyst's firm, that can also be persuasive.) If not, you have a choice between continuing without them or obtaining their input under less-than-ideal conditions. With individual interviews you'll usually get useful information even after identifying the sponsor. With focus groups, advance knowledge of the sponsor's identity would interfere with the group dynamics, so proceeding on that basis isn't viable.

Now you know what analysts want in general and how to find out what they want specifically from you. In the next chapter we'll see what you can do with this knowledge.

3.3. A Day in an Analyst's Life

Competition in the advising business is stiff. Though the demand for advice and guidance on IT products, technologies, issues, providers, trends, and markets is high, industry analyst firms fight for their share of the end-user and provider client markets. The Web has caused many firms to reinvent their services to meet customer expectations in this area. And economic conditions in recent years caused many research firms to fall short of their growth targets, forcing them to struggle to avoid laying off the personnel they so carefully hired in anticipation of this growth (or laying off any more than necessary).

At the same time, provider consolidation has cut the number of possible clients. In the 1990s research firms could sell to Tandem, Compaq, Digital and Hewlett-Packard. Then Compaq bought Tandem and Digital, before being acquired by H-P. Result: one potential client where there used to be four.

In 2013, with the recent economic slowdown, research firms fight over fewer client dollars. The research industry has been consolidating for years. Forrester's purchase of Giga, then Gartner's of META are the most visible examples. Old firms such as Hurwitz Consulting and Strategis have gone out of business. New ones, often founded by analysts who lost their jobs, are joining the fray.

The role of the industry analyst is changing as a result of increased competition and evolving technology. Besides being a subject matter expert in an extremely dynamic industry, the pressure is on for them to develop business, attend to more clients, publish more research and increase their visibility with the media. Kensington Group research showed the *average* analyst work week to be 60–65 hours!

How analysts spend their work day

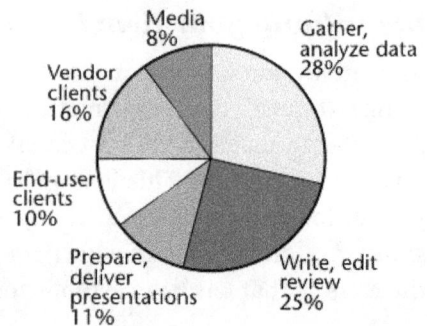

Media 8%
Gather, analyze data 28%
Vendor clients 16%
End-user clients 10%
Prepare, deliver presentations 11%
Write, edit review 25%

Analysts spend their time in many types of activities. A 2006 Lighthouse AR study found a typical day breaks down like the figure. A more detailed breakdown might be:

Research

- Reading trade press, business news, financial reports (online and paper)
- Interviewing customers and providers
- Attending briefings and provider events
- Hands-on product evaluation
- Finding, absorbing information on the Web
- Attending trade shows and industry events
- Writing and editing
- Team meetings to share knowledge, assign work, develop positions and discuss events
- Travel time

Client support

- Responding to client inquiries (may require additional research)
- Consulting with end user clients (often an extension of research)
- Consulting with provider clients (reviewing product development, roll-out plans, channel strategy, ...)
- Provider client briefings and events (even if no current work will use the information)
- Travel time (again)

Business Development

- Speaking at company and industry conferences
- Talking with the press and media
- Accompanying sales representatives on customer visits
- Client presentations
- Attending trade shows and industry events
- Conceiving, defining and creating new research product offerings
- Travel time (a third time)

Administrative

- Attending internal business meetings
- Interviewing, hiring
- For managers: creating and maintaining schedules, supervising subordinates' work
- The administrative side of any job: expense reports, activity reports, requesting time off, keeping one's computer running properly ...

A not-unusual day on the calendar of a US-based analyst might look like this:

7.30am	Conference call with U.K. analysts for global research update
9.00am	Meet with vendor to discuss previous quarter's shipments
11.30am	Update database with latest data, generate draft market shares
12.30pm	Lunch with vendor to discuss marketing strategy for new product
2.00pm	Meet with colleagues to review research project methodology
3.00pm	SWOT analysis of vendor positioning to respond to client inquiry
3.30pm	Phone call with client to discuss strategy of providers on short list
4.00pm	Review and edit draft research note for colleague
5.00pm	Internet search to gather content for client presentation
5.30pm	Respond to voicemails on train home
8.00pm	Conference call with Singapore vendor to discuss contract renewal

More and more providers are aware of analysts and their impact on the company's bottom line. They are strengthening their efforts to get on analysts' radar screens by increasing their analyst relations budgets and staff, developing analyst tools such as focused Web sites, engaging them for paid consulting, and more. While all this is intended to help analysts (and often does), the e-mail messages, phone calls, teleconferences, and meetings to at least consider even if one doesn't attend, also add to the demands on their time.

Analysts are pressed for time, now more than ever. Analyst relations efforts have to be more than just "good." You need to *compel* analysts to pay attention to your company. Since you can't order them to do this, you must create compulsion by what you offer.

4 | Goals of an analyst/consultant relations program

This chapter will cover:

1 The overall goals of any analyst/consultant relations program

2 Three specific types of goals: what is *yours?*

3 Messages in support of your goals

The goal of any analyst or consultant relations program should be to utilize analysts as effectively as possible to further your company's business objectives.

This can be via improving products and/or strategies, improving messages, moving markets in what it considers to be appropriate directions, and last but not least improving sales when analysts and consultants send positive messages to prospects.

Many support programs focus only on the last of these objectives. While it's important, using analysts solely as a marketing channel is transparent. Nobody likes to be treated as a tool whose value is only in helping others reach their objectives. Analysts are no different. They will push back if they sense that this is how your company sees them. It may work for a while, as analysts won't be sure of your motives the first time they meet you, but this approach will inevitably produce poor results in the long run.

4.1. Who are you trying to influence—and how?

Any communication activity in business should start by asking and answering this question: *What behavior change do you want to see, and in whom?*

Your sales-related analyst/consultant relations goal is simple: to increase the fraction of situations in which consultants, when your product/service or a competing one can fill a need, recommend yours; or analysts, when discussing products and services in your area, praise yours relative to others. The figure on the next page shows how this works.

The top split in the chart separates analysts and consultants into two groups based on their field of interest. Some work in your field. Some don't. If you have the greatest Web site security system in the world, don't waste time telling an expert on business intelligence about it. There are gray areas, there are generalists whose interests span many fields, and there is that rare product with something for everyone. But most advisors either do or don't care about what your firm or division does. Focus on those who do.

The second level deals with analysts and consultants in your space. Ideally, you'll zero in on those who will be in a position to write about your company or recommend it in the next 18 to 24 months or so, and ignore those who won't. (Anyone who won't care about your product in the next two years can be dealt with later.) In practice, you can't be certain someone won't be in a position to say something about your company for 2+ years unless he or she has been sentenced to at least three years in prison. You must cater to everyone in your industry segment, knowing that some of your effort will be wasted.

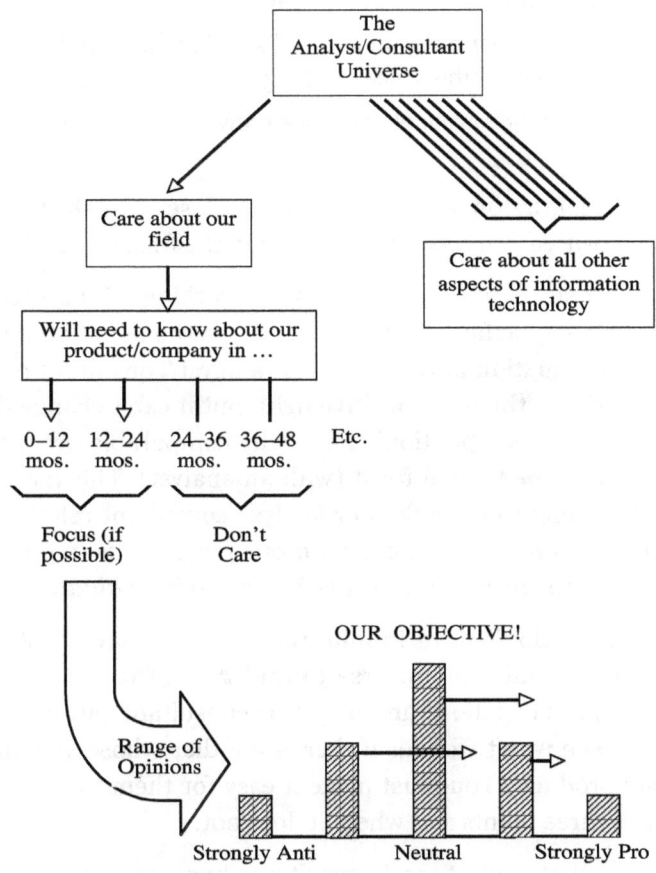

Figure 4-1: Program Objectives

Time frame is more of an issue with consultants than with analysts, because analysts have more need for on-going information than consultants do. You can assume that any analyst who follows your field at all will care about you in the next 24 months.

The third level is where the purpose of analyst/consultant relations comes into focus. At any moment analysts and consultants hold opinions about your firm and its products. Their opinions range from "It can do no wrong, everyone should use their products" to "Hearing its name makes me see red." There is little anyone can do about the extremes. Extremists, for or against anything, are irrational. You want to move the mass in the middle to the right.

How to do this ties into the analyst/consultant "hot buttons" in the previous chapter. They'll ask "How will I look, in a month or a year, for having taken this position?" To answer this question positively, he or she must feel that:

- Your **product or service** meets the client's need (consultants) or the overall needs of many potential users (analysts). If it meets them better than the alternatives, so much the better. In any case, it **must** meet them adequately.

- Your **company** will meet their needs in terms of stability, support, training, maintenance, successor products, and every other issue in a long-term relationship.

- Your **resources** will be made available to address any problems that arise.

If an advisor feels your product or service falls short on any of these, it won't be recommended. It's that simple. Miss on any of these and you lose. Pass these tests and you will usually be discussed positively in reports or make it to the final evaluation stage.

Your success in the last stage, when a consultant is working with a specific prospect or an analyst is evaluating a specific scenario, depends on the situation and on the merits of your offering in that situation at that time. An analyst/consultant relations program can help put these merits in the most positive light, but it can't change the facts. If your price is twice as high as the competition's for a fully comparable product, you'll usually lose (with a consultant) or be faulted for it (with an analyst). This has everything to do with your price and nothing to do with your analyst/consultant relations. *The most realistic objective for an analyst/consultant relations program is to get your product to where it can compete on its merits and to have those merits evaluated fairly.*

Consultants and analysts don't have infinite time. If they have fifteen products that meet a need, they won't comb the universe to find #16. (That's one reason Web sites must be easy to find and navigate. If an analyst or consultant can find enough suitable products easily, he or she won't wonder if there's another whose site didn't lead quickly to the appropriate product.) You must make it easy for them to see where your offering satisfies the above three points and where it does not.

In doing so, remember that analysts and consultants know your product can't do everything. Knowing that no product is all things to all people, analysts and consultants need to know where yours fits. Tell them, *honestly*. Tell them where it *doesn't* fit, too. Openness and honesty increase credibility. Credibility has two benefits with consultants:

1. It increases the likelihood that your product will be selected where it fits.
2. It increases the likelihood that it will be ruled out early where it doesn't. That's good too, because it would usually have been eliminated later anyhow, after your sales force wasted time and effort in a lost cause. Or, you could have made the sale, ending with an unhappy customer and a consultant who will never recommend you again. (Some salespeople are so motivated by the thought of an immediate commission that they don't think about next year, but those aren't the salespeople that most companies want to keep.)

Credibility is equally important with analysts, for different reasons. See Section 8.3.

The same principle applies to support. Different firms have different support programs to suit different types of users. Does your price include much support? Fine. Point that out. At the same time, concede that self-supporting prospects who want a bargain might do better elsewhere. If you're on the other side of that fence, be equally open. The prospect who has money and wants help at every turn might do better with the first vendor. "Tell them where you fit *and where you don't*" applies to both analysts and consultants.

To summarize these points:

- No product or company can be all things to all people. That includes yours.
- Credibility helps.
- Sooner or later, analysts and consultants will learn what you can't do. Sooner is better for all concerned.

Your ability to mobilize resources is critical. This doesn't mean your firm's resources must be infinite. Analysts and consultants are realistic. A start-up with a $199 software package is not going to put four people onto a plane to sell three, or thirty, copies. Tell analysts and consultants what your available resources are, under what conditions they can be brought to bear, what a customer or a customer's consultant has to do in order to get them, and (for those who might have to do it) how to make it happen.

Example: a computer company was known a while ago for confused support. Users could get a great deal of help by making noise. There was no consistency. This firm eventually wrote down and distributed its policies. The new policies were, overall, more restrictive than the unwritten ones had been. They resulted in less support for most users and a net revenue increase to the firm. Still, all were delighted with the new policies. Why? Because, now, they knew where they stood.

The moral applies to your firm. If analysts and consultants know how to access your firm's resources and do not know how to access a competitor's, it is as if your firm has resources and it does not. For example, if they know how to arrange a demo of your system but not how to arrange one of a competitor's, you are more likely to get a chance to demonstrate. Make sure they know what to do, who to call, and what buttons to push.

This will lead you to a successful analyst and/or consultant relations program. In the next few chapters we'll get more specific regarding building blocks to make it happen.

4.2. Three types of consultant relations program goals

Your program goals should depend on where you are in analysts' and consultants' minds before you start. Each possibility leads to a different program. It's important to do an objective reality check to see where your firm is in terms of these needs before you plan your program. You can't rely on what colleagues think (they're not objective), what friendly analysts say (they may not be typical) or what you knew when you worked at a PR agency (which may not be true today). The three:

- Few or no analysts and consultants know of you. You need a ***building*** program.

- Analysts and consultants know your firm, but (for whatever reasons, which may be unfair) their opinions are often unfavorable. Your firm needs a ***corrective*** program.

- Analysts and consultants generally know your firm, and their opinions range from neutral/objective to favorable. Your firm needs a ***sustaining*** program.

A building program should focus on recognition. Who is your firm? What does it do? Why are its products or services wonderful? (Innovative technology is part of this.) What are they good for? What are they *not* good for?

A corrective program should focus on the negative perceptions. For example, if the issue is Chapter 11 reorganization, anything that implies financial stability is important. If it is poor support, focus on steps your firm is taking to improve that (did you, perhaps, hire an executive from a firm known for good support?) and how they are bearing fruit.

A sustaining program should reinforce your firm's strategic strengths: technology, price, training, or anything else.

4.3. About your program goals

Analyst relations program goals should:

- Be strategic
- Mirror your overall corporate goals
- Be measurable
- Be realistic

Be strategic

Planning your program should not begin with what you'll do this afternoon or next week. Start with what you hope to achieve over the coming months. *Near-term actions can only be planned properly in the context of longer-term goals.*

The strategic point of view also means seeing analysts as more than "mouthpieces." (This is the concept of the AR Compass model in Chapter 1. We'll go into it more in Chapter 9.) Even if your company doesn't need the advice of a particular analyst, a strategic view of the relationship may tell you that this analyst's view of your firm will improve if his or her advice is solicited. In this case the strategy—the best way to improve this analyst's opinion—helps determine the tactic, to solicit advice. That will, in turn, determine specific actions: what advice to solicit, how to solicit it, who should make contact, and so on.

Finally, being strategic means thinking about what's going on in your market segment. For example, suppose established providers in one segment are expanding into a related area which smaller providers now dominate. This has happened many times. An example is ERP vendors' adding business intelligence (BI) modules. What each must do, in terms of analyst relations, depends on that firm's strategic position:

- If it is among those entering BI, it must convince analysts that the advantages of an integrated package outweigh the product plusses of software from someone else: your product will soon catch up, but the hassles of dealing with multiple vendors (if a customer takes that route) will long remain.

- If it is an independent BI vendor, it must persuade analysts that you will keep ahead of integrated packages' BI modules. By the time they catch up with where you are today, you'll have moved on. Integration, you can say, is done once per release, but your software's advantages pay off every time anyone uses BI.

- If it is an established ERP vendor that is *not* expanding into BI, it must convince analysts of more or less the same thing. It might ask them "Why should we waste effort doing something poorly, when someone else already does it well?"

The latter two types of firms may find common cause in getting this message out. You could explore this with your management if you find yourself in this situation.

To get out in front of analysts' needs effectively, you must know where the industry is going and plan in that context. Talking with analysts is a good way to do that, and shows them that your company appreciates their strategic insight.

Mirror your overall corporate goals

Your company can only reach its business goals if every part of it works toward them. For you to do this, you must know what those goals are and relate them to your program.

For example: If your company has a corporate goal of penetrating new markets, you should identify analysts who cover those markets and reach out to them. If its goal is to maximize market share in existing markets or maximize earnings in declining ones, your time would be better spent working with analysts in those markets. If you reach out to new analysts they should be new to your present fields, not in another area.

Asking your management about strategies as in either of the two preceding sections, then discussing their implications for analyst or consultant relations, also demonstrates business savvy. That never hurts!

Be measurable

It is often said "if you can't measure it, you can't manage it."

Your management wants measurements to verify that you are doing what you said you would do and that your program is having the desired impact.

You need measurements to gauge progress against goals and improve your program. The subject of measurements is taken up in more detail in Chapter 12.

Be realistic

Your goals should reflect reality. This includes the time frame to achieve results, the budget you'll need to achieve them, and realism about your company's history with analysts. They can be a bit of a stretch, but overpromising leads to underdelivering. Miracles are not part of your job description. Don't let anyone talk you into promising them.

4.4. Your messages in support of these goals

Having defined your goals, it is now important to figure out what messages you want to get across to analysts and consultants. (Focusing solely on messages does not reflect analysts' strategic value, as you know, but messages are still important.) That will let you direct your communications toward supporting these messages rather than sending random signals with correspondingly random effect.

Consider, for instance, a write-up of your new automated production line. It can be written to reinforce any of these messages:

- **Technology leader:** you use the latest automated manufacturing technology, showing your commitment to technological leadership.
- **Low-cost producer:** this line incorporates the latest automated equipment, permitting you to manufacture at the lowest cost and pass the savings on to your customers.
- **Quality vendor:** automated equipment eliminates human error in manufacturing, leading to improved product quality.
- **Responsive vendor:** computer-controlled equipment can be linked to online ordering, reducing the response time to produce exactly what a customer needs.
- **Niche specialist:** The new production line was custom-designed for the needs of your target niche.

BUT: while a story can reinforce any of these, it can't reinforce all five! Nobody will remember more than one, at most two, key ideas from it. If *you* don't decide which those should be, chance will decide for you. Unless you trust chance more than you trust your knowledge of your company's strategy, the outcome will be better if *you* do the choosing.

In addition to relating to your program goals, your analyst and consultant messages should have these four characteristics:

Market-driven

Your messages should reflect what your markets want. Great technology, for example, is irrelevant if people in your market don't care about technology. Analysts and consultants care what your products and services can do for their clients. Your messages must reflect that.

Unique

Everything today is Web-enabled, cloud-based, object-oriented, transparent, scalable... Your firm's products and services must have the right buzzwords, but these are not the stuff of which persuasive messages are made. "Me-too" messages don't help your cause, since your audience hears them from every provider in your space. Your messages must show what's different about you, not what's the same as everyone's (unless you need to overcome a perception that you lack something basic).

Analysts and consultants refer to " 'insert vendor name here' presentations:" with a new logo, any provider could use them. Ask: could one of your competitors use the same message, changing the name? If the answer is "yes" or "maybe," find a new message.

Supported by fact

You should be able to tie every aspect of your message into a provable fact. That gives it credibility.

You may feel that some messages don't tie into facts. For example, your R&D vice president says "We designed our Mark 3 gizmo for near-field communications, because that's where we feel gizmos are going." Where's the fact here?

The source of confusion is that gizmos may or may not be going to NFC. Nobody knows for sure, though any number of analysts will be happy to swap their opinions for your money. The fact here is that this VP thinks they are. That's enough.

Long-lasting

You don't want to change your message just as your audience "gets" it. It should stay stable long enough to be repeated many times under different circumstances.

Specifics will change. Change is a given. What you have in six months will be better than what you have now. But the basic message, why users should do business with you rather than a competitor, should outlast version numbers and technology upgrades. It shouldn't change just because you upgrade from 2.5 to 3.2 exablats or replace Version 17 with 18.

For example: BMW autos are promoted as "The ultimate driving machine." While car buffs may debate the accuracy of this tag line, it has remained constant through generations of automotive technology because it transcends specific products. Strive for the same longevity with yours.

4.5. Momentum

Momentum is the tendency of an object to maintain its speed and direction. An object with momentum will ride through or over minor obstacles and keep going. An object without it will slow down and stop.

You want your analyst/consultant relations program to move in a positive direction and then to develop momentum to keep moving. Some actions you can take might help it move initially, but could also keep it from developing momentum. An example is treating analysts as "mouthpieces," mentioned earlier. It can be tempting to go for the quick fix, managers may press for it to boost short-term results, but it's not a good idea in the long or even the medium run. Such an approach will start quickly, then stall out.

In this book we'll focus on approaches that build momentum that pays off for months and years down the road. If you find yourself in a situation where a quick fix is necessary, you shouldn't have any trouble using these methods to create a short-term program. Just focus on activities that can be done without a great deal of lead time.

Summary

Your objective is to move analyst/consultant opinion by creating messages that meet the criteria of this chapter and getting those messages to your audience as effectively as possible. The next chapters will discuss how you can get them across.

5 | Means of a consultant/analyst relations program

This chapter will cover:

1 Three dimensions of how analyst/consultant programs achieve their goals

2 Analysts' and consultants' work processes

3 Elements of each of the three dimensions

The previous chapter discussed goals of analyst and consultant (direct advisor) relations. After setting goals, we must ask: Now that we know our goals, how will we reach them?

That's what this chapter is about. It will discuss the means to that end, in general terms. Each of the next three chapters focuses on one category of those in concrete detail.

Any consultant or analyst relations program has three dimensions:

1. Your firm provides *information content* and/or materials for their work.

2. It provides the content and materials through specific *channels*.

3. In doing so, it conveys an *attitude* that transcends these specifics.

Example: An executive responds to an analyst's briefing request about your firm's strategy. The content is the strategy. The channel is direct (in-person or phone) contact. The attitude is willingness or reluctance.

Example: Your employer, as a matter of policy, declines to provide an analyst with information about discounts offered to users of competitive products. The (missing) content is discounts. The channel is probably a phone call from the analyst liaison. The attitude can be anything from arrogance to regret.

We can define a program in terms of 23 elements: eight types of content, twelve information channels and three attitude descriptors. We'll discuss each of these at an overview level here. The next three chapters, one per category, will cover them in more detail.

This isn't the only possible list. The right number might be 21, 24 or something else. But this list has been used in over 1,000 analyst/consultant interviews for more than a decade. It has been refined to reflect evolving tech-

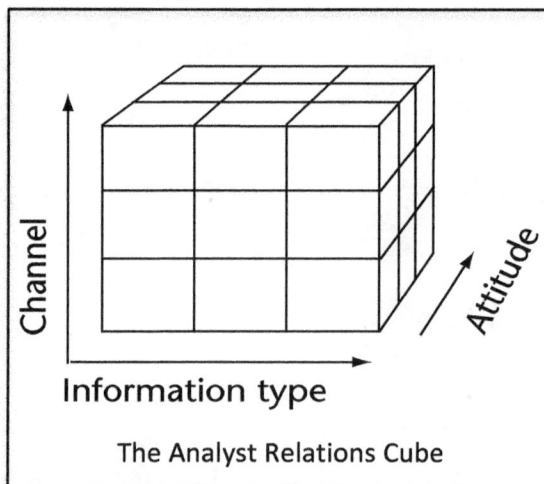

The Analyst Relations Cube

nologies and the evolving roles of consultants and analysts. Providers and advisors of all types feel that it captures the essentials without being too long.

Before getting into the factors, we'll discuss the processes analysts and consultants follow in their work. That will help fit each factor into its context.

5.1. The Process for Analysts

1. ***Keep up with emerging technologies, trends, user needs, and solutions.*** This involves reading, Web surfing, talking to providers, talking to users, talking to researchers and more. Analysts' top complaint is information overload.

    You can help here. One of the most valuable services you can perform is to clue analysts into new developments.

2. ***Evaluate technologies and products most likely to meet user needs.*** This is based on perceptions of those needs. You can put analysts in touch with users whose needs your products and services meet, as well as by giving them information.

3. ***Report assessments to clients.*** As discussed earlier, research firms vary in how and how often these assessments are reported.

4. ***Recommend choices.*** These are generally not phrased as "Get X." Rather, it's a list of candidates, or statements such as "If you have A you should probably get X, but look at Y too."

Some firms present recommendations through structured methodologies. Gartner, for example, positions firms on its *Magic Quadrant*: a chart giving their assessment of the firms' vision along one axis, their evaluation of its current offerings on the other. Other firms use other charts, checklists with ratings on product aspects, or a three-dimensional graph that can be rotated on a computer screen. The list is endless.

5.2. The Process for Consultants

Consultants' work process differs from this, so their information needs do as well. We'll focus on them in Chapter 10, "The Consultant Difference." It generally looks like this:

1. ***Determine client requirements.*** This may take minutes or months. Defining ERP needs for a multi-billion, multi-national firm may involve a whole team.

2. ***Define solutions to meet them.*** Consultant expertise comes into play here. They seldom contact providers to help define conceptual solutions; they think they know enough to do that themselves. If you want one to consider your innovative approach, it's essential to reach that consultant ahead of time.

3. ***Develop a preliminary provider list.*** Names reach this list from many sources. A good consultant knows the major industry players. Analyst reports, trade press articles, ads, and Web directories are also used. Get into as many of these as possible.

4. ***Screen providers down to a short list.*** Analysts need information from you here. You may get a general Request for Information first, more focused requests later. Usually,

don't supply more than requested. Extra information can get in the way. It won't improve your chances of making it to the next step.

5. ***Analyze short-listed providers/products***. Now it's time for details. Consultants may need contact with specialists, visits in one direction or the other, or other types of support. If the consultant isn't working with your field sales force yet, make that contact now. You and the local pre-sales staff should coordinate your activities to make sure you don't duplicate effort, leave anything uncovered, or seem disconnected.

6. ***Recommend choices***. This is out of your hands. If you handled the previous steps properly, your "hit rate" will be higher than it would be otherwise.

But they won't tell me who the client is!

Sometimes a consultant won't identify the client (your prospect). There can be several reasons:

- The client doesn't want to be bothered by salespeople. (Telling you "Make sure your rep doesn't call my client yet" will probably prevent any calls, but the fear persists.)

- The consultant doesn't want provider salespeople involved until after some preliminary groundwork. (Ditto.)

- There is no client. The consultant is collecting information for his or her files, maybe for one of your competitors. It's even possible that this "consultant" works for a competitor, using a false company name. This is usually discovered. Word gets around. It causes long-term damage to the reputations of the firms and individuals involved, but that doesn't stop optimists from trying it once in a while.

The first two are annoying but not damaging. The third is rare, but worth protecting against. The best way is to ask for information that will help you serve the consultant. For example: what industry is the client in? What is its approximate size? What existing IT infrastructure will your product or service have to work with? A consultant should have this information, or be willing to get it, and won't have a problem sharing it as long as it can't be used to identify the client. If there's no client, answers will often be hesitant and inconsistent. A few good actors can pull off this scam, but not many.

If a consultant gets upset at this and threatens to hang up if you don't quit the grilling, there's a good chance there was no client in the first place. Real consultants with real clients welcome the opportunity to share as much as they can. They know this helps you help them and are pleased when you take the time to find out. They draw the line only when answers would be too specific.

5.3. Information Content

There is probably nothing about a provider that some analyst or consultant, somewhere, sometime, hasn't needed to know. These form the first dimension of the consultant/ analyst relations cube. Content falls into these categories:

Information about strategy. What is the firm's strategy? Why this strategy, not another? Does it differ from last year's strategy? If so, why? (If a firm has multiple lines of business, each LOB will have a strategy of its own. These are equally important to analysts who follow each line.)

Information about products. This includes the plethora of technical specs associated with any high-tech product. If a firm doesn't have a tangible "product," such as most services providers, this item covers the specifics of whatever it offers.

Information about pricing. The basic content here is the list price, where this is a meaningful concept. Pricing structure is also important: so much per port, seat, server, location, or usage unit. Consultants and analysts also want to know "deal" or "street" pricing: what do customers *really* pay? This is a sensitive area, even more so in services where it's hard to define what the price is for.

Information about shipments. When did your firm first ship its new product? How many has it shipped, in what regions, with what total revenue? What are the trends over time—how quickly are orders for Rev. 10 replacing orders for Rev. 9? This information is vital to "market watchers" who provide data to all providers.

Information about the organization. Who heads a new business unit? What did he or she do previously? Where does it report in the organization? This is important because of what it implies about the division's claim on top management attention, its priority for corporate resources, and likelihood of its long-term existence.

Information about competitive positioning. Every offering has competition. What's yours, and how does what you sell differ from it? (It may not be a similar product from another company. It may be solving the problem another way, not solving it at all, or not upgrading from your previous release.)

Information about technology. Known as *backgrounders, white papers,* or by other names, this type of content orients its readers to the technology, strategy, or market trends underlying a product.

Reference accounts. Who uses your products? Who uses the specific product being evaluated? How long have they used it? And who can I contact to learn what they think of it?

5.4. Information Channels

The second dimension of the cube reflects the channels through which this content is provided. The major channels are listed next. We'll discuss them in detail in Chapter 7.

Some channels are more appropriate to certain types of information than others. You won't ask your CEO to provide detailed background on the technology of a new product (unless he invented it and people really want to hear him discuss it). A white paper on the Web is normally a better vehicle. All the channels are useful some of the time. In choosing one, consider the content, the audience, and your objective in providing this content to this audience.

A central point of contact. This is where analysts and consultants go when they don't know where else to turn. Your company may also want them to use this contact even if they do know. (This may be you.)

Contact with executives. A provider's top managers are a prime source of information about strategic direction and other high-level issues. Access to executives is important to analysts who care about these. When it is needed, there is no substitute.

Contact with other staff members. There are things other people know better than executives. Your marketing VP is unlikely to know the API for updating the Priority field in a message control block.

Visits to the analyst or consultant firm. When you want to make sure all relevant people at analyst or consulting firms get updates on your strategy or your new announcement, taking this information on the road is the best way to do it. Fortunately, geographic concentrations of advisors—especially analysts—make this practical.

Visits to you. Bringing analysts or consultants to your facilities gives them access to more of your people, including executives who might not be able to travel and specialists you can call in on short notice.

Multi-firm briefings (analyst or consultant "days"). Instead of hosting one firm at a time, why not invite several of them in and meet with them jointly? This has pros, such as improved efficiency from the provider's point of view, and cons.

Teleconference briefings. Analysts can often be briefed efficiently by phone. A good "telebriefing" includes visuals sent ahead of time and Q&A with experts.

Web site. This is an excellent way to make product, technical and corporate information available to analysts and consultants 24/7 when the personal touch isn't mandatory.

Social media. There are many ways analyst relations programs can take advantage of social media to connect with analysts and extend their reach.

Outbound written communications. You'll probably send periodic updates to your analyst/consultant targets: new products, services, and customers; organizational changes and strategic initiatives.

Detailed reference material. Manuals are an important source for technical advisors assessing products in detail. Some firms also have an overall reference manual for consultants and analysts, with in-depth information about the firm and its products.

Demonstrations. If a picture is worth ten thousand words, what is a live demo worth? At times, especially for products that can be appreciated visually, a lot.

5.5. Attitude Descriptors

The third dimension of the consultant/analyst relations cube describes the attitudes in which this content is provided. The major attitude factors are listed here. They're discussed in depth in Chapter 8.

Try to keep your dealings with analysts consistent in terms of the attitude you convey and authentic with respect to your corporate culture. This affects analysts' overall impression of your "brand."

Keeping the analyst/consultant informed. This refers to proactive aspects of your program. Your firm should maintain awareness over time through regular outreach.

Responsiveness. This is the "flip side" of proactivity. When analysts or consultants call, how long does it take to get back? Do the answers fully address their questions? Remember: advisors' only first-hand basis for evaluating responsiveness is responsiveness to *them*. When they get slow support, they learn that your firm responds slowly. A hundred customers swearing that you respond quickly won't dent that knowledge.

Candor and honesty. Analysts and consultants have long memories. If they ever find out that your firm was less than totally honest with them, it will take years to rebuild their trust—if it can be rebuilt at all.

These elements combine to support consultants and analysts. None stands alone: responsiveness without content is as useless as content without responsiveness. Put them together and you will get the most positive reports, recommendations and press quotations that the merits of your products and services call for.

The next three chapters give specifics and best practices for analysts. Chapter 10 then discusses how consultants' needs differ.

6 | Information content for analysts

This chapter will cover:

1 Eight types of information content for analysts
2 Each type of analyst's needs for each type of content
3 Best practices for providing each content type

This chapter opens our discussion of the nitty-gritty of analyst support: how you should support them in their work and thus win them over to your firm. As you read in Chapter 5, we can divide information content for analysts into eight major categories. At some point every firm will be asked to provide all of them, though the emphasis will vary.

This chapter focuses on analysts, as they are the more important target for most (though not all) IT vendors. Chapter 10, The Consultant Difference, discusses how a consultant relations program differs. Therefore, we'll use the term "analyst relations program" here. Read it as "analyst or consultant relations program, whichever you have."

This chapter's eight sections cover the eight content types of Section 5.3 in more depth. Think about them in terms of the analysts your firm must reach (Chapter 1) and what motivates them (Chapter 3).

6.1. Information about strategy

> **BEST PRACTICE**
>
> Strategy information should be presented by executives who can address it with authority, should be concrete rather than merely stating goals, and should present an integrated view across a firm's product lines and/or business units. Demonstrate timely execution of strategies to make the message believable and reinforce credibility.

Strategy information is, according to all studies, one of the most important types of content a provider can provide analysts. They use it to assess how firms and products are likely to evolve in the future. If two firms' products are equally suitable for one type of user today, but A's will evolve along lines those users need while B's will diverge from them, that's important. (This may not mean that A's plans are better. B's may be better for different users, perhaps even for a larger and more important group of users.)

Analysts want to know, first and foremost, *what* your firm's strategy is. Then, they want to know *why* it chose that strategy, not some other one. They want to know if it has changed from last year and, if it has, what (technology, market, executive changes, or simply realizing that last year's strategy wasn't working) led to the change.

If a firm has multiple lines of business, each LOB (division, sector, whatever your firm calls it) has its own strategy. These are important to analysts who follow each line. Any discussion of LOB strategy must reflect the others in two ways:

1. How does this LOB's strategy tie into the others'? How do they support each other? What synergies exist? Even if there's no connection, it's important to explain why rather than ignore the subject. Saying nothing is, to an analyst, the same as saying "we don't know." Giving analysts the message that your strategy spokesperson doesn't know this sort of thing is not a good idea.
2. How does this LOB strategy tie into and support the corporate strategy? It is possible, but unlikely, that there is no connection. Some corporations are essentially holding companies that operate a collection of loosely connected subsidiaries. If that's you, say so. Don't leave analysts wondering. Again, not saying is the same as saying "we don't know." You don't want to say that.

Making these connections isn't just a theoretical exercise. Analyst practices don't break down along the same lines as your company's organization. Any analyst's slice of the IT spectrum probably includes multiple elements of your firm. This means the analyst will hear multiple LOB strategy messages. Presenting an LOB strategy in isolation from the others and from the whole creates the impression that your firm doesn't have a coordinated strategy.

A corporate strategy shouldn't change from one day to the next, even from one month to the next. It is therefore not necessary, or even advisable, to brief analysts on it frequently. Once a year is enough unless there are major changes. If you visit or host the same group of analysts more often than that, you don't need detailed strategy discussions each time. A brief "we told you about it last time, nothing has changed" reminder may be in order, if only so that the new person in the room will know you're not ignoring the topic, but don't spend more time on strategy unless something has changed.

Two don'ts in presenting your firm's strategy

The most common analyst criticism of strategy presentations is *confusing goals with strategies*. "To double our market share in two years" is not a strategy. That is a goal, an objective. The strategy is how your firm intends to reach that goal: what products it will develop, why they'll be superior to what the competition develops in the same time, what resources it will use to reach it, what it will do differently in the future than it did in the past—in other words, the framework that will guide its tactics and actions, and the commitments that make the goal achievable.

Second, analysts often find strategy statements so generic that they could be made by any firm in a market segment. If yours is like that, it needs revising. If you're charged with analyst relations, you probably can't revise the strategy itself. However, you can *and must* help those who will present it understand that it must be stated with specifics. If it isn't, analysts will be quick to catch on. If the analysts don't say anything during the meeting, which can be embarrassing, they'll say it later in reports, customer recommendations, and comments to journalists. That's worse.

Who cares about your strategy?

Some analysts care deeply about strategies. To them, today's products are transitory. In dynamic markets providers leapfrog each other, each taking its turn in front, so who's on top at the moment is irrelevant in the big picture. These analysts see their job as advising clients for a two-to-five-year time frame. They don't care where your firm is in the leapfrog game today. They have to know where it plans to go. As one such analyst told a vendor, "I care more about what your CEO eats for breakfast than about today's products."

Others feel that any strategy is at best conjectural. Anybody can give a fine speech about where a company plans to go, but even if the speech reflects today's intentions honestly, many factors cause plans to change before they become reality. These analysts say "the only reality is today's reality." To them, strategy discussions are hot air, a waste of time.

Neither position is right. Neither is wrong. Each is appropriate to some analysts and some of their clients. The important thing is to know that both positions have merit and matter to some clients who will choose between your products and your competitors'.

Analysts will tell you which type they are and what they want. This isn't altruism. It's self-interest. They want to get information they need as efficiently as possible without wasting time on information they don't need. This means telling you what they need.

It may be hard to get this message through to colleagues. They all think their work is important. (It is.) They all think that everyone, including analysts, ought to care about it. (Perhaps they should.) So, they all want to tell analysts about it. You may have to tell them that this meeting isn't the right time, or this group isn't the right audience.

This isn't difficult with product-level staff members. You don't have to schedule them if their work isn't of interest to a given audience. It's more difficult with executives. An executive welcome is a common (and valuable) part of many analyst meetings. Executives care about strategy. You must sometimes say, tactfully, "yes, but these folks don't."

How to present your firm's strategy

Ways to present your firm's strategy include these, discussed in the next chapter.

- Webcasts and other remote briefings
- Analyst events
- Executive visits to key analysts and/or firms
- Executive meetings with analysts who visit you
- "Buddy programs," round-robin calls

What different types of analysts need in strategy information

Research Agenda-Driven	Strategy for LOBs whose products/services will be covered in up-coming reports, how this ties in with corporate strategy
Event-Driven	Strategy for LOBs whose products/services are the subject of an announcement or are otherwise newsworthy, how this ties in with corporate strategy
Calendar-Driven	Generally less interest in strategy, except as background for or explanation of market share changes and future expectations
Client-Driven	General background to come up to speed quickly when details are needed in a specific area to respond to a client inquiry

6.2. Information about products

> **BEST PRACTICE**
>
> Since much product information is already available via other channels, AR should focus on adding value: make sure analysts have exactly what they need, break down "solutions" by components, clarifying what is different. The analyst relations group also should facilitate meetings and contacts to fill the gaps, and brief analysts proactively on new developments.

The previous section mentioned analysts who don't care about strategies. Those analysts care about products. (A "product" need not be a product. It's whatever your firm sells. This section applies equally to services.) What, precisely, do yours do? How do they do it? How fast are they, how easy to use? How do they interface with each other and with related products of other firms? Of the features this analyst considers important—many analysts have checklists for various products—which does it have, and how well does it implement each?

The specific questions vary with the product or service. The need for answers does not.

A big difference between strategy information and product information is that product information is available from a variety of sources without your intervention.

The most important is the Web. Your firm's site has information about its products. It probably also has a link to request more detail. Some sites even have the full text of spec sheets, perhaps also reference manuals, or provide ways to download them.

In addition, your firm probably has channels through which anyone can get product information in hard copy. Sales offices often have marketing literature in stock and can get anything else in a day or two. Acquaintances within your firm, including experts whom analysts have met in your meetings, can provide documents that don't contain proprietary information. Your users probably have a set of manuals on hand and will share them with professional colleagues.

For all these reasons, Analyst Relations doesn't play as big a role in providing product information as it does for strategy information. It plays a key part, though, as a facilitator—getting the right people in front of the analyst to discuss products, getting documents to them as needed, acting as go-between to find answers to questions or set up discussions between the analyst and the people who have these answers.

The analyst relations role in providing product information will generally consist of:

1. Telling analysts what product-related material is available. A periodic list, perhaps sent via e-mail, handles this nicely.

2. Responding to requests for specific items. Most requests will come soon after your list goes out, with analyst interest triggered by seeing something in the list.

3. Putting analysts in touch with specialists who have information that does not exist in prepared form. Depending on the information, this may range from a brief telephone call to a week-long visit to your firm.

The role of NDAs in providing product information

Analysts often ask about unannounced products. Knowing something about them is part of their job. If their clients are considering committing to a product line for several years into the future, analysts want to know at least what the next quarter will bring.

"Unannounced products" covers a lot. It means what you'll announce on Tuesday, which has been covered accurately on Web rumor sites for weeks. It means the breakthrough your Advanced R&D department just sketched out, which may or may not become a product in five years. And it means everything in between.

Analysts must often sign a **non-disclosure agreement** to get this type of information. An NDA specifies that they won't discuss the information with anyone outside their organization, discuss it with anyone within their organization who doesn't agree to be bound by the same conditions, or release it publicly. It specifies its topic in enough detail not to prevent them from discussing other subjects freely. And it usually specifies a time limit after which it can be discussed publicly, or "until the information is made public by other sources." Any corporate legal department is familiar with NDAs. Many have a standard form to fill in: product or topic, name of research firm, names of individual analysts, date, etc.

Many providers and analysts work with firm-wide NDAs. These cover any information that is described as being not for disclosure in any contact between the two firms. These save the trouble of signing a separate NDA every time a future product is mentioned.

Analysts take NDAs seriously. They know that word of violations gets around quickly and their trust can evaporate immediately. Therefore, NDAs are often an appropriate solution to the problem of discussing "futures" with analysts, especially in the U.S.

Outside the U.S., NDAs are less used. Many non-U.S. analysts are offended by a request to sign one. They feel it says the provider can't trust their word. Some have had enough experience with the "litigation-obsessed" U.S. culture that they don't take it personally, but others aren't that understanding. Outside the U.S., use them only when necessary.

You may hear the term **embargo** in this context. An embargo is a short-term NDA with a specific end date, typically the announcement of a new product within a week or two. If your firm uses embargoes, make sure they don't put the analyst in the awkward position of being legally barred from discussing the subject with a journalist who has also been briefed—and who may have been told, by your management, to call that very analyst!

Some analysts won't sign NDAs. They prefer not to know about anything they can't discuss with clients. They give several reasons:

1. It's hard to remember, in discussing multiple topics, which are OK to discuss and which aren't.

2. Suppose an analyst is briefed on a product to be announced in two months which represents a major improvement over what you offer today. Then a client calls to ask about buying today's version. The analyst is over a barrel. He or she can't in good faith recommend today's, knowing it will soon be obsolete, but can't talk about the next one either. One way out is to recommend a competitor whose product is better than what you're shipping now, even if it's not as good as your next one will be.

3. Many NDAs are over-restrictive, keeping information private long after it has effectively become public. While these may be legally unenforceable, getting a court to agree is time-consuming, expensive, and can damage analyst relationships.

4. Outside the US, as mentioned earlier, many analysts feel NDAs reflect mistrust. If a firm doesn't trust an analyst, they ask, why brief that analyst in the first place?

What different types of analysts need in product information

Research Agenda-Driven	Lots of detail about products that fall into the area of a report. They'll know these areas months in advance. Regular contact will give you lead time to collect information and make technical experts available.
Event-Driven	Enough about your announcement topic to analyze it. Comparisons with your earlier products and/or competitive offerings are helpful.
Calendar-Driven	Generally less important, but make sure they have your products properly characterized in terms of their breakdowns of the marketplace.
Client-Driven	General background to come up to speed quickly when details are needed for a client inquiry. Be sure they know how to access product information quickly when a need arises.

6.3. Information about pricing

> **BEST PRACTICE**
>
> If you are constrained by policy or management direction not to divulge pricing, tell analysts the situation; stick to your guns; and try to provide as a minimum an explanation of your firm's structural approach.

The analyst's job is to point out strengths and weaknesses of information technology providers and their products. To the purchaser, price is an important part. A package that is a bargain at $500 might be in the thick of the competition at $5,000, priced out of the market at $50,000.

Analysts need pricing information because they have to discuss prices in reports. If you don't tell them, they'll get their information from reference services, their files, or talking to users. Reference services, if they exist for your field, get out of date. Analysts' files aren't updated until you update them. Users can only say what they paid when they bought, months or years before your prospects read an analyst's report. Meanwhile:

- If your prices have gone down (the usual case, especially in hardware), out-of-date prices will make your firm seem to be at a competitive disadvantage that isn't there.

- If your prices have gone up (as in services and other labor-intensive fields), your new prices will ultimately be reflected in your bids. Nasty surprises then can embarrass an analyst and can't possibly help you. They may cost a sale that a higher price, if known early on, would not have prevented.

This being the case, analysts want to know how much your products cost. Unfortunately, this simple request is clouded by a host of real and imaginary issues:

- There is seldom a single "cost." Unless your firm sells shrink-wrap software, options and variations in configuration, services, and bundling affect the item being priced.

- The cost to one user may not be the same as that of an identical product or service to the next. Quantity discounts, competitive situations, special situations such as educational pricing, and customer negotiating skills all affect the "deal" or "street" price."

- Prices change rapidly. Today's numbers may be wrong tomorrow.

- Providers may feel that disclosing selling prices will reduce their bargaining power with prospects, who'll want a better deal, and upset customers who didn't do as well.

The result is often a policy of refusing to disclose pricing at all. This is an over-reaction. One can give analysts information they need without "giving away the store." How?

First, you may have sample prices. This lets analysts calibrate the range in which your prices fall. For many purposes they don't care if it's $500 or $600. They have to know if it's $500 or $5,000.

Second, if you have list prices, it can't hurt to give analysts those. They know street prices will be lower. They'll calibrate how much lower by talking with your customers. This doesn't tell them anything they couldn't find out otherwise. It just makes their job easier. That makes your firm easier to deal with. Isn't that what you want?

Third, analysts are often more interested in pricing structure than actual figures. Tell them you have a base price per system plus a cost per seat, or whatever. Tell them when you change the structure—say, to a higher base but no add-on per seat, or a higher price per seat but zero base. And explain the strategic reasons for the change.

In discussing pricing with your management, keep in mind that analysts talk to your customers. Your firm can't prevent this. Analysts *will* get street price information from them, whether your firm gives them this information or not. The only thing you *can* control is whether that is their only source. If it is, you force them to do more work than they feel they should (they'll resent that) and miss a chance to influence them.

What different types of analysts need in pricing information

Research Agenda-Driven	Enough detail about products that fall into the area of a report for whatever tables are to be in the report. Discuss their needs ahead of time if possible
Event-Driven	Enough about your announcement topic to position it in its market. Complete sample configurations are helpful for announcement reports.
Calendar-Driven	Generally less important, but make sure your products are properly positioned for market segmentation if price is a factor.
Client-Driven	They may have a client need with little advance notice. Treat them like consultants in this case. (See Chapter 10, "The Consultant Difference.")

6.4. Information about shipments

> **BEST PRACTICE**
>
> Decide in advance what you'll provide to analysts and what you won't. Tell them what this policy is, and make sure everyone in your company understands it. Make sure analysts give you sufficient lead time for this information and tell you how it will be used.

Some research firms are "market watchers" who assess market sizes and product/provider shares. The two largest are Dataquest (part of Gartner) and International Data Corporation. There are smaller firms that focus on individual segments of IT, such as Dell'Oro Group in the U.S. for telecommunications, or Paul Budde in Australia in the same field for that continent and its neighbors. Many founders of these firms previously worked for one of the "big two:" Tam Dell'Oro of Dell'Oro Group, for example, was at Dataquest. These break down the computer and communications industries into a variety of segments and often also look at regional breakdowns around the globe.

Part of the reason they do this is to report how well different firms are doing. This helps financial analysts forecast earnings, and technology buyers choose providers who appear to be winning. (Whether or not this is a good policy is a separate issue.)

Comparing one period's data with that of earlier periods also enables these firms to study the overall growth or shrinkage of market segments. If trends show nobody will buy laptops with less than 1TB storage next year, that's important information to folks who make disk drives, folks who make laptops, folks who sell software and others.

These firms try to publish their analyses as soon as possible after the period they cover. A report on first-quarter sales in an important market segment will typically appear in mid-to-late April. This means they need information within a very short window. Before March 31, it's not available. After mid-April, it's too late. You need procedures in place in advance for getting this information as quickly as possible, putting it in the form the research firms need if necessary, and shipping it out.

There is a reluctance on the part of firms with small or declining sales to share information that will be used for some of these purposes, especially by prospects who want to bet on a "winner." Still, consider this:

- If you don't tell analysts, they'll guess. They purposely guess low. If your market share is small, this may lead them to drop you off tables. If it's dropping, this will make it seem to be dropping faster. This rewards cooperative firms, penalizes the others.

- They can find out if they need to. As with pricing, you can make their job harder but you can't stop them from doing it. Why go to that trouble to offend someone who influences your sales?

- Without good data from all sources, forecasts are worthless. This hurts all providers alike, including your company, since your business planners use these forecasts.

- Many firms use this information only as part of industry-wide or segment-wide aggregates. These firms will agree to use your numbers only as part of totals from which individual providers' sales figures cannot be extracted.

Some firms play a "high-low" game: they don't give the analyst numbers, but respond to analyst guesses until a guess is within an acceptable range of the answer. If you and your management find this acceptable, it won't be new to the analyst. However, unless you head the analyst relations group, don't try it without your manager's knowledge.

We know you can't overturn corporate paranoia and policy on this topic by yourself. Press for the maximum disclosure that your management will allow. One firm developed a relationship with a business school to solve this problem. A team of students was commissioned to estimate numbers for the firm, and its competitors, that the firm itself could not publish. Working with an advisor who knew the firm, the researchers were able to estimate the numbers in a different way from the analysts. By giving these students' data to the analysts, this vendor helped analysts without violating its policy.

What different types of analysts need in shipment/volume information

Research Agenda-Driven	Generally little need. They'll use market watcher data when they need it. Gartner analysts use Garter Dataquest data, their direct competitors tend to use IDC data, others use either or both.
Event-Driven	They can get "market watcher" data, but because their work tends to be done under time pressure, you can help them by supplying it.
Calendar-Driven	This is the basis of their work. Their cycle repeats every quarter and year. Find out what they need and when. Then establish regular procedures to provide it.
Client-Driven	They can get "market watcher" data, but because their work is often done under time pressure, you can help them by supplying it here too.

6.5. Information about the organizational structure

BEST PRACTICE

Focus on specific types of infrastructure information that demonstrate how

> the organization is positioned to accomplish its strategic and revenue objectives, weeding out any that do not meet analysts' needs.

Analysts don't care directly about your organization or who's managing it. They do, however, care about what your organization means to them, their work, and their clients:

- Suppose you announce a strategic business unit for hydroponic circuits. If this new SBU reports to your CEO and is headed by a well-known hydroponics circuit pioneer whom you recruited from a competitor at a great cost, it suggests a serious commitment. If it reports to the head of janitorial services and is run by someone whose previous job was assistant cafeteria supervisor, it suggests something else.

- Suppose the manager who spearheaded your successful entry to hydroponic circuits last year has now been named to head your faltering Asian region. What does this mean for its future? Conversely, what would it have meant if the hydroponic circuit venture had been a flop? And what does it bode for your hydroponic circuit SBU? Because of their strategic impact, analysts need to know the reporting structure of your key business units and the backgrounds of the people who head them. They need to know about things that affect your customers, because they advise those customers. Keep them updated on these.

This is an opportunity to sell your company's strengths, but don't overdo it. Analysts don't care where the new manager of your Springfield branch attended school, or even if this worthy attended school at all. Unless this person has another claim to fame, such as an Olympic medal, ignore this promotion. This applies to executives, too. Unless your new CFO is important for a specific reason, such as bringing stability to a previously chaotic finance situation, most analysts don't care about him or her.

The second type of organizational information analysts want is how it impinges on their clients (your customers). Is your sales force organized by geography, industry, some other basis, or a combination? Tell them, so they can inform their clients about the kinds of salespeople those clients will deal with. A salesperson who sells to everyone in the client's locale will have one set of strengths and weaknesses. One who covers the client's industry in ten U.S. states and half of Canada will have a different set. Your prospects want to know what to expect, analysts want to tell them, and it's not a secret.

Tell analysts when this changes, too. If the sales organization moves from a regional to an industry focus, ends direct sales to small customers to eliminate channel conflict with resellers, or decentralizes technical support to its branches, tell them this too.

That is because each of these moves has implications. The sales relationship will improve for some customers, stay about the same for most, and perhaps get a bit worse for a few. Analysts must figure this out to write informed reports and advise clients. Their ability to do so depends on understanding these aspects of your organization.

The third type of organizational information they need is about the analyst relations function, since it affects their own work. Who's in it? Who heads it? Where does this person report? How does it support analysts in different regions, specialists in different technologies, access to your various divisions? Tell them all about this. (This isn't in the table below, because it applies equally to all analysts and firms.)

What different types of analysts need in organizational information

Research Agenda-Driven	Usually not a top priority. May need information related to product(s) or service(s) in a report. You will generally have plenty of lead time to meet this need.
Event-Driven	If they're reporting on a major reorganization, all you can get on people and divisions involved. Otherwise, usually little need.
Calendar-Driven	Generally little need for this type of information.
Client-Driven	Depending on client needs, perhaps sales force information.

6.6. Information about competitive positioning

> **BEST PRACTICE**
> Present your assessment of your competitive position to support your announcement, strategy, or marketing programs. Be objective, find out what your audience has written on this topic, and address disagreements with them frankly.

Even companies with dominant market shares, such as Microsoft in desktop operating systems in 2013, have competition. It may come from unexpected sources, such as the emergence of the Web and the cloud as a computing platform. It may appear in the form of inertia: To those who would have to pay to upgrade, replace applications, and train users in a new and different interface, Windows XP and 7 compete with Windows 8.

Analysts need to understand your competitive position because they have to tell their clients how different products, all of which meet the same general user need, compare. In most cases this does not mean calling one "good" and another "bad." It means identifying strengths and weaknesses of each one, then identifying the types of users for whom each is best suited.

They also need to understand your competitive position to predict how the industry will evolve. This includes predicting who will rise and who will fall. This is not always pleasant, especially if they see your firm as falling. There is an element of self-fulfilling prophecy here: since negative analyst forecasts can have a chilling effect on customer purchases, companies may fall because analysts say they will. (Providers in this situation can console themselves by noting that even the best analysts sometimes miss a call.)

While analysts have to understand your competitive position, some don't want to hear about it from you. They say "It's my job to figure that out. That's what my clients pay me for!" Most, however, are interested. Even if they do their own analysis when they get back to their offices, they want to hear what you have to say about it because:

- It gives them a starting point.

- It tells them something about the thoroughness of your market research and the realism with which your firm approaches its markets.

- They may use parts with which they agree. (Cut-and-paste is their friend.)

Don't expect analysts to agree with everything your firm says, or to present it as their own. They know your speakers will "spin" your position. Just don't overdo the spin to the point that you lose credibility.

Before explaining your position to an analyst who writes about your firm, read what he or she has written about it. Don't repeat it as part of your (or your firm's) presentation: analysts know what they wrote and will resent this waste of their time. Don't rebut it point by point, either: you're not there for a debate, though some analysts enjoy the intellectual pleasure of debating. But your presentation should reflect awareness of what the analyst has said. If you feel he or she is seriously off target in key respects, say why you feel that way and what evidence you have for your position.

Analysts are especially negative about feature checklists (except their own, of course). You know these: features down the left, products at the top, and a check where the product has the feature. They're used from tents to TV sets. The column for the vendor who created the checklist is dense with checks. The others have a scattered few.

Analysts don't like these because each vendor picks features to make its product look good. A basic word processor capability such as "Supports italic type" looks no more important in a feature list than a trivial one such as "Can position toolbar on left or right." They're also subject to interpretation: a hub could be unchecked for "Supports 16 Ports" when it supports 20, if 16 isn't a valid configuration. Unless there's a generally accepted list of features that every product of this type should have, such as Codd's twelve criteria for relational databases, leave checklists at home when you visit analysts.

Analysts are more sophisticated than sales prospects in seeing through semi-trickery. It reflects negatively on a vendor who uses it. To take an example from the automotive world, consider Nissan's commercials which cite a research firm's report that it has the best V-6 engine. The average person considering Nissan and BMW would think this means that Nissan's six-cylinder engine is better (in that firm's opinion) than BMW's.

An analyst, however, would know that BMW uses an inline 6 (I-6), not a V-6, and was therefore not in the comparison group. This analyst would probably find the Nissan ad deceptive, though not exactly incorrect. Since most car buyers don't use analysts, analyst reaction to a Nissan commercial probably won't hurt Nissan sales. Your prospects, however, ask information technology analysts what to buy. You don't want analysts to associate your firm with deceptive tactics.

Finally: telling analysts about your position does not mean Marketing 101 on topics they follow. Most find this a waste of time or even a professional insult. Say enough to establish the basis on which you developed your plans and figure your position, but don't go into agonizing detail. Ask yourself: "How much about this do they already understand, if they belong in this room in the first place?"

What different types of analysts need in competitive information

Research Agenda-Driven	As much as possible in the area of their report, as most reports compare multiple providers. You'll have time to assemble this.
Event-Driven	Very helpful when they have to analyze an announcement in a short time frame.
Calendar-Driven	Seldom much need, but lists of competitive products can help them check their market segmentation.
Client-Driven	If they have a specific client need with little advance notice, treat them as consultants.

6.7. Information about technology

> **BEST PRACTICE**
>
> Inventory what your firm has available, especially white papers written by your specialists, and make them available. Don't use scarce resources to have white papers written by outsiders just for analysts/consultants.

Some analysts understand your firm's technology as well as, or better than, your engineers. It would be nice if all did, but sadly that's not the rule. Most understand it pretty well, but have gaps. Those who follow its business use, its markets, or the providers in it, have bigger gaps those who focus on technologies as such.

That being the case, reducing those gaps pays off in several ways:

- The analyst will be grateful for the education.
- The analyst, by understanding your technology better, will understand your products and their merits better.
- Where multiple technologies can meet a need, analysts favor those they understand—and hence the companies who use it.

So, it helps to provide analysts with material explaining your technologies, how they work, and their merits. This material is usually called a *backgrounder* when it's at an elementary level, a *white paper* (the term comes from 19th-century explanations of British foreign policy) when it's deeper.

A white paper, in pure form, is an objective description of what your company does in an area and why. It provides technical information, not a marketing message. Analysts come to white papers to obtain a better understanding of why certain products were developed or why certain services are offered, why trade-offs were made in one way and not another, in a depth that would otherwise require long discussions with specialists. They read them to understand how a product works, since that level of understanding can help them draw conclusions about how it will fit a user need in a new situation. They also use them to learn quickly about new technologies, or technologies that are new to them even if not new overall.

Well-written white papers have high credibility with analysts, though those written by firms that compete directly with a given analyst's firm usually do not. (An analyst from such a firm will think "I could have written a better one," or, if the subject isn't that analyst's field, "My colleague Kim could have written a better one.")

Such documents are usually written by members of your technical staff, or by others with a technical background. They are written for a variety of audiences. Backgrounders are important to the press. Many customers or sales prospects, especially those with a technical bent, want the understanding that comes from a white paper. They are also used for internal training and may appear in company-sponsored or independently published magazines and journals.

There is little you can do to make sure that such documents are written, besides adding your voice to the others asking for them and perhaps suggesting an analyst who can help if someone says they need a capable writer. Then, keep on top of what is being written and be sure analysts know about it. Some won't need it or want it. Some will. Those who do will appreciate it.

The Web is a good way to disseminate white papers. With it, analysts can get them whether or not you're on the job. (Aside from scheduled absences, which you can arrange coverage for, analysts often work irregular hours and can be anywhere in the world, so they can be at work when you're asleep and may observe different holidays.)

The biggest drawback of white papers is that abuse has tarnished their reputation. During the 1990s, providers realized that white papers have more credibility than marketing materials. They created materials that looked like white papers and were called white papers, but were thinly disguised sales material. This eventually made all white papers suspect. Analysts will still look at them, though. If they read yours and think "this one is for real," your firm will gain respect.

What different types of analysts need in background information

Research Agenda-Driven	Probably don't need much, since analysts who write reports generally know a lot about the subject, but can use explanations of innovative technology.
Event-Driven	Analysts who report on announcements are often called on to cover a wide range of topics, so these may need these on short notice.
Calendar-Driven	Seldom much need here, though many analysts in these firms enjoy learning more about the technologies they track.
Client-Driven	Like event-driven analysts, these people are often called on to cover a wide range of topics, so they also may need these on short notice.

6.8. Reference accounts

> **BEST PRACTICE**
>
> Analysts need customer references. Have a list in place of pre-approved references organized for easy access. Don't overwork the same names. Try to include users who had a problem or two which you've fixed.

As the saying goes, the proof of the pudding is in the eating. The proof of an IT product or service is in the using. It has to solve real problems for real customers. Technical elegance, a cutting-edge Web site and top-notch sales reps aren't worth much if it can't.

Analysts therefore want to know what users it solves problems for and how well it solves them. The best way for them to learn this is to talk to those users.

Analysts can find people who use your product. They talk to their clients. They meet users at professional gatherings. They have MIS executive directories. They read articles and call people quoted in them. They Google pages that contain your product name and the term "CIO." The list goes on. They still use providers for references:

- They may be able to find people who use product X, but it's harder to find people who use version A on platform B in industry C and region D. A vendor can do this more easily.

- A provider has access to its entire customer base. An analyst's sources, no matter how much digging he or she does, are more limited.

- A provider can often supply the name and contact information of a person to talk to. With other methods it can take several steps, each involving delays.

- The analyst learns something about the provider by seeing how the request for references is handled and what sort of references are supplied.

- It saves the analyst time.

Therefore, analysts request providers to supply customer names and appreciate them when they are supplied. Specifically, they need:

1. Name of organization.
2. A little background: platform, applications, services, etc., and about the product (version, configuration, time in use, etc.) if those weren't part of the original request.
3. Name and position of individual to contact within the organization, with contact information.

Once they have this, they'll call the reference and ask questions. These usually start with procurement: What were your requirements? Which products did you consider? Why did you pick this one? They'll ask how well the product performs: Is it reliable? Responsive? Easy to install, to use? Well supported? What problems have you had, if any? How were they resolved? What features do you use? Not use? How well does it meet the expectations you had when you chose it? (This is for products. They'll ask similar questions in services.) The call will probably take 30 to 60 minutes. They may say at the beginning that the individual's and firm's names will not be used. Or, they'll give the user the option to speak for the record or anonymously.

Analysts don't always call all the names they get. They ask for more than they need, knowing that some people will have left their firms, be out of town, or be unable to participate. They call until they have what they need, then they stop. If you tell a customer "Analyst H.B. may call you as a reference," be sure to explain that H. B. also may *not* call.

Sometimes, analysts ask for names of sales prospects who did *not* buy your product or service, so they can find out why. This helps them get a balanced picture. This isn't information that most companies keep readily available. If you're asked for it, you'll have to decide if it's worth the effort to dig it up. (Don't worry about "airing your dirty laundry in public." They'll also ask your competitors about *their* losses. Those will include some of your wins. Overall, things even out.)

Analysts take provider-supplied user names with a grain of salt. Some feel that many reference accounts have received consideration to agree to be used, and cannot be trusted. Others, while not that suspicious, expect the reference account list to be screened to eliminate users with major problems or who are dissatisfied for other reasons. (They're right. It should be.) They still want names. They know that even the happiest customer tries to paint an objective picture. And, even if provider-supplied reference accounts define the "best case" situation, comparing the best case across providers is valuable.

The need for reference accounts also depends on the analyst's field of specialization. Analysts who follow hardware or networking/telecommunications need them less. Analysts who follow software or services need them more. This reflects how well a product can be evaluated on the basis of design, specs and limited exposure, versus needing to live with it for an extended period before being able to assess it.

The content of your reference account database is discussed in Section 11.1.

Verifying names

Confirm reference names before giving them to an analyst. This lets you make sure their contact information is current and that they are still reasonably pleased with your product or service. (Every analyst has talked to references who said "it crashed two weeks ago and they still can't make it work!") It also gives you a chance to spread the burden of talking to analysts across as many customers as possible.

Verifying can mean calling the customer, the sales rep responsible for the account, or both. Start with the sales rep. He or she has a personal interest in the customer relationship. Some may prefer to contact the customer themselves rather than having you do it. They may tell you how to contact the customer if they don't do it themselves. They may even know of a reason the customer shouldn't be contacted, saving time and trouble.

If time is pressing and you can't reach the salesperson, try his or her manager. Third choice is the account's technical support team if it exists. If you can't reach any of these, you may have no alternative but to contact the account directly. If you do this, leave an "audit trail" of voice mails, e-mails or messages documenting your efforts to go through channels, with your deadlines and saying you'll have to contact the account directly if you don't hear back by a certain date and time. This isn't to be arrogant or nasty. You have to do your job. Part of your job is to give analysts reference account information. If you can, though, find a different account in preference to bypassing the sales force.

What different types of analysts need in reference account information

Research Agenda-Driven	Very important. This section applies most strongly here. Many firms won't publish a research report without user comments.
Event-Driven	Including names of beta sites in announcement kits can be helpful, but make sure they're not swamped with calls right after an announcement.
Calendar-Driven	Little or no need.
Client-Driven	Varies with client requirement, but can help. They may have little advance notice of a need, so you may not have much lead time.

6.9. Financial information

Financial information wasn't included in Section 5.3. This isn't a real section, either. Analyst Relations is seldom, if ever, called on to supply this information. It's already available from other sources. Publicly held firms, in the U.S. and most industrialized countries, publish annual and quarterly reports. These are often supplemented by more detailed filings with regulatory authorities. Privately held firms may publish public reports as well, though their requirements to do so are less stringent or non-existent.

Beyond these documents, financial results of major firms are reported in the business press as fast as or faster than AR could disseminate them. And most publicly held companies of any size have an Investor Relations group that provides this information to anyone on request. They don't even care if the requester owns stock in the firm. After all, he or she might buy some.

So, feel free to include financial highlights in analyst communications if you want, especially if they're something to brag about, but don't worry about this. For once, there's something you can let someone else do.

7 | Information channels for reaching analysts

This chapter will cover:

1 Twelve information channels for reaching analysts
2 Each type of analyst's needs for using each channel
3 "Best practices" for providing information via each channel

Chapter 5 gave an overview of the information channels analyst relations programs use. All allow wide variations in how they are put in place. Analyst support can be a part-time job for one person, or a full-time job for a dozen people in the field and another twenty at headquarters. What suits a global firm that is a major player in many segments of the computer industry is wrong for a focused start-up. Here, we look at the major information channels and how you can implement them at your firm.

As you read in Chapter 5, there are twelve major information channels. Some are mandatory for any firm. Others are optional. The content of each varies with the size of your firm and the nature of its products.

Read this chapter in the context of the previous one. The channels covered here are how the groups you support obtain the information discussed there.

Like the previous chapter, this one focuses primarily on analysts. Chapter 10, "The Consultant Difference," suggests when and how a consultant program should use additional or different elements. Where this chapter mentions consultants, the content is identical or nearly so for both groups.

As you plan and implement these building blocks, think of analysts (and consultants) as extensions of your sales force. That may be hard at first. You don't pay them a commission. You can't tell them what to do. They may seem to work against you. But working against you is not their intent. They work for their clients, their firms and themselves.

Analysts should be, and usually are, provider-neutral. No company has a permanent monopoly on the best products or services. It is unrealistic to expect analysts to favor any firm, yours or a competitor, consistently. If they feel it is in their and their clients' interest to give opinions that work against you in a given situation, they will give them. This doesn't mean they're against you. Conversely, if they feel it is in their and their clients' interest to say things that favor you in a given situation, they'll do that. This doesn't mean they will continue to say such things in the future, though you hope they will. The easier it is for them to create favorable opinions of your firm, the more often they will. The most effective way to make it easy is to give them the tools they need to do so, and to convey an attitude that encourages it.

The best way to make analysts work with you is to make them feel part of your team. If you treat them as part of your team, they will feel and act like part of your team. If you treat them as outsiders, they will feel and act like outsiders. If you treat them as prospects, with a negotiation-based relationship, they will feel and act like adversaries.

One guideline transcends all other considerations as you plan your analyst support programs. *Don't start anything you can't follow through on.* Reliability and predictability are vital to trust. Trust is vital to analyst endorsements. As noted earlier, analysts favor a product they know is adequate over one they think might be fantastic. Start-stop programs, no matter how outstanding their first steps are, convey unreliability and unpredictability. The damage this does will outweigh any benefit your firm might obtain from them. (This is related to the momentum concept at the end of Chapter 4.)

The following twelve sections cover the analyst communication building blocks of your program. As you read them, think of them in terms of the analysts your firm must reach (Chapter 1) and what motivates them (Chapter 3). Also, think about what type of analyst relations program your firm needs: building, corrective or sustaining. Consider your firm's resources and existing market programs. Develop a preliminary concept of what you should offer or do in each area. If your firm already has an analyst relations program, write down what should be cut, enhanced, or changed.

The twelve sections on communication channels are followed by one that pulls them together in the context of launching a new product or service.

A note on regional differences

In most respects, information channels are global. There is one regional difference.

All else being equal, analysts in Europe and the rest of the world are hungrier for personal provider contact than are North Americans. (Because of the geographical distribution of the analyst community, research has focused on North America vs. Europe. Limited data suggest that Asian analysts resemble Europeans.) This may be because they get less of it, especially from the North American providers who at this time dominate global IT. It may be that greater time pressure causes North Americans to accept impersonal communication. It may be cultural. In any case, survey after survey has found that Europeans want visits, meetings, analyst days, and social events more than North Americans. North Americans ask for telebriefings and other "get to the point and get off" contacts.

7.1. A central point of contact

> **BEST PRACTICE**
>
> A central contact point for analysts and consultants is vital. This person must see the role as more than just facilitating access, but as developing relationships and driving high-value communications externally and internally. He or she must keep analysts and consultants informed of major ini-

> tiatives, strategy/product updates and key personnel changes, and updated on the status of pending requests and inquiries.
>
> The central contact(s) must know the company's business, market, competition and how its products and services meet customer needs. This aids meaningful discussion and helps identify areas where an analyst could be useful to the firm, adding value to the AR function.

Large organizations are confusing enough to people in them. Imagine how confusing they are to people on the outside who have to figure them out, and who also have to figure out several other comparably complex but different ones. That's the analyst's problem in trying to find information in your firm.

When analysts need information from a firm with no analyst relations program, they pick up the phone or click their "New Message" icon. If they know someone there, they'll contact that person. Otherwise, they'll try a local sales office, corporate HQ or the "info" e-mail address on the corporate Web site. The usual result is frustration as a series of phone transfers or e-mail replies slowly brings them closer to the person with the answer—who is out of town for three weeks. Other outcomes include:

- "I'm sorry, there's nobody here who can help you" after the fourth trip to the main corporate phone number.
- Reaching somebody who has the answer, but is noticeably upset at being interrupted to discuss it with a total stranger.
- Reaching an engineer deep in the R&D organization who e-mails confidential specs of the next release as the quickest way to answer an innocent technical question.

The alternative is a central contact. The person or people who staff this function get information for analysts, arrange meetings and demos, obtain copies of documentation, and do anything else that will enhance the relationship between analysts and your firm, with proper confidentiality procedures.

Most information technology providers therefore designate one or more individuals as primary analyst contacts. Their job is to provide guidance and information, and to manage the other information channels discussed later in this chapter. He or she has a title such as "analyst relations manager," "analyst relations director" (usually where there is a supporting staff) or "analyst liaison" (usually for a member of such a staff.) The title *analyst relations manager* is often used for individual contributors. It means that they manage relationships with analysts, not that they necessarily supervise others.

This person, whom we'll call an analyst liaison, provides a contact for analysts who need something and don't know where to get it. Sometimes analysts are asked to contact the liaison even when they *do* know, since channeling all requests through one point ensures that one person has a full picture of that analyst's contacts. Analysts appreciate such a person. In every industry segment, they consider a central contact one of the most important information channels a provider can provide.

The analyst support team may not arrange demos, meetings, presentations, etc., themselves. They have to know how and through whom they can be arranged. They can then make contact with those parties and stay in touch until the activity is completed to everyone's satisfaction.

Designating one or more analyst liaison(s) is not an added expense. *What an analyst liaison does has to be done anyway.* If an analyst calls, someone has to take the call. Having a person whose job is to take such calls *saves* money by having someone who knows how to do it well and has learned how to do it efficiently. If there is no analyst liaison, this work is spread over many people. Those people were hired to do something else, are paid to do that, do that better, and would rather do that. Identifying an analyst liaison makes the expense visible on someone's budget, but doesn't increase it.

Analyst liaison name(s), phone number(s) and e-mail address(es) should appear in everything your firm sends to analysts: mailings/e-mails, invitations, announcement kits, newsletters (if you have them; see Section 7.9), and answers to inquiries. They should be easily found from the home page of your company's Web site. People who answer your phone at HQ and at every sales office should have them handy. Your sales force and marketing staff should know they exist and how to find them. Voice-mail greetings and e-mail auto-replies should tell analysts of any absence longer than one business day.

Reviewing analyst reports

The analyst support team is responsible for making sure anything analysts write about the company is reviewed for factual content. If you're on top of the analysts who cover your segment of the IT industry, you should know when any of them is preparing a report on you. They will have called you for information, probably spent some time on the phone with one or more product specialists, often have met with you at your offices or theirs. They will tell you what sort of report they're preparing and when it is to appear.

Any reputable research firm will give you a chance to review what they write. This should be a mandatory part of the process. You'll be able to point out factual errors, which they will correct. (They don't want mistakes in reports any more than you do.) You can take issue with their conclusions, but unless you can show that they were based on an error or misunderstanding, you probably won't change their minds.

The catch is that research firms operate on tight schedules. Review time delays report issuance and allows competitors to get theirs out first. You'll probably have very little time for this, often just one business day.

So, line up reviewers ahead of time. The research firm will tell you when a draft will be ready. For products with technical content, get at least two reviewers: one in marketing/management, one in R&D. Prefer people who have spoken or met with the research firm, but if they're not available, find someone else. Make sure they understand the urgency and are ready to drop almost everything when the draft shows up.

Then, make sure these folks know what is needed here. They're not proofreading, copy-editing or debating the merits of green buttons versus blue. It's not their task to say their part of an announcement didn't get enough attention. They should review the draft for errors of fact—your blades support 16 processors, not just 8; you really do have an office in China—and for mistaken conclusions based on such errors. If they want to disagree with anything else, "We feel differently because ..." is OK because it respects the analysts' right to draw any conclusions they like.

Organizational issues

Small firms don't need a full-time analyst liaison. The task can be assigned to a marketing support professional in addition to that person's other duties. What's important is to make sure someone knows it's his or her job to work with analysts. As analyst activity and the firm grow a full-time person can be assigned, then perhaps two or three.

A new firm should establish an analyst contact point as soon as it hires its first marketing support person, if not sooner. That recognizes that analysts *will* call, whether or not anyone is assigned to work with them. Given this fact, calls and e-mails should go to someone who expects them and knows what to do.

A typical high-tech firm assigns a full-time analyst contact when it reaches an annual revenue level of about $100 million, though firms fall in a wide range on either side of this figure. From there up, the number of people in analyst relations grows more slowly than corporate revenue. Its full-time equivalent headcount typically doubles each time revenue grows by a factor of 6. Thus, the typical $600 million firm would have two people on this job; the typical $3.6 billion firm, four. A bit of interpolation says that three people correspond to a size of about $1.5 billion. It's impossible to be more precise than this since so much depends on the firm. For example, a firm with products in many segments of information technology might have to work with more analysts, and would therefore have a larger analyst relations staff, than a firm with the same annual revenue but where that revenue all comes from one segment of IT.

We'll discuss where analyst relations can fit in the corporate org chart in Chapter 13.

Qualifications

What sort of person is best suited to this job? Analyst liaisons should have as many of these characteristics as possible:

- A personality that enjoys working with different people, making new contacts on a regular basis, and keeping in touch with dozens of people regularly.

- A positive attitude toward a supporting role: one in which he or she solves problems for other people, to facilitate their work.

- An understanding of business concepts to understand where analysts fit in the industry "food chain."

- Communication ability, orally and in writing.

- Willingness to work hard and spend time on the road.

- An understanding of the firm, how it works, and its people. (This develops over time.)

- Enough technical savvy to understand what technical questions mean and relay them without misinterpretation or distortion.

Should analyst liaisons be technical experts in their own right? On the one hand, such people can often answer questions directly, without going to the R&D staff. When it's time to call in the real experts, a technical background can save time and reduce internal miscommunication.

On the other hand, knowledge gets out of date. Such people may give wrong answers without knowing it because things have changed since they worked on them. Engineers and programmers have succeeded in AR, but it's not required. Analysts don't expect it.

What different types of analysts need in a central contact

Research Agenda-Driven	Insight into the organization to set up teleconferences and meetings at the level of detail required for in-depth reports
Event-Driven	Proactive announcement information, ideally in pre-briefings tailored to each analyst's professional orientation and focus
Calendar-Driven	Ability to put a standard process in place to get the required information quarter after quarter, year after year
Client-Driven	Rapid responsiveness to unpredictable needs

7.2. Access to your executives

> **BEST PRACTICE**
>
> You must provide access to executives as required, primarily to discuss strategy and obtain a sense of your firm's ability to execute it. Exposure to top management can result in positive relationships. However, executives must be protected from excessive demands.

Sometimes an analyst has to talk to the "big cheese."

Perhaps she needs an authoritative view of corporate strategy.

Perhaps he needs to know how the provider will respond to a competitive development, a new technology, or a government regulation.

Perhaps she needs to understand the corporate commitment to a business area.

There are times only the president, or someone in the president's inner circle, will do. Responsiveness in such a situation comes down to making the right executive available to the analyst.

Analysts find executive access important. They rate it as one of the top three information channels in importance. However, its importance varies with analyst orientation. Analysts whose work is strategy-oriented place it at the top of their list. Those who focus more on products tend to say "let me talk to people who *really* know something." The type of person an analyst wants to talk to depends, in other words, on the information that analyst needs.

Analysts are realistic about executive availability. They won't call Virginia Rometty at IBM or Steve Ballmer at Microsoft over a detail. They know executives have things to do besides waiting for analysts to call. They do, however, expect executives to be aware of analysts' importance in the industry and to their firm's sales. They expect executives to understand situations in which people further down the hierarchy won't do. And they expect executives, in those situations, to make time available to talk with them.

For executives to be accessible, they must understand analysts' role in the industry and the impact even a short discussion can have on their opinions. They must know that any analyst of importance influences more business than the firm does with its top customer. Therefore, the analyst deserves the attention and priority this customer would get. If an executive would free up time for a phone call with your largest customer, given reasonable notice, that executive ought to free up time for an important analyst too.

This is not analyst arrogance. It's an objective fact. Executives who don't understand this make analysts wonder what else they don't understand. Having people who influence customers decisions wonder what your executives don't understand is not helpful.

The first contact between analyst and executive often takes place during a scheduled visit, analyst program or teleconference (see sections 7.4–7.7 below). Once a relationship exists, some analysts will contact executives directly. If one doesn't want this, he or she can make this clear (politely; most executives know how to be polite) at the first offense, asking the analyst to schedule contact through analyst support channels. As long as those channels (you?) are responsive and meet requests without undue delay, most analysts will comply.

Occasionally, analysts will ask to speak with an executive for no reason, perhaps to stroke the analyst's ego via "I got to talk to Ms. X today!" More likely, the analyst saw her name in the paper as general manager of your Widgets Group and doesn't know anyone else there. Either way, unless this is an important influencer with an ego that needs stroking (they exist) Ms. X is the wrong person for the call.

The chance of this is one reason some executives want analyst requests filtered. If you get a request for contact that doesn't appear justified, you can say you *could* get Ms. X on the phone, but "with all due respect to her, she doesn't know a thing about how our widget works with HTML5, and she'd say so herself. Why don't I set you up with the product manager? She'd have to ask him what to say anyhow. This way you'll get it direct. If you still have questions [you know the analyst won't!] call me back and we'll take it from there." Properly phrased, such an offer is hard to turn down.

Executive Attitudes

Executives below the president/CEO level take their cue from the top in terms of availability to analysts. If the "head honcho" understands analysts and their value, the others will follow suit. If this person refers to analysts as "slimebags" in the competition's pocket, that will be copied.

If executives aren't fully aware of analysts and their place in the industry, an analyst liaison can't just waltz into their offices and complain. Education must be slow and steady. It can consist of actions such as:

- Start with requests to meet with analysts whom you know are personable and non-confrontational. (Analysts with a provider clientele tend to be less confrontational than those who serve mostly users.) Make sure the meeting has a topic the executive is qualified to discuss. Strategic issues are usually good candidates, if the analyst has a real interest in them and is reasonably current on their published aspects.

- When this analyst writes something positive about your firm later, send the executive a copy with a note of thanks for his or her contribution to the favorable "ink."

- Send him or her press clippings or reports in which an analyst says something favorable about an executive of a competing firm. Mention that the competitor's executives spend a lot of time with analysts and you must "fight fire with fire."

- Give the executive more opportunities to talk with analysts in groups or one-on-one.

Most analysts are intelligent. They understand the issues executives deal with. They can often offer insights and suggestions that will make the executive's job easier. Exposure will lead to comfort and mutual respect. Using analyst insight this way has two benefits:

1. For the executives, the benefit of the analyst's insight into industry issues.
2. For the analyst, the feeling that "this firm cares about me."

Telephone programs

Two useful structured ways for executives to connect with analysts are *buddy programs* and *round robin calls*.

In a buddy program, each participating executive has a small group of analysts with whom to stay in touch on a regular basis. This includes proactive calls about once a month, being the person to give these analysts a "heads-up" about upcoming news, and being available within reason for telephone or e-mail contact. For such a program, choose analysts for common interests with the executives in question.

In round robin calling, the responsibility for calling key analysts rotates among executives. Less of a personal relationship is created, but the analyst may get a better view of your firm as a whole, a personality conflict doesn't create a problem that needs resolution, and nobody is stuck forever with an analyst who's a pain in the neck (or lower).

Both of these require willing executives. If your CEO sets an example, others will follow. Otherwise, you'll have to work with those who want to work with you.

Sitting In

In some firms the analyst liaison sits in on in-person or telephone conversations between analysts and executives. This has several purposes:

1. To know what the analyst was told, without extra work on anyone else's part.
2. As a result, to enable the analyst liaison to brief others about what the analyst has already been told prior to future meetings.
3. To take notes, so the executive can focus on the conversation.
4. For the analyst liaison to follow up on action items without a separate request or introducing an additional, error-prone step into the communication process.
5. To protect executives, who may not be used to dealing with analysts and their penetrating questions, from being drawn into discussions they'll regret later. An analyst liaison who recognizes the signals can cut off a line of questioning. (The liaison may have to "take the heat" later from the analyst for this, but that's part of the job.)
6. To ensure consistency in what different people tell analysts, or, if this is not possible without embarrassing on-the-spot disagreements, to resolve differences later.

Despite these reasons for sitting in on conversations, some executives don't like it. It can inhibit free discussion, no matter how well its reasons are explained. One or both parties may feel they're not totally trusted. It makes scheduling more difficult, since three people must be available at the same time (and, for in-person meetings, in the same place). Finally, many cultures teach that listening to other people's conversations is rude.

Ask each executive if he or she minds your listening in. Give the above reasons and others that come to mind. If he or she refuses, there's not much you can do. Arrange for a short debriefing later to learn what areas were covered and if there's any follow-up to handle.

Some firms require analyst liaison participation in all contacts. If yours does, you're fortunate. However, it can be difficult to enforce such a policy with executives. You or your manager may have to take this up with the executive suite if you see problems here.

What different types of analysts need in executive access

Research Agenda-Driven	An executive meeting is a common and valuable part of writing an in-depth report on a provider and its products, or about an area that includes such products.
Event-Driven	Executive statements about the strategy that led to a new product/service, or answers to questions about it, may be required.
Calendar-Driven	Seldom any need, but may help mobilize resources to meet these analysts' needs.
Client-Driven	Depends on the situation, but may be helpful for reassurance about the stability of strategic directions or commitment to a product area.

7.3. Access to your firm's staff

> **BEST PRACTICE**
>
> In addition to executives, analysts need access to spokespeople such as product managers, marketing managers and technologists. Develop technical and marketing spokespeople who can address specifics of your offerings without violating policies or revealing proprietary information. Keep your list updated as people's responsibilities evolve and to distribute the workload.

Executives are analysts' main source of strategy information. For product information, though, lower-level staff members matter more.

Issues involved with making staff members available to analysts are:

1. **Finding.** Organizations have few executives, many staff members. You must find one who can answer an analyst's questions.
2. **Briefing.** You may have to start from the ABCs: who analysts are, why talk to them. They may not be as tuned in to confidentiality concerns as senior management.
3. **Scheduling.** These folks aren't necessarily busier than executives, but they're often more tightly scheduled with deadlines and meetings that are not under their control.

Many staff members work well with analysts and enjoy the opportunity to interact with them. After a while you'll come to know who these are and get a sense of how often they're willing to help out. This will make your job easier.

Reasons for sitting in on discussions apply more strongly at this level. These people are less likely to be sensitive to the implications of what they say, less likely to be aware of what's proprietary, less able to put their comments into perspective. Fortunately, the "I'm important, you can't tell ME what to do!" attitude that may come up with executives is rare here. Try to sit in (in person or on the phone) whenever possible.

What different types of analysts need in non-executive staff access

Research Agenda-Driven	Intensive meetings during work on a topic related to your firm. At other times, occasional contact to answer client questions.
Event-Driven	In-depth contributions to announcement briefings or pre-briefings, with rapid response to answer questions about the announcement before press and client calls
Calendar-Driven	Focused on those who can provide shipment data, to a lesser extent those who can help them categorize your product
Client-Driven	Rapid response to questions asked on behalf of clients

7.4. Visits by your firm to analysts

> **BEST PRACTICE**
>
> In-person meetings with analysts are an important way to start relation-ships, and are often the best way to convey specific information. Go on tours when you have a reason to do so, customize your agenda for each firm you visit, and allow time for genuine interaction. Conversely, invite analysts and consultants to visit you when they need information that can-not be obtained in a more time-efficient way.

In-person contact between analysts and members of your organization has a "stroking" effect: it makes analysts feel you care about them. It helps establish a relationship that will pay off over and over. Some things are hard to do at a distance, even with interactive multimedia. Therefore, meetings are important.

Since you can't brief every relevant analyst at your events or theirs, from time to time you must "hit the road" and visit them. Plan a regular visit schedule, at least once a year to major firms. These can coincide with an announcement, which makes a natural dis-cussion topic. (See Section 7.12 for announcement-related activities.) If analysts are on a calendar schedule, tying visits to the previous year's or quarter's results works well.

Meetings can also be held at your facilities. (They can also be at a neutral site such as a hotel, but most meetings between providers and analysts are at the offices of one or the other.) Reasons for meeting at the analyst's office include:

- Saves the analyst time and money.
- Analyst staff less fatigued from travel.
- Can reach more analysts than could visit the provider. This is important where several analysts cooperate on a report, or where your firm works in several practice areas.
- Provider staff less likely to be interrupted.

Conversely, reasons for meeting at the provider's facilities include:

- Provider personnel less fatigued from travel.
- Can involve more provider employees than could visit the analyst. This includes those on the agenda and specialists who can be pulled in on short notice.
- Can show facilities and equipment that are impractical to transport.
- Analysts get "the smell of the place," a sense of your firm that no meeting in the research firm's conference room can provide.
- Analysts less likely to be interrupted.
- The meeting takes place when the analyst wants it, not when the provider goes on tour or is in the area. Analyst tours driven by an announcement are appropriate for analysts whose work is driven by industry events, but may not meet the needs of others.

As a rule, analysts prefer to have providers visit them. This is primarily to save time, which is scarcer than money. There are three major exceptions:

1. When the provider is a client and the trip is part of client support.
2. When an analyst needs specific information, access to people, access to equipment, etc., that are impractical to bring to the analyst.
3. When analysts don't work at the firm's office. If they have to go somewhere, they might as well visit the provider.

The section after this one (7.5) is devoted to analyst visits to your facilities. The rest of this section is for when you and your colleagues are the ones who get on the plane.

How often should you visit a research firm? Once a year is usually enough. More than twice a year is never called for. If you have a major announcement, a visit centered on it can be added, but you should know about really big ones far enough in advance not to make a regular update visit within a month or two on either side. After the tour you can continue contact by phone or e-mail, since each participant will then have a sense of who is on the other side of the connection.

Factors to consider in planning a tour

Consider these items in planning a tour:

- **Which firms to visit.** Select firms who influence your users, are important to your strategy, influence trends in your markets, or in whose good graces you want to be for any other reason(s).

- **Geography.** Take advantage of local concentrations of research firms in areas such as the Boston area, southern Connecticut, "Silicon Valley" in California, along the Thames Valley west of London, or Amsterdam. Ideally, visit firms on both U.S. coasts and in Europe. (If you want to go further afield or your markets justify it, there are analyst clusters in Sydney, Singapore, and a few other places.)

  Many analysts work at remote offices or at home. If you can't schedule your meeting for a day when key "targets" will be in the office, arrange for a remote hookup. (Firms may do this as a normal procedure if they have many telecommuters.)

- **Participants.** A group of three or four is usually about right. Include an analyst liaison, an executive or senior marketing person, and a subject matter expert. If you'll visit several firms, you may have to travel with more because one size does not fit all. Trying to cover a subject area with people who don't fit is penny-wise and pound-foolish. If you bring a large group, it's OK to leave some out of a meeting: you don't want to overwhelm your hosts.

- **Materials.** Analysts will need copies of your presentations. If you'll use a computer projector, bring your own as insurance against the research firm's being out of order or not working with your computer. Many models cost and weigh no more than a laptop.

  Review materials in advance for analyst suitability with minimal hype. Prepare a slide set for each firm you plan to visit. Even if their content is identical, the title slide and footers should identify the research firm and give the date of the meeting.

Follow up by giving analysts soft copy of these files. Not only are they more likely to be used if they are on the firm's intranet, but some analysts will import them into meeting reports. Flash drives with your firm's logo are inexpensive in quantity, make nice gifts, are easier to carry than piles of paper, and can include additional information on the topic of your visit.

- **Training.** See Section 11.6 on training speakers to talk to analysts. It will help cure them of the compulsion to use all their slides. Having a dialogue is more important than going over the API of every module in Release 8.2. (Analysts who really need to know what every API in Release 8.2 does won't be bashful about asking.)

- **Closing.** Ask the analysts what they think of whatever you discussed. Is there is anything they expected to hear that they didn't? What would they say if a reporter called them tomorrow? If the answer is negative, don't put them on the list of analysts you give the press. You can't stop reporters from calling them, but you don't have to encourage it! (Make sure PR takes them off their list of briefed analysts, too.)

- **Follow-up.** After the tour:
  - •• Thank analysts for their time again by e-mail or on the phone.
  - •• Find out if there is any more information they need.
  - •• Take care of any action items.
  - •• Track their reports and press quotes to see how your information was used.

What analysts don't like about provider visits

Analysts aren't always thrilled about these visits. Some call them "seagull tours:" the provider flies in, drops something, and flies away with no further contact. Assuming you know better than to do this, their biggest other complaints about provider visits are:

1. They take place on the provider's schedule.
2. They follow the provider's agenda.

There isn't much you can do about the schedule. If you're going to bundle three VPs onto a plane, you'll make sure they visit all the analysts they can. Some of those analysts might have preferred a different time. That's life. If they can't meet, they can't. Don't press too hard. Two things can happen if you do. One is that you still won't have a meeting. In this case, you've upset them to no avail. The other is that you'll have a grudging "mercy meeting." That can be worse.

You can, however, do a lot about the agenda:

1. Ask the research firm what they want to hear. If there will be several analysts in the meeting, ask the most senior. Many firms have guidelines ready to e-mail.
2. Ask your speakers to focus on what these analysts need—no matter what they'd like to cover, what their prepared materials are on, or what they'll cover with other firms on that trip. Confirm that their talk is on topic for each firm when you review it.
3. Allow ample time for Q&A. Interacting is more important than getting through 80 slides. (Some people even suggest not bringing slides to a meeting at all, unless they are specifically requested, but that great a departure from what speakers are used to

can make them uncomfortable. You don't want your speakers to be uncomfortable.)

An option is to go to a city near many analyst firms, get a hotel conference room, and invite analysts to visit you there. This makes the trip more efficient for the your firm, as you don't have to spend time shuttling among offices. It also allows you to set up systems that are not easily portable, perhaps involving a server and four laptops on a LAN. In terms of analyst time, this is almost as good as going to their office.

The major concern here is that hotel conference rooms are not as hospitable as research firm offices. Furthermore, analysts are more likely to arrive late or leave early when a meeting is at a hotel. We recommend this only if time is extremely tight or if demos can't be set up as easily as logging into a Web site or opening a laptop. Otherwise, visiting analysts in their offices is worth it for the relationship.

What different types of analysts need in visits from providers

Research Agenda-Driven	The detailed information they need for reports is usually better obtained by their visiting you, timed to match their research. Visits to them can remind them of your interest in them and keep them aware of how you might fit into future research.
Event-Driven	An important way they get information to analyze announcements. Visits should ideally be before the announcement, to allow for answers to questions by people who must be contacted after the meeting.
Calendar-Driven	Help establish relationships for smooth procedures to get shipment and related data. Also helpful when products change sufficiently to enter or leave tabulation categories.
Client-Driven	Good for establishing relationships that will permit rapid response later as needed.

7.5. Analyst visits to your firm

> **BEST PRACTICE**
>
> See "Best Practice" nugget of the previous section. Invite analysts to visit you when they need information that can't be obtained, in another, more time-efficient, way.

These visits are the counterpart of analyst tours: instead of your going to them, they come to you. This happens when they have a specific information need that doesn't coincide with an announcement or another reason for you to go on the road.

Analysts may visit you for the three reasons given in the previous section, plus these:

4. The analyst flew in to visit many providers. If you're in an area with a concentration of computer firms, analysts visit it periodically to meet with as many providers as possible. Prior contact can get you on their itinerary even if they wouldn't visit you otherwise.

5. The provider invited the analyst and it seemed reasonable to go.

6. Some analysts, especially those who work from home, prefer to visit providers. As with many other things, analysts will tell you what they prefer.

Arranging a visit by analysts to your facilities differs from arranging an agenda for visiting the analyst in at least three ways:

1. They're the only analyst firm on the agenda. You don't have to meld the needs of several firms into a program that can be handled with one group of people, etc.

2. You have more flexibility in choosing your firm's participants, since you can use people who can't leave the office for a tour.

   This lets you customize an agenda more than you could if you were visiting the analyst. Since analysts often visit because they need something they can't get from a road trip, this works out well. However, expect to spend more time working your way through Marketing and R&D to find the perfect people.

3. You have to handle the logistics—conference rooms, coffee and snacks, and putting their name on the welcome board in the lobby.

Many firms have a visitor center to organize and host visits. These usually serve sales prospects and customers, but can handle other audiences as well. Its services come in handy when analysts come for a general briefing. When the focus is on technical details, an R&D conference room may be a better choice. Analysts who care about technology like rubbing shoulders with engineers and programmers in their pizza-box-strewn lairs.

In these days of wearing T-shirts and shorts to the office, tell the visitors what your dress code is. If it varies from day to day, as in "casual Friday," tell them what it will be when they visit. The intent isn't to make them blend in, but to avoid embarrassment if they find themselves out of step (either way) with everyone else. This is especially important with visitors from other countries, who may be used to different practices.

Hospitality is an element of these visits. An executive welcome is usually in order. Depending on the length of the visit, a meal is often appropriate. It's also a nice touch to provide the visitor(s) with the use of a telephone, or at least a private location for mobile calls, and facilities to check e-mail (especially if your internal Wi-Fi isn't unprotected).

Don't stretch a visit longer than necessary. Hosts may think "They came way out here. We have to make it worth their while. Let's set up twenty meetings, serve lunch, take them to dinner and show them we're great hosts." Twenty meetings, lunch, etc., may be perfect. They also may *not* be, especially when analysts are in your area to meet with several vendors and want to fit you in. Don't fall into "great host" mode automatically. Ask the visitors what they want to cover and how much time it will take to cover it. Your estimate may end not match theirs exactly, but don't pad it to a day when an hour is called for.

Who picks up the tab?

Should you pay for analysts to visit your firm?

There are two issues: paying for their *time* and reimbursing their *travel expenses*. Paying for analysts' time, whether in cash or by using inquiry time that your firm has bought as part of a research subscription, is not appropriate for a briefing. Analysts allocate some unbillable time each year to learn about firms and products. This visit is part of that. They expect it to benefit their work. If they didn't, they wouldn't come.

If a meeting is part of consulting for your firm, it is billable to that engagement and covered by their fee.

Paying for travel expenses may be appropriate if a visit is in lieu of your visiting the analyst. Your firm would have to buy plane tickets and a hotel room for someone. These cost the same either way. (If you're worried about an analyst lacking cost-consciousness, perhaps using a more expensive airline to earn elite frequent flyer status, get tickets through a travel agency that knows your travel policies. As long as these policies are reasonable, analysts can hardly object.)

However, lack of expense reimbursement is seldom really a factor in an analyst visit. The more critical issue is usually time out of the office—away from client calls, away from colleagues, not producing as much. Expense reimbursement doesn't address this.

Exceptions to this generalization:

1. Some small research firms must, in fact, watch every penny.
2. Some firms use travel budgets to control the amount of time analysts spend on the road. Their general policies aren't always right for each individual analyst, but every analyst is still bound by them. (Exceptions usually require the approval of a senior manager and are more hassle than most analysts usually want to go to.) If reimbursement makes a visit practical, some analysts will come who otherwise will not.

If you reimburse travel expenses, make sure this isn't seen as an inappropriate incentive which your firm expects to be repaid by positive coverage, or as a precedent for the future or for other analysts. Partial reimbursement can be a good compromise.

Conversely, some research firms have policies against expense reimbursement because they're concerned with the appearance of impropriety. These tend to be firms that get most of their revenue from users.

Also, reimbursement practices differ in different geographic areas. European analysts usually expect providers to cover their travel expenses, especially if they're traveling to another country. North Americans, under identical circumstances, generally don't.

What different types of analysts need in meetings at your facilities

Research Agenda-Driven	This is how they get much of their information for reports. Since they have a budget for preparing each report, no reimbursement should be expected.
Event-Driven	You may want to invite key analysts to learn about announcements. If so, travel expense reimbursement will often be appropriate.
Calendar-Driven	This is seldom necessary unless an analyst is so far off the beaten path that he or she is never included in your own tours. If the visit is instead of being visited, expense reimbursement may be appropriate.
Client-Driven	Often necessary to get detailed information in a hurry. Since their client is paying for their work, reimbursement is never required.

7.6. "Analyst Days:" multi-firm briefings

> **BEST PRACTICE**
>
> These are a time-efficient way to reach and develop relationships with more analysts than you could otherwise, and are expected of major providers. Provide one-on-one time with executives and senior specialists, contact with users and partners, and a chance to see your latest products.

If analysts know you, they'll feel comfortable with you and will trust you more than if they didn't. Meetings for analysts to learn about your firm and its products and meet some of its people are an excellent way to create this comfort. They are particularly important for smaller research firms. You can't visit every research firm that exists, or even all that cover your markets, but you can invite them all to multi-firm events. Smaller ones know that their size doesn't justify personal briefings and are likely to show up. (Some small firms are influential beyond their size and are exceptions to this generalization.)

Why have an analyst briefing event? Because:

- You can reach more analysts than you can in a private meeting
- You can compress the impact of multiple visits to a shorter time frame
- You can get undivided attention for longer than you could in a meeting
- You can justify more resources than you could for a meeting with one firm

These are all good reasons. Before scheduling an event, know which of them (or many others) are *yours* for *this* one. Also, be clear on your objectives. Possibilities include:

- Building relationships with analysts
- Conveying strategy information or perspective
- Conveying product information
- Building corporate or product credibility
- Meeting analyst expectations that providers of your stature will hold such events

While all these can be achieved via an event, *they cannot all be achieved with the same event*. You must choose your primary objective. It won't be the subject of the whole event—a product-oriented event will include some strategy sessions and will help build relationships—but it guides your focus.

To benefit from an event, you need an audience whose size and quality will justify its cost. This means a large number of senior people from a wide area, despite these barriers:

- Analysts are busy. They won't come just for good food and a pleasant time.
- In today's economy, many firms watch travel costs closely.

- The value of demos isn't what it used to be, as many of today's products can be demonstrated via the Web or (for software) shipped to analysts on a CD or provided as a download, for them to install and use themselves.

- Analysts from major firms know you'll visit them within the next few months.

- Many analysts are reluctant to ask questions in front of their competitors.

- Specialized analysts may find only some of your sessions of interest.

- If you invite financial analysts or the press, industry analysts will be less interested in attending. (A few like these interactions, though.)

Once you know your objective, determine the message you want the attendees to take away. That you're a technology leader? Your executives have strategic vision? Customers love your support? Your products are easy to install and use? Your firm keeps its promises? All these and more may be true. You could build an agenda around any or all. But, if you try to give them equal time, you'll end up with little to show for your efforts.

The greatest value of analyst get-togethers is to give background information efficiently to many people at once, to provide an opportunity for one-on-one meetings without imposing an undue travel burden on your executives, and to provide a comfortable environment in which to start a relationship between an analyst and your firm. Therefore, focus on agenda items that provide these.

Conversely, these meetings are not good places for "pressware." Don't give material that could be found on your Web site, except as a brief introduction to a deeper discussion. The emphasis should always be on value that can't be obtained elsewhere. Demos, especially accompanied by an opportunity to interact, try the system, and ask in-depth questions of experts standing by for the purpose, are one way to provide such value.

Some analysts are reluctant to ask questions in front of competitors, lest they disclose what they're thinking and lose a competitive edge. One can argue with their logic, but winning a debate won't change this feeling. That being the case, provide for one-on-one discussions between analysts and members of your firm. These should include executives, for strategy analysts or those who just want to meet one, and technical experts.

This reluctance to speak up is more of an issue in North America than in Europe. European analysts tend to be more collegial. (Sadly, this attitude may be changing, especially in the U.K. as its analyst community grows.) Europeans *will* often ask their best questions in front of competitors, knowing that those competitors will likewise ask theirs, that nobody has a monopoly on insight, and that the net result benefits everyone present.

Some of this difference may be due to cultural factors. Some may be due to the generally smaller size of European firms (or European branches of U.S. firms), which reduces the opportunities to interact with colleagues in the same practice area. Some of it may result from a dearth of visits by U.S. providers, causing Europeans to take advantage of any available opportunity to meet with them. Whatever the reasons, you should expect a more positive response to multi-firm briefings in Europe than you'll get in North America.

Even if you provide opportunities for individual meetings, many North American analysts won't come. Those from major firms, or with strong individual reputations, prefer private meetings and can usually get them. They'll come to a broader one only if it offers a chance to meet with executives who wouldn't otherwise be available or another concrete reason.

Location

In setting up a meeting for longer than a day, it's tempting to pick an attractive site where attendees can combine business and pleasure.

Tempting, yes. Tempting, as a way to attract analysts who might not come just for the content but would be lured by the combination of content and other activities. And tempting, as a way to give your own colleagues (and, let's be honest, yourself) a trip to a garden spot at corporate expense.

The desirability of such a venue depends on who you want to attract. Junior analysts will vie for the "paid vacation" even if they have to attend a few sessions. Most experienced ones say "Been there, done that." If they want a holiday, they'd rather be with family or friends than with you—no matter how well you get along. They're busy and don't want to take three days for content that could be conveyed in one. You may get some, if your meeting happens to hit a rare slow spot in their schedule and the location is attractive to them, but a fancy location is generally not a big plus to this group. (Not everyone golfs, not everyone loves wine.)

Your senior executives may differ, perhaps recalling analyst events of the 1990s. Back then, major and not-so-major high-tech firms would "wine and dine" analysts at the choicest spots. The world has changed. Analysts' schedules are more congested. There is more pressure on their time. Practices of the '90s don't reflect 21st-century reality. Today's analysts want to show up with minimum travel time, get information with no distractions, and be back in the office before still more work piles up.

This doesn't mean Spartan surroundings. If your event is in San Jose, don't book the Days Inn. The Fairmont is a lot nicer, and not too far from SJC airport. (The Doubletree is nice enough, and right at it.) Asking people to drive to Carmel is too much. Travel adds a day of unbillable time. Unless you know that key people want that spot, don't.

Expense reimbursement must be considered. Here the expense is larger because more analysts are involved, and consistency is necessary because people compare notes. Unless there's a clear reason for different reimbursement levels, such as one analyst flying across an ocean and another driving across town, differences will upset those who shell out more. Partial reimbursement may be a good compromise. IBM, for example, pays (or did, shortly before this was written) all expenses from landing at the nearest airport until they drop the analyst off there for the return trip. Getting to that airport is at his or her expense. While this gives an advantage to analysts near the conference, it saves IBM thousands of dollars compared to full reimbursement. (Their having analyst conferences in many parts of the world neutralizes this advantage somewhat.)

Schedule

There's no ideal time. Someone will have a conflict for any choice. Some guidelines:

- For a meeting of half a day or less, avoid Monday mornings and Friday afternoons. (Some suggest Friday mornings, so participants can start their weekend early by taking the rest of the day off, but most analysts are too busy to take advantage of that.)

- For a full day, avoid Mondays and Fridays.

- Most product announcements take place on Tuesdays or Wednesdays to avoid Mondays while giving reporters time to write them up for Friday's weekly trade press deadline. If you want to give analysts a last-minute preview, this suggests Monday afternoon or Tuesday morning. (Ideally, you'll have pre-briefed as many as possible during the preceding weeks. That also gives your firm a chance to fine-tune materials if analysts find problems. The day before is too late to do more than fix typos.)

- Some firms schedule half-day events for about 10 a.m. to 3 p.m. with lunch. This is done to let analysts from outside the immediate area, but not too far away, attend with just one day out of the office. A Boston firm, for instance, might do this for people from the analyst-rich southern Connecticut shore or New York City, or who fly in from Chicago.

  We don't recommend this. For every analyst who takes advantage of it, two will resent taking a full day for a half-day meeting. If you do this, be sure to explain why. Local folks may not be happy, but at least they won't wonder.

- Multiple-day events can be scheduled at either end of the week. This lets analysts minimize time away from the office by traveling in one direction off company time. If the location is attractive, it also lets them extend their stay through the weekend. (However, remember the caution about deliberately scheduling analyst events for vacation spots. This suggestion applies to events whose natural location happens to be in or near a spot that people might find attractive for a short holiday.)

Tracks

If your firm just makes multi-protocol routers, anyone who shows up will care about multi-protocol routers. You can devote your agenda to them and get undivided attention.

If you have a broader product line, this won't work. Larger firms, even if not on the scale of IBM, H-P or Microsoft, have more variety. No analyst will be interested in all of them. And analysts don't like to sit through discussions of topics of little or no professional interest. It wastes their time. Time is their most valuable commodity.

One solution is multiple tracks. H-P, for example, could have tracks on servers, printers, personal computers, network-related topics, and so on. Analysts can go to sessions they care about. Throw in an executive introduction, a social hour at the end, and you're set.

The problem is that, as mentioned earlier, no analyst practice breaks down the same way as any provider's structure. There will be times when two sessions of interest conflict. At other times, nothing useful (to that analyst) will be going on.

One solution is to schedule each session twice, opposite different sessions in the other tracks. This puts an added burden on presenters, but not an excessive one. An analyst still may want to go to three sessions and be unable to schedule them all, because A is opposite B once and opposite C the other time, with B's and C's second offerings opposite each other. That's life. No solution is perfect. This one, if you can persuade most of your speakers to give their talks twice and have enough rooms, comes close.

Another solution is to send analysts a list of possible sessions in advance and ask which each plans to attend. (These are plans, not commitments.) Then you can schedule them to minimize conflict. It's a bit of work to figure out the ideal schedule, but it gets easier with practice. This also lets you fit room size to each session, and cancel sessions that don't generate interest instead of letting a vice president show up to empty seats.

The second problem, nothing useful going on, isn't a problem. Analysts can arrange meetings for those times. Gaps also give them a chance to catch up on phone calls and e-mail, renew old friendships, do some low-key recruiting (or job-hunting) with other attendees, or just go for a walk.

Mixing analysts and consultants with other groups

It can be tempting to mix customers, prospects, analysts and consultants (they're close enough here) to reduce planning and save money. If your expected audience is small you may have no alternative. A program for just analysts is better, though, because:

- The issues analysts care about are not the issues that prospects care about.
- Analysts appreciate recognition as a group in their own right.
- Analysts feel more comfortable asking questions away from present or potential clients.
- What you tell analysts in confidence might leak out, but what you tell the others surely will—faster, and more visibly.

If you invite analysts or consultants to customer/prospect seminars, customize their invitations. Explain "this is what your clients will hear; you may be interested too." This shows that you recognize the differences between analysts and customers, and prepares them for a customer-oriented agenda. If they come, they know what they're in for.

There is one situation where inviting analysts and consultants to customer/prospect seminars is desirable: when it puts them in contact with potential clients. This occurs most frequently in specialized, often vertical, markets. If you run a briefing for financial industry executives, analysts who follow the market for financial industry systems and consultants who work with the financial industry will want to attend. The basic principle still applies: to recognize these groups for what they are. Invitations for analysts or consultants should not be the same as invitations to customers or prospects.

A different temptation is to mix analysts with the press, especially for product announcements. This is almost always a bad idea because:

- Analysts hate being confused with the press. It happens so often that they become over-sensitive and suspect it even when it's not the case.

- Analysts want to be briefed enough in advance of the press that they can collect their thoughts, ask questions, get answers, develop a position, and respond intelligently when the press calls. They can't do this if they and reporters hear about it at the same time.

  (Inviting pre-briefed analysts to an announcement press conference as a reporter re-source is a separate issue. This is a good idea, but expect to pay for their time.)

- There is no such thing as "off the record" in a press conference. This can make it difficult for analysts to pursue lines of questioning that could ultimately result in a more favorable position on your product.

It may seem more logical to group industry and financial (stock market) analysts. While they have more in common with industry analysts than either group has with reporters, this also usually works out poorly.

One reason is personalities. Industry analysts as a group tend to be reflective and intro-verted. Financial analysts, perhaps used to the "rough and tumble" of securities markets, are the opposite. The result is a perception on the part of industry analysts that "pushy" financial folks monopolize discussions, executive time, Q&A sessions and even social interaction in cocktail hours. This leads to resentment.

A second reason is that financial analysts, in a mixed group, will naturally ask industry analysts what they think. While this is often just to be friendly, industry analysts may see it as "pumping" for what other clients pay for. As with so much else, it's a matter of per-ception. Industry analysts feel they're being pumped. Short of requiring financial analysts at a mixed meeting to wear a muzzle, the best solution is not to mix the groups.

If you want to take advantage of the overlap between these two groups' areas of interest, then take most financial topics out of industry analyst meetings and let industry analysts attend financial analyst sessions instead. While financial analysts may hog the limelight there too, any industry analysts who attend will consider it their right to do so.

Analyst Event Dos and Don'ts

To have a productive event that justifies the resources that went into staging it, which leaves analysts feeling happy about having attended and positive about your firm, try to do as many of these as practical:

- Provide lots of lead time. Analysts' schedules typically fill up at least six weeks in ad-vance. If you expect them to set aside two or three days of time for you, allow two months. (If analysts don't have enough time to plan to attend, nothing else matters.)

- Keep a balance between high-level and nuts-and-bolts sessions.

- Try to have more and/or higher-powered executives and specialists at the event than would normally travel to visit a research firm. If possible, have more than an analyst could normally visit even if he or she came to your headquarters.

- Have breakout sessions for one-on-one meetings with these executives and specialists.

- Invite customers for analysts to meet. (They don't have to be there the whole time.)

- Create a demo that can't travel or be accessed effectively remotely. (Even if the technology could travel, maybe the folks who explain what's behind the screens couldn't.)

- Pack your event with *content*. Don't schedule morning sessions with an afternoon of golf, a harbor cruise or a visit to the local distillery. That will attract junior analysts with nothing else to do. The people you want prefer to get in, learn what they came for, and leave. If you want to plan social time beyond meals and evenings, schedule it before or after the main event for analysts who can come early or stay on.

- Allow time for socialization: dinners, lunches, a cocktail hour where analysts can mingle with executives. Aside from relationship-building value, it gives analysts a chance to see them in action in a less formal session than a strategy presentation.

Your event plan should cover:

- *Timeline.* In addition to the event itself, include when to send invitations to analysts, when to call, when to remind and when to confirm.

- *Agenda*, with times for group sessions, breakout sessions, meals and other activities.

- *Venue.* See above. Your company may have event planners who can help. If not, there are services you can use if this is not your area of expertise.

- *Spokespeople.* Plan a balance between executives and hands-on people. Make sure most can stay around for one-on-one discussions and socializing during meals.

- *Other staff.* Staff a conference desk during sessions and at other times when people may arrive or need help. Have two people there if possible, more if your event is large, so it won't be unattended when someone must handle a problem or take a break. You'll also need technical staff for audiovisual equipment and videotape key sessions. (Many conference sites can provide these, though the daily rate may be so high that it pays to bring your own.) If demos are on the program, they must be run and supported.

- *Topics.* Start with an executive welcome and strategy overview. It should recap what was said last year, compare that with what happened, and explain differences. (Analysts will do this anyhow. You might as well give your view.) Any recent announcement is another "must." Beyond that, look at topics from your customers' perspective, since that's what analysts do. Case studies and testimonials are compelling.

- *Speaker training*—e.g., to keep spin and hype under control. (See Section 11.6.)

- *Private meetings* should be in the plan. Take requests ahead of time. Pre-schedule as many as possible. If a request can't be accommodated, tell the analyst *before* the trip. Most will come anyway, but it's infuriating to get off a six-hour flight and find out that the main reason for being there won't happen. This will not endear your firm to that analyst. He or she won't be bashful about telling the story.

- *Q&A sessions.* Allow a third of each session for this. For example, a 90-minute session would consist of a 60-minute talk (including brief clarifications) plus 30 minutes of Q&A. Questions that would take too long to answer, or whose answer wouldn't interest anyone but the questioner, can be met with an offer to answer them privately afterward.

- *Handouts* should include copies of all the presentation materials, plus white papers, product briefs or other documentation. Hard-copy handouts allow analysts to take notes, soft is better for later use, so try to have both. Package them attractively.

- *Gifts.* Analysts usually get a memento of the occasion. Unfortunately, it's hard to come up with novel and appropriate ideas. Anyone who's attended more than a few of these (the people you want!) already has two of everything. A marketing promotions professional can help with this quest.

  We won't make suggestions here, since analysts would soon have six or seven of whatever we listed. Effective past gifts have included a samurai sword (to just a few analysts, because of cost), less expensively but still at the high end a watch with the corporate logo (at least one analyst wore hers regularly on visits to that firm's competitors), and, at a lower price point, a beach towel. That one paid for itself in free seaside advertising.

- *Follow up.* Gaining trust requires repeated contact. One event, no matter how well organized and informative, can't do the job. Following up offers another touch point. So, call or e-mail to learn if analysts received everything they wanted, what suggestions they have for next year, and if you or a speaker can provide anything else.

- *Report back.* Aside from the facts, assess the event's value. Who showed up? How influential are they? What topics came up in Q&A? What feedback did you get? Did your messages show up in press quotes and/or research? What recommendations for improvement do you or anyone else (including analysts) have for future events?

What different types of analysts need in analyst events

Research Agenda-Driven	Useful background, can suggest topics for future research or that this provider be included in reports scheduled to be written
Event-Driven	Good way for small firms to hear about announcements in depth, especially (under NDA if need be) before public announcement
Calendar-Driven	Useful as general background/perspective on the provider
Client-Driven	Useful as background, to be able to "hit the ground running" in future engagements

7.7. The teleconference alternative

BEST PRACTICE

Use audio/video teleconferences and the Web to deliver messages interactively with no need for travel, particularly when relationships are already established. Provide materials and notifications well in advance. Train speakers to use these media effectively. Try to include someone in each briefing whom at least some of the analysts have met in person.

Can't get everyone together in one place? Have an announcement that needs an hour, not a day? Don't have two months lead time? Can't get people away from their offices? Use audio teleconferencing, video teleconferencing, interactive webcasts and other technology to work effectively and cost-effectively.

Remote briefings are increasingly popular to get information to many analysts at a time. Analysts who have an existing relationship with people at your firm often prefer this time-efficient approach. Those who have not yet met them, who have no mental image to invoke, will also usually be practical enough to realize that it can't always happen.

An effective teleconference is accompanied by visuals. Analysts must be able to view these while on the phone. There are several ways to do this:

- Send them ahead of time via postal mail, courier service or fax.
- Put them up on a Web site, for viewing before or during the briefing.
- Provide them in downloadable form for analysts to print or view.

These all have pros and cons. For every analyst who wants to take notes on paper, there's one who likes to file materials electronically. For every analyst who wants to surf related Web pages during a briefing, there's one who finds that distracting. For every analyst who likes the flexibility of on-screen viewing, there's one who prefers the higher resolution of print. Try to offer a choice, say between PDF (usually best if you must pick one format) and PowerPoint. (In 2013, .pptx files are as acceptable as the older .ppt.)

Web technologies support animation, let a presenter use the screen interactively, and generally do most of what can be done in a conference room. If you're in a position to use these technologies, that's a powerful argument for using the Web. If you take advantage of its capabilities, even analysts who prefer hard-copy materials will see the its value for communication.

These technologies demand bandwidth. Research firm offices have high-speed connections, but not necessarily analysts participating from other places. Some will call in from home. Even in 2013, not every home has really fast Internet. Others will be in hotels: most provide high-speed access, but not all, and it can fail. Make it possible for people who can't access the interactive online content to participate, even if not fully.

A teleconference agenda should be to the point. Getting acquainted isn't the purpose of this session, nor is this a good medium for it. A product-related agenda could be:

- Open the briefing. Give the purpose and agenda, introduce the first speaker.
- This speaker is someone such as a program manager who can speak to its market, its relationship to other products and/or earlier versions, and its place in your future.
- Handle Q&A for this speaker and introduce the next. (Or, do group Q&A at the end.)
- The second speaker discusses the product itself and its technologies. This could be its R&D manager, its system architect, etc.
- Conduct a Q&A session with the second speaker (or with both, if you didn't do the first earlier). You may want others on hand in case a question calls for their expertise.
- Close by offering one-on-one calls between interested analysts and either speaker. Analysts can be just as reluctant to ask questions in front of their competitors in a teleconfer-

ence as they are at an event. This also recognizes that analysts may have questions later, after they've had a chance to think over what they've heard.

It's nice if all the speakers are in the same room, to signal each other or pass notes, but this isn't mandatory. You can e-mail back and forth during the teleconference, use instant messaging or have an online chat room for your firm's participants.

You can also let analysts e-mail questions, or send them via interactive chat, instead of asking them on the phone:

- You can screen questions, combining duplicates or near-duplicates.
- Analysts can ask questions anonymously. This may reduce a barrier to asking.
- You can answer pre-planned questions even if no analyst asks them.

If you don't want to answer an e-mailed question you don't have to, but the analyst who sent it will know you didn't. You can apologize on the air for not having enough time for all the questions, send that analyst an e-mail explaining why you didn't, or do any number of other things, but you have to do something. You can't ignore it.

Many firms have teleconference facilities. If yours doesn't, your telecoms manager has probably set up teleconferences using outside suppliers. If you do it yourself, there are many firms you can use, including your phone company. They provide a call-in number and a conference code to key in. Cost depends on duration and number of participants. (If participating requires anything beyond a phone and a Web browser, such as software to download, tell analysts in advance.) Some Web-based teleconferencing services include voice, via participants' computers or by providing a phone number.

Allow ample time for the teleconference. Reserve more than you think you'll need if you use a service. The cost of a few more minutes is nothing compared to hearing "I'm sorry, your time is over" as your CEO sums up the rationale for your new strategy.

Schedule teleconferences well in advance. They interrupt as much as a visit. Participants may not have to travel, but they have to clear their calendars. They can't be in a meeting, on a plane, or doing anything else. So, don't think "it's just a phone call" and tell analysts the day before. If it were a phone call, they could say "Can't do 1. How about 2?" You'd then say "OK" or "Kim's busy at 2, how about 3?" Teleconferences don't work that way. Give analysts the same notice as you would give them for a visit. If you wouldn't say "I'll be at your office tomorrow at 1; if you want to hear about X, be there!" don't do it for a teleconference either.

Take time zones into account if you expect analysts outside your home region to participate. And don't forget the date line: One firm scheduled a teleconference for late Friday at its Massachusetts HQ so a Sydney analyst could participate, only to learn that it was indeed 8 a.m. in eastern Australia—on Saturday!

Finally, European analysts tend to like teleconferences less than North Americans. They prefer more personal visits and analyst events. Keep this in mind in allocating resources among ways to maintain analyst contact.

What different types of analysts need in analyst teleconferences

Research Agenda-Driven	Can be a useful update, especially if in an analyst's area of specialization. Consider the analyst's research schedule.
Event-Driven	Excellent way to brief, or preferably pre-brief, analysts whom it's impractical to visit.
Calendar-Driven	Generally little interest
Client-Driven	As with analyst events, a good way to get background in an area in preparation for possible future engagements

7.8. Online information: your web site

> **BEST PRACTICE**
>
> A site or portal specifically for analysts and consultants, with access control and visitor tracking. It should contain easy-to-navigate, low-graphics paths to content pages, analyst/consultant briefing materials, recordings or transcripts of executive speeches, and contact information.

Your firm surely has a Web site. Even local pizza shops post menus and hours on the Web. The IT world is even more Web-oriented than society in general.

Web sites have much that analysts need to know: background information, financial results, product specs, contact information, press releases. Many also contain technical details, white papers (to read online or download), animated demos or downloadable demo software, executive bios and more. Analysts often go there before anywhere else.

The typical provider Web site, however, was not designed for analysts. Issues include:

- Product information is organized by the provider's view of the structure of its offerings. This may not match the analyst's view of how things fit together. That's OK for customers, who don't have to cope with a dozen other provider sites too, but analysts *do* have to cope with them.

- It may have promotional information that most analysts would rather skip.

- It may not be designed for frequent visitors, requiring multiple steps to reach a desired page. (Bookmarking pages doesn't always solve this problem, as URLs often change when information is updated. Old bookmarks may generate "page not found" errors. Worse, they may take an analyst to out-of-date information, with no alert that current content can be reached by laboriously following the links on the site.)

- Being designed for occasional visitors rather than frequent users, its design emphasizes graphical attractiveness over speed of loading and rendering. A site need not be ugly, but analysts prefer simple designs that load and render quickly.

- You may not want all your analyst information on display to the Googling or Binging public.

An analyst-only web site

An analyst-only site is a good way around these issues. Such a site doesn't duplicate all the information on the main site. It replaces only the top two levels or so of that site. From there it points to the same information. For everything except its unique content, it's more of an alternate entry point and means of navigation than an alternate site. Its unique content can include:

- Analyst support names, areas of responsibility and contact information
- Briefing materials, such as those for teleconferences
- Organization chart, including names for at least the top couple of levels
- Strategy and top level product or services descriptions, with key messages
- Company history and background (can be a link to elsewhere on your company site if this information already exists there)
- White papers (see Chapter 6, Section 7)

An analyst site can be protected. If there's no information on it that isn't also on the main site—that is, it's solely a faster path to existing information—there's no need to protect it. Analysts may feel privileged if they need a password to get in, but they may also get upset at the delay. Once they catch on that its content is public, which won't take long, they'll wonder why it's necessary. If the site contains information that is not available to the general public, protection is necessary, with steps to prevent search engine bots from including it in their travels.

Using this site for analyst teleconference visuals will acquaint analysts with it, if they're not already aware of it; force them to register, if it's protected and they haven't already done so; and get them into the habit of using it. You can then leave the materials up after the briefing so participants can share them with colleagues.

The Web site is, in many ways, today's version of the Consultants' Reference Manuals many firms had in the '80s and '90s. You may still want one, so Section 7.10 in this chapter is on that. Some suggestions there can also help you plan an analyst Web site.

Things to avoid in analyst web sites

1. **Time-consuming graphics.** Analysts' most precious commodity is time. It's what they sell. They spend a lot of that time visiting provider Web sites. They don't want to wait for a full-color rotating Flash image of your headquarters building to load.

   Analysts do not always work under the ideal Web-surfing conditions that site developers enjoy on the job. They may be in a hotel room, using a laptop that was fast years ago, with a slow and noisy connection, paying $1 a minute and needing information before a client shows up. If every corporate Web site developer had to use his or her work under those conditions, full-color rotating Flash would vanish in—well, a flash.

2. **Confusing layouts.** Analysts use multiple provider sites. They're all organized differently. None of the organizations matches how the analyst's mind works. They use different search engines and different terminology.

That being the case, provide multiple easy-to-find paths to information. And ask analysts what they like about the site, what they don't. A feedback button never offends.

3. Material that must be downloaded before a reader can get a good idea of what it is. Downloaded files cannot be viewed at all until they have been transmitted in full and often decompressed and opened with another application—which may not be on that laptop). Provide brief summaries of downloadable files along with a statement of their size, and provide them in multiple formats. Not everyone has a PDF reader, or the latest release of even the most popular application.

4. Pages that can't be bookmarked. Analysts want to get to useful information quickly. They use electronic files of URLs as alternatives to paper file cabinets. If the information can't be bookmarked, or as a minimum isn't one click away from a bookmark, they get frustrated. Where possible, avoid dynamically created URLs and frames. Web developers love these, though in 2013 frames are somewhat "old hat," but their benefits to those who visit a site to get real work done aren't as compelling.

    Put an "OUT OF DATE" notice on any page that is made obsolete by later information. You may not want to remove the page entirely, since people may want to refer to it for historical purposes, and there may be reasons not to give the new information the same URL, but this way site visitors will know that newer information or products exist.

What different types of analysts need in analyst events

Research Agenda-Driven	Details, depth. They often visit several providers' sites for a report, so make it easy for them to find content on yours.
Event-Driven	The ability to find out as much as possible, quickly, on what you just announced and anything else they must understand for perspective.
Calendar-Driven	This may be a place to post data they need. That will put all "market watchers" on a level playing field.
Client-Driven	The first two levels down about almost anything. If they need to go further and your site doesn't have the information, they can ask for it.

7.9. Social media

The phrase *social media* is a blanket term for a host of sites that enable people to connect with each other. It's part of a phenomenon often called *Web 2.0*, though that term is usually taken to include many types of sites that focus on user-provided content. Since both analyst relations staffers and the analysts themselves are people, it follows that social media can help them connect with each other. While enthusiasm for social media has cooled off a bit since they were overhyped in the early 2000s, they are still a valuable part of the analyst relations toolkit.

Blogs

A *blog*, short for *Web log*, is a series of related posts organized in reverse chronological order. Blogs provide a channel through which people can express thoughts on anything from Android apps to zombies. The eBiz MBA knowledge base reported in February 2013 that the top seven blogs each had 10+ million unique visitors per month.

Most blogs allow readers to comment. That creates interactivity, increases the connection between the blog and its readers, and makes blogs true social tools rather than just a way to format one-way communication.

The collective community of all blogs is called the *blogosphere.* With over 150 million blogs in existence (perhaps 200 million by the time you read this), people need a way to find specific ones. Among the sites you can use to search for blogs are Technorati (*technorati.com,* the earliest blog search engine and still among the largest), Bloglines (*www.bloglines.com*) and Google blog search (*blogsearch.google.com*).

Many research firms blog. (The word *blog,* as a verb, means "to write a blog.") Some are official firm blogs, some are written by the analysts in a specific service, and some are written by individual analysts. Firms may provide an incentive for analysts to blog, but generally don't require it because not every analyst has the personality to be an effective blogger. Research firms often collect their blogs on an index page such as *blogs.gartner. com* or *blogs.forrester.com.* Their customers pay attention to these blogs. So should you, since information often appears in them before it shows up in a formal report. If you see something in a blog you disagree with, you can catch it before it takes on permanent form. You may be able to comment on the blog, and you can always contact the blogger.

Analysts read blogs to keep up on firms and topics in which they're interested. Some firms have official blogs, such as Intel Software at *software.intel.com/en-us/blogs.* There are also unofficial blogs about providers, such as *www.ifoapplestore.com* about Apple's retail stores. (That's not a typo. The domain name starts with *ifo,* not *info.*) Analysts who follow that topic can go there for the latest unofficial information, or (as with many blogs) set up RSS feeds to alert their browsers to new posts.

If you think analysts might want to follow your blog, first see if your employer has a corporate blog or a blogging policy. (If it has a corporate blog, it almost certainly has a blogging policy as well.) Find out what you are allowed to do and not do. Then, set up your blog within those guidelines.

If it doesn't, you can create a blog easily using a popular blogging site such as Wordpress (*wordpress.com*) or Tumblr (*tumblr.com*). Both of these and many others are free. Once you've made a few posts, send the blog URL to all the analysts on your list. Some won't follow it, but a large fraction will.

Your firm may consider blogging to be "publication" for legal review purposes. If it does, have your posts checked out before you put them up. People have gotten into trouble over poorly thought out posts.

If you write a blog, consider the Abercrombie & Fitch blog as an example of what *not* to do. In late 2012, it had a single post—from July 2007! Mercifully, it was taken down in early 2013. Maybe clothing buyers don't care if a company follows through on what it starts, but industry analysts do. You don't have to post every day or even every week, but you should be able to find at least a few posts per month even when things are quiet. If you find yourself posting that your firm's accounting manager cleaned his aquarium last week, you might want to reconsider the blog idea.

Facebook

When people in the street hear "social media," Facebook is usually the first site that comes to mind. In October 2012 it reached one billion members—about one of every six people over age 13 in the world. (The minimum age for Facebook membership is 13, though it's hard to enforce.) However, not all its members are people. Many companies have Facebook pages, such as Dell's at *www.facebook.com/Dell.*

Facebook, as you probably already know (given that it has a billion members), enables members to create profiles with information about them and update their pages with information about their activities. Members may request other members to *friend* them. If the second member accepts the request, each has access to content on the other's page that is not available to the public at large.

The Like button is an important feature of Facebook. It indicates that a member (such as an analyst) approves of another member (such as you). Liking differs from friending in that friending is two-way (If I'm your friend, you're mine) but liking is one-way (I can like you without your liking me). Many consumer sites have Facebook Like buttons, by which visitors to that site can indicate their approval on Facebook, and may offer incentives (such as a discount coupon) for visitors to click that button. You can add a Like button to your firm's analyst Web site to let analysts show approval of your analyst support, but they aren't likely to take advantage of that opportunity. They might be concerned that your competitors could see it as favoritism.

A Facebook site is a valuable addition to an analyst relations program. It lets those who care about your activities keep updated on them. If you'll be at Gartner's Symposium in Florida in October 2013, you can post that information there. Others who want to meet with you can set up appointments for the conference or arrange to meet at a nearby bar.

Facebook has groups built around communities of interest. Some are business-related. However, most tend to be at the personal level: Lady Gaga fans, Nikon camera users. For analyst relations LinkedIn discussion groups (see below) are probably more useful, though you should join any Facebook groups that are related to your company.

Facebook is an excellent example of how the social media landscape changes rapidly and why one must stay on top of it. Not many years ago, this section would have discussed MySpace. Today, MySpace is history as a general social network. (It still has users in its original focus area of music, is used as a music streaming service, and as of early 2013 may reposition itself on that basis.)

LinkedIn

LinkedIn has been described as "Facebook for business." That misses the point. Facebook is designed to keep members updated on people they know and are in touch with.

LinkedIn has moved in that direction under competitive pressure, but it was designed to help members find people they *don't* know and locate people they've lost touch with.

People, including analysts, use LinkedIn to make contact with others in specific positions at specific companies. Suppose I want to talk with Meg Whitman at H-P. I don't know her. However, by logging into LinkedIn and entering her name into its search box, I find that we have an acquaintance in common. If I really need to contact her, I can e-mail him and ask for an introduction.

Not all searches produce such a useful result. Dominick Cavuoto, head of the technology, consulting, and integration services business at Unisys, is one step further away. I know five people who know someone he knows, but I don't know who the links between them and Cavuoto are. I can contact my five friends to see if they feel comfortable asking their connections to introduce me to him. Not as good as a mutual acquaintance, but better than nothing.

LinkedIn doesn't always do even that well. It found no connections between Steve Ballmer at Microsoft and me. Larry Ellison of Oracle and Michael Dell of Dell didn't even turn up in a member search.

LinkedIn is of value in analyst relations precisely because it helps people find people they don't know. You want people you don't know (analysts interested in your company) to be able to find you. When I entered "analyst relations dell" (without the quotation marks) into LinkedIn's search box, I found several people who could be useful to an analyst wanting to establish contact with that firm. I could contact a senior manager of AR in Texas with whom I have two acquaintances in common, or scan the list further for a better match or a closer connection.

You also want to be able to contact people you don't know. Suppose you read a quote by an analyst about your firm and want to contact that analyst. LinkedIn may enable you to make that connection more effectively than "I'm in AR at XYZ Technostuff, and ..."

Third, LinkedIn has professional groups. The Association of Analyst Relations Professionals group, the IIAR (Institute of Industry Analyst Relations) group and the Influencer Marketing and Influencer Relations group all have discussions that can be both interesting and useful. There are also groups, such as the Association of Technology Analysts and Influencers, that consist primarily of analysts but where analyst relations professionals can participate.

Twitter

Twitter, as you also probably know, lets people publish snippets of information up to 140 characters long. (This was originally to fit within the limits of a mobile phone text message.) Others who *follow* that person receive those snippets, called *tweets*. They may get them immediately on mobile devices, when they log into Twitter at their desks, or in other ways. They will then be up to date on what the person they follow is doing, what he or she thinks is important, or whatever else he or she wants to tweet about.

The most frequently followed people in the "twitterverse" are of largely personal interest. Justin Bieber passed Lady Gaga as the most popular in early 2013, with each having over 33 million followers. The top non-entertainer was Barack Obama, in fifth place with 26 million followers. (You can get the latest numbers at *twittercounter.com/pages/100* .) Twitter can be of value in analyst relations as well, though you're unlikely to be quite as popular as any of those three people. You can use it in three ways:

Following

Many research firms have twitter feeds. If you want to find out what people think at Forrester Research, have your Twitter account follow @forrester. It has about half a dozen tweets in a typical day, most of them with links to more information on their topic. In addition to tweets by a firm, individual analysts also often tweet. You can often find that information on their Web pages, or you can search for them within Twitter.

Being followed

You can tweet about what's going on in your firm that may be of interest to analysts, such as analyst relations activities, and put a "follow me on Twitter" button on your analyst site. Many analysts who care about your firm will follow you. Some won't, so make sure that your tweets are never the only way an analyst can get important information.

If your firm has several product lines, you can set up Twitter accounts for each. There is no limit to the number of Twitter accounts you can have. The only restriction is that each account must be associated with a different e-mail address. That shouldn't be a problem in a business.

Hashtags

Another way that Twitter lets you keep on top of a topic is via *hashtags*. A message can include a keyword prefixed with #, as in *#cloud*. Anyone who posts on that topic can include a hashtag in a tweet. Others who are interested in that topic can receive all tweets with that hashtag, regardless of whether they follow the person who tweeted them or not.

Companies follow their own hashtags to find out what people are saying about them. Online discussion groups are full of stories about people who tweeted about an airline problem with the airline's hashtag, and who were then contacted by the airline to resolve the problem. Your company may already be following its hashtag for that reason. You can create a hashtag for analyst relations, too.

What different types of analysts need in social media

Research Agenda-Driven	Information on opportunities to stay current with little effort, such as newly scheduled telebriefings or someone's visit to their area.
Event-Driven	Information about announcements and other events.
Calendar-Driven	Little professional need, but some like to stay in touch this way.
Client-Driven	Keeping in touch to facilitate contact when the need arises.

7.10 Updates: E-mail and more

> **BEST PRACTICE**
>
> Regular updates, e-mail or hard copy, can maintain analyst awareness of your firm and reach out to more analysts than you can contact personally. Keep each "mailing's" objectives in mind as you produce it.

There are two sides to analyst support: responsiveness and proactivity. Most outbound proactive contact with analysts involves written material in one form or another.

7.10.1. General Principles

One purpose of analyst communications is to "show the flag" on a regular basis. It reminds your audience that you exist and that you care about them. Hard information can usually be provided better by your Web site, with an option to request more information or a different medium if and when it's needed.

You do this because influencing people takes repeated exposures. Would you recommend a product after one mailing? If it's a $3.98 vegetable slicer, perhaps. If it has a major impact on its user's life, no way. It takes about seven exposures, over 12 to 18 months, to get the impact you want. Your communications are an important part of this. Those that come on a regular schedule also reinforce your image of reliability.

This vehicle can be paper or electronic. If it's paper, include the entire content in one package, which you can think of as an analyst newsletter. If it's electronic, the content will be on the Web, most likely in pages linked to the update's main page. In this case, send analysts an e-mail message when a new issue of your "Webletter" appears. Reasons not to include the entire content in the message or as attachments to it are discussed in the section headed "E-mail attachments" toward the end of this section.

Another purpose of analyst updates is to announce new products or services, or convey other important news. By sending announcement kits or the other news to all potentially interested analysts, you cover those whom you weren't able to include in your briefing meetings or weren't able to participate.

7.10.2. Regular updates ("newsletters")

Content

Plan content to tie in with your marketing strategy. Your firm may want to be seen as a technology leader, a quality vendor, a low-cost producer, the primary provider for a particular market niche or something else. Choose materials with this in mind. In writing, keep your basic analyst or consultant messages firmly in mind, along with the message concepts discussed in Section 4.4. The example of a new automated production line in that section is especially apt for a mailing. (The word "mailing," here and in general business usage, doesn't necessarily mean the postal service. Today, it usually doesn't.)

Choose topics with audience interests in mind. These interests are not necessarily the same as yours! The purpose of your mailing is to influence analysts and consultants, not to stroke your corporate ego. Look at each article from the viewpoint of someone *outside* your organization. Where possible, sound out an analyst about proposed topics and possible approaches to them. (This is one way to use extra inquiry time in analyst contracts.)

For example: articles about corporate reorganizations, complete with a photo of every vice-president, are a staple of some updates. They shouldn't be. Why not? You care about your corporate organization because it affects your life, but it doesn't have the same impact on an analyst's life. Your VP won't determine an analyst's next salary increase, promotion, or project. Analysts care about your organization to the degree that it affects *their* lives: on your firm's ability to develop products that will solve their clients' problems, bring those solutions to market, and support them in a way that promotes the client's satisfaction. Unless you can relate the reorganization to these concerns, don't bother with it. If you must run this story to keep your job, give it the minimum prominence you can politely get away with.

Keep financial information to a minimum for the same reason. People who care about it get it from the Web or *The Wall Street Journal* before your message reaches them. Yes, you can brag if your sales tripled over last year. Analysts care about your financial stability. Tripled sales are a good sign of this. Just don't treat this tidbit as "news."

Also, remember that analysts and consultants aren't customers. Their needs and interests are not the same. Topics on which you want to convince them are not the same. For instance, you want to show existing customers new uses for your products, or related uses for related products, so they will buy more. Analysts and consultants are more interested in the suitability of your products for someone who doesn't have them yet. An article on how to create a pull-down menu from data in another file will interest customers and contract programmers, but not system selection advisors.

It's tempting to use the same articles for multiple audiences. Sometimes it may even be a good idea, but not always. Think carefully about the impact of the article on both publics before you do.

What are good update topics? Try these. As you think of ideas, remember your messages:

- **How your firm's products and/or services solve real problems.** Be specific as to the need and how your products/services met it. Also, discuss parts of the need that were met by other products/services. This will help clarify what your offering is by pointing out what it isn't. For example, if you sell tools for developing artificial intelligence applications, mention the parts of the overall solution which you didn't supply, too.

- **How your firm's products work with related products that are market leaders in their areas.** The next time a reader needs an optimization package for Excel data, he or she will think of you.

- **Information of value for selection or sizing.** Performance data is such information. If your studies show your server can support fifty typical database users, say so. If you have graphs, put them in.

- **Factors to consider in system selection.** This is especially helpful if your product is in a new area with which analysts may not be familiar, or if its new approaches make standard evaluation factors out of date. Of course, you'll emphasize factors that correspond to strengths of your firm's products. If your firm sells neural network software, give them a list of key factors in choosing neural network software—stressing ones where yours shines.

- **How your firm has worked with analysts and consultants in various situations.** These can be test sites if your firm, or the product you're discussing, is new.

- **Your support policies and how they work.** What you will and won't do, free and for a fee. What are the fees? Don't be coy. Analysts (and consultants) are not prospects, whom you may want to persuade before you reveal the costs. Provide straightforward information.

- **New technology and the people who make it possible,** if technological leadership is part of your strategy.

- **Your analyst/consultant relations programs and how to use them.** Contact names, phone numbers, e-mail addresses and, if more than one person does this, each one's area(s) of responsibility.

- **Statements of direction about future products.** Go as far as you can without impacting sales. It gives advisors confidence that you're serious about your plans, and gives them information they need for their two-to-five-year planning horizon.

- **Lists and summaries of articles** about your firm and its products that have appeared in the press, or professional papers and conference presentations by your staff.

- **Corporate resources that can be of value to the reader's clients.** Do you have a custom systems group? What does it do? For what types of customers? On what typical schedules? How does one get a quote? What are their facilities? What are the qualifications of their staff? Also: do you have benchmark facilities? Demo centers? Speakers who can talk to professional gatherings? Any such resource can be the topic of an article. Tell analysts what it does, with examples of past successes, and how to access it.

- **Lists of newly published documentation with ordering information,** including press releases. If the documents are on the Web, give their URLs or the URL of an index page. If your analyst "mailing" is electronic, make these live links.

- **Training course and seminar schedules.** Don't put your whole training catalogue here. Just tell readers how to get it—again, with a URL if it's on the Web.

Still need ideas? Go back to Section 4.1 and reread the three points (product, company, resources) that analysts and consultants must believe to recommend your firm. Write about anything that addresses one of them.

Your firm doesn't have to write the entire newsletter itself. If you can get an analyst or consultant to write an on "How Acme Data helped me keep my clients happy," it will make an excellent addition to the articles by your firm's staff. Most consultants will be glad to, since the article can help in their marketing efforts. Analysts are less likely to help. Their desire for publicity will be balanced by a concern that the article will be seen as indicating bias. They'll also expect to be paid for time spent writing it.

Encourage reader feedback and publish it. What you hear can be of value to your marketing. When analysts read what others wrote, they'll feel a stronger bond to your firm.

Consistency is important in your update. You already know it should appear regularly. Consistency should also mark its content. Plan a regular mix of content: some sections every month, a certain number of longer articles in regular places, feedback, a list of your firm's analyst contacts. This consistency reinforces your image of reliability.

Some firms send customer magazines to analysts. This is nice, but analysts aren't customers, so their content and approach don't reflect analyst needs. One firm resolves this dilemma nicely: it sends its customer magazine to analysts with a card reading "Compliments of Analyst Relations" to remind them where it came from. You can add a handwritten note to the card for your "A list" analysts if you want to, keeping in mind that their "B list" colleagues might see it and wonder why they didn't get one.

Frequency and Timing

Your analyst update should appear once a month to once a quarter. If it appears less than once per quarter, readers will forget it from one time to the next and you will lose the cumulative impact of regularity. More than once a month, and analysts who suffer from "information overload" will resent the imposition and may discard it unread. You'll also have trouble getting enough meaningful information for greater frequency.

If you'll use your update for announcement information, monthly frequency is mandatory. If it arrives any less often, announcement information will be "old hat." A quarterly update must be supplemented by other contacts to give your firm seven exposures within analysts' and consultants' 12-to 18-month "window of awareness."

Coordinate the content of your update with your firm's announcements. In the months before an announcement run items about its general product area, its importance to the information technology world, and your firm's prowess in it. At announcement time you can discuss the new products and how they address user needs better than earlier products, yours or anyone's. Intervals between announcements are good times for articles about how your firm's products are being used to solve real problems.

Other considerations

Updates should be literate. Misspellings, poor grammar and other errors in the mechanics of standard English will ruin your image. Copy-editing doesn't have to cost a lot. Your firm's PR department or agency probably has a copy editor on staff or knows of freelancers. If you're a new startup on a tight budget, English teachers at local schools often do this sort of thing to earn extra money.

Size. Less than four sides in print or a PDF download, or less than four pages of content on a Web site, aren't much of an update, though a small one is better than nothing if your firm is new and you don't have the resources to fill more. The upper limit is the readers' patience. If you go over eight pages in print or a single electronic document, make sure important material is easy to find. Instead of going over sixteen, publish a short newsletter plus one or more magazine-format publications. The magazine format provides more room to treat topics in depth and, on quality paper, makes a good physical impression. The upper limit isn't a concern for Web sites. Having lots of links doesn't create the same impression of bulk that the same number of pages does in print.

Production. If you print your updates, in today's era of $250 color laser printers there is no excuse for lesser print quality. A small firm can prepare a newsletter masthead once, run off masters on this paper, and have the result reproduced by photo-offset. While low-cost color ink-jet printers offer high resolution, the slightly feathered edges of ink-jet print on most paper scream "cheap" subliminally even if readers aren't conscious of why they feel this way.

Typesetting is desirable if you have graphics, since the difference shows up there more than with text. Even untrained eyes subconsciously associate more quality with a typeset product. Larger firms should invest in typesetting and should use 11" x 17" high-quality paper folded and stapled in the middle. Once you have the procedure worked out, going outside to obtain typeset masters from page layout software won't add more than a day to your production cycle.

An analyst newsletter doesn't need glossy paper and four-color printing. Save them for magazines if you have them.

Considerations for Web publication are different. Keep to the palette of 216 "Web-safe" colors, though this is less important with newer browsers, and compress graphics as much as possible without losing quality. (It doesn't take long to check a graphic at two or three JPEG compression levels to decide how far to go.) Test your pages with the current versions of Chrome, Internet Explorer and Firefox, to make sure they display properly with all of them. Ideally, you should also test with IE 8, the last version that runs under

Windows XP (still used by over 20 percent of all personal computers in early 2013), and with Safari, at least on Macintosh.

In creating a document to be read online, whether in PDF or word processor format, design considerations are similar to paper. However, the lower resolution of computer screens means type should be larger and graphics can't show the same level of detail. (They may still print in full resolution, depending on their format, but that's not reading the document online.) Most soft-copy preparation software lets you create internal hyperlinks so a reader can navigate within a document by clicking.

Design and layout is a profession. You don't have to be a pro, but you must pay attention to pros. As a minimum, try to get professional help for overall design and layout. Your marketing communications department may have the necessary skills. Your PR or ad agency may offer this service. Many free-lancers can take over the entire job or a part of it. Some desktop publishing and Web page creation software comes with a set of layout templates. If you'd rather do it yourself, start with a book on layout from your local library. Continue by attending a seminar, reading magazines and Web sites on design, paying attention to examples that cross your desk, and surfing the Web for ideas.

A final note. Two things should appear in every newsletter or update but are easy to overlook. One is your analyst support contact information. The other is a way to submit changes and additions to its distribution list.

Form

You have several options:

- **Within the body of an e-mail.** This is limiting if the size of the e-mail is to be kept within reason. However, you should use e-mail to notify analysts that it exists (optional if you send it on paper), with a summary of its contents in the body.

- **A PDF or word processor file** to download. This gives you better control over layout and graphic elements than you have on a Web page. It also makes it easier for analysts to save the document, to read later or to refer to in the future.

- **A Web page.** Most people are used to accessing information this way. Drawbacks are that the reader has to be online to access it, and Web browsing (even with a fast link) is slower than moving around a PDF document.

- **Hard copy.** While most analysts prefer soft copy, this is not universal. Some (not all over fifty years old!) like paper: it's tangible, has higher resolution than any computer screen, can be read anywhere, is easy to make notes on, and can be carried. Mailing a paper document also lets you enclose items such as sales literature for a new product.

- **Fax.** Avoid this. Your other faxes, if you still use them, will lose urgency if you fax non-urgent content. Faxes also lose urgency when office support staff put them into an in-tray or mailbox mixed with everything else. Finally, their appearance does not present a good image. They are in black-and-white, at low resolution, and often with transmission data at the top and/or bottom. In short, faxes have all the drawbacks of hard copy with none of its advantages. If you want to send paper, send *real* paper.

Most analysts, as just mentioned, find soft copy easier to manage, file, search, forward, and perhaps incorporate into other documents. Ask each one, keep his or her response in your database, and ask again from time to time because the answer may change.

Issues

Analysts have these major complaints about providers' periodic updates:

1. **Duplication.** They get an e-mail, then they get a fax with the same material, then it arrives by courier, then it comes in the mail ... All too often, the end result is a practice of discarding (for instance) every letter from a provider on the assumption that it duplicates an earlier e-mail. Once in a while it won't, but the analyst has no way to know which are "new" without opening all of them—which he or she has already decided is a waste of time.

2. **Irrelevance.** As noted earlier, few analysts cover every aspect of a multi-product firm. High-level corporate strategists who care about every side of the firm don't need details on any. None want updates on topics they are not interested in. If they get used to the idea that what you send them is generally irrelevant, they may get into the habit of tossing it all.

   The solution is simple. Find out what information each analyst wants and what form he or she prefers. Then send that information, in that form.

3. **E-mail attachments.** Analysts find these aggravating for several reasons. They often can't read any e-mail without downloading all their messages (including attachments) in full because their e-mail reader works that way. They can't see what the attachments are ahead of time, a problem made worse by the all-to-common practice of giving attachments file names that are meaningful only to their senders. They can't stop a download without terminating the entire e-mail session. And, especially on their laptop in a hotel room but even in their office, they often can't even open an attachment because they don't have the right platform, program, or plug-in.

The solution is simple here too. Put material on a Web site or other place that gives the analyst a choice about whether, and when, to get it. Provide enough information about the file to allow them to make an informed decision as to whether or not they want it. As a minimum, summarize its content, tell them how big it is, and, if it's anything but straight text or PDF, what software it requires. If practical, provide multiple versions such as PDF and Microsoft Word, since no software package is universal. (If a new release of a package such as Word introduces a new file format, as Word did in 2007, stick with or at least offer the previous format for another year or so.) Avoid Windows-only files, including .exe files; Macintosh and Linux market shares are higher among analysts than in the world at large.

Some e-mail software has a "download the first N KB of attachments" setting. When the analyst uses this, short documents including Web links will probably be downloaded, but full PDF or other files may not be. Again, having the full document on the Web or on an ftp site solves the problem.

Another reason to put your updates on the Web is that you can tell who read it and which pages they viewed, using fairly simple methods that your company's Web design team or consultant should know. You can't tell who opened an e-mail attachment.

Having put the document on your Web site, give analysts its URL. Few things are more annoying than being told "it's on our Web site," period. You know where it is. Why keep that a mystery? Analysts would have to search for it, often using a search tool they're not familiar with on a site that's not organized the way they think. Tell them.

7.10.3. Specifics for announcements

Analysts want to hear about your announcement from *you*, not read about it. It makes them feel that you care. (Announcements are good opportunities to further your relationship with consultants, too.)

Another reason for telling analysts about announcements is so they'll hear about them before the press. Reporters call analysts for opinions on announcements. If they don't have time to reflect on them, and ideally to get answers to their questions, they won't be able to express an informed opinion. What they say then won't please your management.

So, send announcement information to analysts whenever you have an announcement and a list of analysts. You can do this electronically or with paper. Each has its advantages, so you may want to use both.

A good way to "push" announcement information, or even less significant events, to interested analysts is via an RSS feed. This technology a list of new materials on subscribers' browsers whenever they care to check, with an instantly available count of how many new entries there are. Any Web designer or consultant can tell you more.

Content of an electronic announcement package

An electronic announcement package should consist of an e-mail message. No more. It should point to more information on your Web site, but the message itself should be short and to the point.

The sample letter of the next section also makes a suitable, if long, e-mail announcement message.

The additional content that should be available on your Web site in this case should mirror the content of the paper announcement kit described in the next section.

Content of a paper announcement package

Many of the materials that are typically prepared for announcements don't lend themselves to electronic transmission. Brochures, photos and other high-quality print materials lose impact on a computer screen, even with technologies such as PDF that reproduce their appearance as closely as the medium permits. While the content of a demo CD-ROM can theoretically be downloaded from a Web site, the time required to do so can make this approach impractical. And the trinkets so beloved of marketers, those mouse pads, light-up pens and Lucite paperweights, have to be delivered physically. For these reasons, courier services work overtime delivering announcement materials even in this age of electronic communication.

A minimum announcement package for analysts can consist of your press release. This is a good starting point for a new firm with limited resources, since the press release contains basic information about what you announced, what it's good for, and how much it costs. If a PR firm or professional develops the release, its grammar and proofreading should be flawless. That's one less worry for the typical overburdened start-up marketing team. If that's all you're going to send out, the paper package isn't really necessary—just e-mail it. Assuming you want more, package content depends on your budget and on how important you consider a particular analyst to be. You can include:

- A cover letter introducing the package. An example is on the next page, edited from one the author received. Note the references to preserving customers' investments and the implication of consistency in mentioning an earlier statement of direction.

  Also, note the URL in the last paragraph. It was impossible to give the URL of the information since it was on a protected site that requires log-in, but the letter told analysts what link to follow.

  A letter such as this could (as noted above) also be an e-mail message.

- Customized press release(s). Word processing makes it easy to customize press releases for analysts. You can have special stationery printed for these if you send out hard copy. Customizing tips are in the next subsection.

- Product briefs or brochures about the newly announced products. You may not have fancy four-color brochures, but at least you have spec sheets. Include whatever you'd give prospects. You don't want analysts to be less informed than their clients!

  Sometimes your announcement will be too large to include all the briefs and brochures. In that case, put in a few of the most important. Then, list what's available and suggest that interested analysts download electronic versions from the Web or obtain hard copy through analyst relations channels. Few analysts will ask for paper copies, but they'll all appreciate the offer.

- You don't have to send the same kit to everyone on your analyst list. One option is to send your "A list" a complete set of materials. Tell the rest what's available and how to get it.

- Price lists (keeping in mind the discussion of pricing information in Chapter 6), either just for the new products or an update of your complete list. Send a complete price list if it fits on one page. Send an update if the list is 40 pages of small type. In between, use your judgment.

(on Computer Company, Inc. letterhead)

May 16, 20XX

Dr. Efrem G. Mallach
Research Firm, Inc.

Dear Efrem,

CCI is pleased to share with you the enclosed information on products and directions to be announced on May 27. They represent the newest ways "CCI Makes It Work" by providing systems that solve real customer problems. They are designed not only to address current needs, but also to provide growth paths for the future.

Our key announcements are in two areas: desktop systems and Web publishing. In both, we are doing more than announcing specific products. We are defining our ongoing strategy.

The first members of the new CC 200/300 family, the CC 280 and 380, meet the highest standards for Windows hardware and software compatibility. Based on the Intel Core 4 and 5 processors respectively, they respond to our customers' needs for compatibility and industry standard solutions while providing extra value. Microsoft Windows 8 will be pre-installed, and the CCI proprietary solutions which have made the CC 100 exceptional in ease of use are available for the new family. CC System Services, Integrated Document Processing with Web Authoring Applications, CC Data Exchange, and Virtual Webstation are all offered for the CC 200/300. Many of the systems have already been installed at customer locations. Response to them has been extremely favorable.

Introducing these systems is only one way in which CCI protects our customers' investment. With this announcement, we are providing an updated software environment for users of a wide variety of desktop systems, as well as the CC 100. The CC 200/300 systems are designed to be the best desktop solutions for the CCI environment. The new versions of CCI software are available for non-CCI Windows systems as well.

We are also announcing new peripherals and software for the CC Series. The CC 100 remains an integral component of our desktop product line, and these enhancements further strengthen its position. The new CCP-25 Color Printer, which features PostScript V and can output up to 25 pages per minute at 1800 dpi, is also available for the CC 100/200/300.

We are also making the first announcement to implement CCI's Web publishing strategy that we announced last December. We are announcing our integrated solution with full and automated access to popular databases, and are issuing detailed statements of direction on a CC-based advanced data integration solution. Our intent is to offer a range of exciting solutions, integrating data and the Web.

Advanced Web Processing will include our powerful page designer with support for all ODBC databases. It will give office users the ability to produce documents with dramatically increased aesthetic appeal, while incorporating database content and requiring virtually no special training. It is designed to be a major advance in ease of use among high-end corporate Web data publishing systems. CCI will sell and support the entire system.

We hope the enclosed material will familiarize you with our directions as well as with these products. There's additional information on this announcement at our analyst Web site, http://www.cciweb.com/analysts. (Follow the May 20XX Announcement link after you log in.) If you have any questions, please call CCI Analyst Relations at 480 555-4CCI.

Sincerely,

Flash

Flash Gordon
Director, Analyst Relations

New firms with few products can include a complete price list in their announcement kit. (This should be done more often than it is.) Firms with more products may find it easier to provide only the prices of new products and those that have changed. If you publish an Analysts' or Consultants' Reference Manual with a price list, replace any pages affected by changes. Asking people to write in changes, when only a few items on a page have changed, is tacky and won't save much money. Lists of changes get lost or are ignored. Analysts are often under time pressure to price products from several vendors to put a new announcement in perspective. They may not check as thoroughly as they should for the latest prices. Make it easy for them to get yours right. If they get a competitors' wrong, that's not your problem.

- Photos help if there is something about your product that photographs well (such as innovative industrial design in hardware) or has a unique visual aspect that is hard to explain in words (such as a user interface concept in software). If product literature in the kits has photos, you don't have to put in separate photos as well. If there's nothing else in the kit to convey a visual message, add photos unless the cost is prohibitive. If it is, tell recipients that they can get photos through their usual support channels, or let them know where to find them on the Web.

- Competitive analysis material. Don't compare your products against a competitive product unless is a commonly used reference point or you're positioning your product as an alternative to a recognized market leader. Unvarnished "I'm better than you" comparisons leave a bad taste in some readers' mouths.

  It *is* appropriate to put your products into a broad context that includes several competitors. Software vendors have done this effectively with cost-per-seat curves, for example.

  Start-up firms in new market areas may not have much competitive analysis material. In that case, don't worry. Edit whatever you give your sales force to avoid disparaging references to named competitors while conveying a positive tone about your own products and services.

- An update to your Analysts' or Consultants' Reference Manual, if you have one. (The manual itself is discussed in Section 7.10 below.) The content of this update depends on how the manual is organized. A note telling people where to file the press release and product brief, and what obsolete material can be discarded, may be sufficient.

  If your manual contains more than indexed press releases and product briefs, you may be able to replace several announcement kit items with one update. Small firms without a formal manual should still remember that analysts (and consultants) save paper materials in file folders. This being the case, include information in your kit as to which products or services are obsolete with your new announcement, and what old materials can therefore be moved to a history file.

- Almost any announcement material written for your sales force, distributors, or resellers, is appropriate for analysts and consultants. Take out anything really proprietary, keeping in mind that much that is labeled as proprietary usually needn't be. Take out contract and policy details too. Analysts don't care if your new product should be ordered on Form 41, or if its distribution code is R3C. Most of what's left is good to send to analysts. Sales strategy material, with statements such as "this product is good for users with clients at multiple sites because..." is especially helpful. It helps analysts see where your product fits.

What you send out in this category depends on what has been written for other audiences. If you don't send the materials themselves to analysts, familiarize yourself with them before you assemble your announcement kit.

Customizing your press release

Press releases are a staple of announcements, and properly so. Sending them to analysts is equally standard. Yet many firms make the mistake of taking press releases as they are and sending them as is. This is a mistake. Analysts are not the press. The basic content of a press release usually meets analyst needs, but the format does not. If you send analysts a release on paper or in an e-mail, it should reflect their uniqueness.

Customizing your press release for analysts (or consultants) is easy to do. Sending analysts analyst releases, instead of press releases, will immediately set you apart from the crowd. (It's not necessary to customize press releases on your Web site, though. When analysts go to a Web site for a press release, they are aware that they're accessing press materials. This is not the case when they open an envelope or e-mail addressed directly to them.) Here are basic changes to a press release to customize it for an analyst audience:

Whether your release is e-mailed or printed:

- Eliminate the "For Release..." line.

  Why? Analysts don't release information. They keep it.

- Change at least some references to "customers" or "users" to refer to "your clients."

- Change the contact name, phone number and e-mail address to those of your analyst liaison. Even if it's the same as the press contact, change the heading above the name to "For further analyst information, contact..."

- Change the standard sentence near the end that says "Acme is a global firm offering a complete line of 64-bit coffee."

  Why? Analysts think they know this. They may not, but cater to their perception. This sentence could be "For more information on Acme's complete line of 64-bit coffee, contact us at 781 555-5555, anrel@acmecoffee.com." It says the same thing, without implying that it's news.

- Add your e-mail address if it's not already there.

  Why? Many newspaper editors are not e-mail fans. Most analysts are. This applies to e-mail if the message's "Reply To" address is not where replies or questions should be sent. If this address belongs to the analyst relations person who should get replies, adding it again elsewhere is redundant.

If your release is printed:

- Use special stationery. If you don't want to print special paper, use your corporate letterhead with "ANALYST INFORMATION" right below it.

- Put the date on the first page. Include the year, though some press releases omit it.

Why? Newspapers don't need the year: they use releases within a few weeks or toss them. Analysts put them in folders and retrieve them years later. (This applies to PDF documents as well. While readers can retrieve the document creation date, it's easier if it's visible.)

- Drop the standard closing sentence that reads "Acme Coffee is located at 23 Highland Ave., Needham, MA 02492; telephone 781 555-5555, http://www.acmecoffee.com."

  Why? This information must be in the body of a press release which is meant to be printed as is or with minimal editing. Editors won't search it out and add it if it's not there. Newspaper readers don't have the original release, but analysts do. Your address, phone number and URL are in plain sight. Don't insult analysts' intelligence by repeating them.

A given press release may lend itself to other changes as well. Look for customization possibilities each time you review a press release for use with analysts. If you do a total rewrite, an analyst information release can be more personal in tone than a press release. An analyst release goes to a human being with whom your firm has a relationship, while a press release is intended to become a newspaper article. In any case, the above changes are basic. They don't require editorial skill or creativity, and take virtually no time with a word processor. They should become automatic.

Money-saving tips for paper announcement kits

A paper package containing all the above items is expensive. It is probably also unnecessary unless your firm is especially sensitive to analyst influences. Smaller firms will have smaller announcements, less material to send out about them, and fewer analysts on their mailing list, so the cost of sending announcement information is somewhat self-controlling. There are also many components of an announcement kit that are not expected of smaller firms and can be left out where cost is important.

You can reduce costs in several ways.

1. Build up in stages. Your initial announcement package as a start-up can be a customized version of your press release. The second step augments this with a spec sheet or one-page product brief. As your firm grows further you can add other components.

2. Reduce production costs. Send the complete package only to your "A list." E-mail others the basic press release or mail them the modified analyst version. Include the URL where they can obtain more information and, with a paper mailing, a card that they can return for more if they prefer it in that form. (Use a card, in addition to an e-mail address or phone number, since checking a box is often the least-effort action.)

3. Reduce duplicate copies when several people from the same firm at the same location are on your mailing list. Many offices have shared provider and product files. You don't have to send complete kits to everyone in them. If your analyst database has several names in one office, decide which one or two people should get the full kit. If you can tell from job titles that some are senior to the others, the senior people should get them. If you haven't a clue, ask. (This is also a good way to find out who's left the company, moved to a different office, or changed to a different area of specialization.) Few will say "Send everyone the full package" if it's not necessary. People who don't get a full set should get the customized press release with an insert telling them who in their office has the rest of the

package. They should also get a card they can return to get the full set of materials if they want it for their personal files.

Including announcement coverage with other materials

An alternative to announcement packages is including announcement information in your periodic updates. This is usually *not* a good idea because:

1. It's less timely. Analysts will have long since read the basic information in the press, or even sooner in a Web news update.
2. It makes your announcement look less special, more another step in the normal course of business.

Using regular updates for announcement information is therefore not a good idea unless your budget is down to its last penny. Consider this only if your updates are monthly, in which case the lag from announcement date to publication date may be acceptable, or if your announcement happens to coincide with its preparation deadline.

If you put announcement material in an periodic update instead of a separate mailing, cover as many of the items mentioned earlier as possible. Differentiate a mailing from press reports on the announcement by including material that was not in the press release and therefore did not appear in press announcement coverage. For example, most press releases and announcement articles give sample prices. If you put different samples in your mailing, it will add value to your analyst support.

If you have a separate announcement mailing, you should still summarize it in your periodic update. Some analysts, may not have received kits. Your update can carry articles on the background of the announcement, internal preparations to support the new product line, its technology, its quality control, its new assembly line, its new uniform documentation look, and seminars that have been scheduled to tell analysts more about it. List press releases and other materials that are available. Give the URL of the new product's main Web page, or if this isn't possible because of site design, the most efficient click sequence from the home page or analyst entry point. Show that your analyst support programs talk to each other by mentioning the announcement mailing in your update. If additional support materials are available, mention them in the update too.

What different types of analysts need in analyst events

Research Agenda-Driven	General background information for their files and to know, when a report calls for it, what your firm offers, what other information to look for, and where to get it.
Event-Driven	Complete and detailed information, as quickly as possible.
Calendar-Driven	Just enough information for them to keep up to date with major changes in your firm's products and/or services.
Client-Driven	General background information for their files and to know, when an engagement calls for it, what your firm offers, what other information to look for, and where to get it.

7.11. Other written reference material

BEST PRACTICE

Organized basic reference material is important to many analysts. Whatever format you choose, Web, CD-ROM or hard copy, it should be oriented to analysts who follow many firms.

Your firm surely has a sales reference handbook for your sales force. This book (we'll refer to it as a "book" from here on, though it may be a CD-ROM or an intranet site) tells sales reps what your firm's products are, what they do, how they do it, and how much they cost. It's an essential reference for them.

In evaluating, analyzing and recommending products, analysts and consultants need much the same information. The more easily they can get it, the better they'll feel about your firm. If you give them the information, you control how it's presented. If they must find it elsewhere, they'll find someone else's version, go to a lot of trouble to assemble it from several different sources, or wait (perhaps under client or deadline time pressure) while your analyst relations team puts it together. None of these is desirable.

For these reasons it can be useful to have a Consultants' Reference Manual (its usual name, even if it's mostly for analysts). This is an analyst/consultant version of your sales reference handbook. It serves a similar purpose and should contain similar information. It need not resemble the sales force version in format, though you may be able to use some of its material after some edits.

If you don't need a full-scale Consultant's Reference Manual, think about a shorter version: a "briefing book" for your firm, its major products, its distribution channels and other important topics. It would include the major areas discussed in this section, without the details. Readers can get those elsewhere, from your Web site or by asking you, if they need them. So, don't automatically dismiss the CRM idea if you don't need the full treatment. A smaller version may still be useful.

Content

A Consultants' Reference Manual or Web site should contain:

- **A company overview:** history, general structure, names and bios of key executives, locations of major R&D and manufacturing facilities, size information such as revenue and number of employees. Include your annual report if your firm is publicly owned. (Most publicly owned firms already post their annual reports in the Investor Relations section of their Web site. If your manual is online, a link to it is plenty.)

- **Product description material.** Product briefs and sales literature describe products in isolation without relating them to each other. This is fine for a sales prospect who only cares about your Model 150, but it's not fine for an analyst who has to figure out how the 150 relates to Models 100 and 200. If existing materials make up the bulk of your manual, add material that relates products to each other and describes their primary uses. Include statements of strategy and competitive positioning information. Leave out "knock-offs" versus individual competitors.

- **Configuration material** if applicable and is not already in the product literature. How many blivets attach to each wingbat? Can a wingbat support four-armed and eight-armed blivets simultaneously? When does adding another wingbat need a high-capacity power supply, different software, or a license upgrade? Test this content: give it to a few analysts, with nothing else, and ask them to configure a few systems. If they get it right, fine. If not, don't tell them how stupid they are. Maybe they **are** stupid—but if they are, so are others. Rewrite it and test it again, with a new group. (You'll probably have to pay for their time if you want them to do this. It's worth it.)

- **Summary charts.** If you have more than two products in a given category, these are a must. List them and tabulate relevant comparative parameters. If your manual has more than a few dozen pages, this chart should also give the section number, page number or URL for more details. Every page should have a date.

- **Price list.** Granted, these get out of date. But analysts know this; they won't use a 2008 list in 2013. Don't put prices with product information, since that makes prices hard to update by themselves. You can update a separate price list as required. Put a date on your price list—**prominently**.

- **Descriptions of support programs** such as hardware maintenance (including available options), software upgrade and/or problem resolution service, training (as specific as possible), a "hot line" for assistance, user groups, and anything else customers benefit from.

- **List of sales offices and analyst contacts.** Put in every phone number an analyst might need to call for any purpose, every e-mail address to which one might want to send a message. If your firm has several contact points, explain when they should call or write to each one. If you have a documentation distribution center that serves people outside your firm, include it in this list.

- **An e-mail address to which readers can send comments or suggestions** about the manual itself, plus (if it's hard copy) a postage-paid reply card on which paper-oriented people can write them.

- If it's in hard copy and has more than a few dozen pages, **binders with tabs**. Custom-printed binders are not expensive in quantity. For even less, you can get loose-leaf binders with transparent sleeves on the front and spine. Have inserts printed for these sleeves and voilà! An instant custom binder on a budget.

- **Information about your Web site.** Even if the manual is printed, analysts have to go online for the latest information. If they must register to access your analyst site, tell them how. If registration involves human review, so there is a lag between an analyst initiating the process and when he or she can use the site, tell them, so they're not taken by surprise when they try to access the site for the first time when it's 3 a.m. in your time zone and they can't get in.

Updating

A reference manual or Web site needs regular updates. There is nothing worse than an obsolete manual sitting on a shelf as a visible reminder of your firm's inability to follow through, a CD-ROM with a three-year-old copyright date, or a Web page with a "Last Modified" date during the first Bush administration. It's better to have no manual at all than to have one that goes for ages between updates, growing more obsolete and reminding analysts of your unreliability. New products must be added, obsolete ones removed. Specs, contact names, and prices must be changed as changes occur.

Announcements are good occasions to send out paper or CD-ROM updates. If you prefer you can send out updates on a regular schedule, every month or every other month.

If you do, your announcement material should mention that an update for the manual will be in the next scheduled update, giving its time frame. Then make sure it does.

Charges

In pre-Web days some firms charged for these, primarily large firms whose "manuals" filled several thick binders. Their production costs were substantial. They needed to screen out the merely curious. An initial cost in the low-to-mid three figures, with a fee for annual updates, discouraged the curious without deterring serious users.

Today's manuals are smaller because much of what used to be in one is now on the Web. In addition, the curious now get instant online gratification. So, charging isn't necessary. The only time you might consider it if you have a soft copy version but offer paper as an option. In that case, charging for hard copy to offset production costs is acceptable.

Evolution

Don't even think about a manual until you have enough products that their materials need organizing. It's a big job. Until that point, let analysts find what they need on your Web site. Chances are it's all there. If your firm is small, it won't be hard to find.

Your first step uses existing documents. Collect product literature, specification sheets, price sheets, sample contract forms, and backgrounders, a corporate overview. Throw in supporting materials such as an annual report. Put them in a loose-leaf binder with an index and table of contents, or list them on your analyst site. If it's on paper, print tabs for major sections and custom inserts for the front and the spine of blank binders. At this point you'll have more than most firms have until they reach half a billion dollars in annual revenue. Keep it up to date and this collection will serve nicely.

Your next step becomes necessary when you have enough different products, or sufficiently complex products, that their relationships are not obvious from the set of individual descriptions. At that point write introductory material for each section of your manual. This material need not be elaborate or extensive. Three pages per section, or five screenfuls, should suffice. Once written, this material should remain valid for at least a year or two with minor updates to reflect announcements as they occur.

You will now have a binder, printed in your corporate colors to look attractive on a shelf, full of carefully targeted material written for analysts and consultants, and updated regularly with each announcement. That's as far as any firm need go. The seven-volume sets some old-timers recall from the 1980s aren't needed today.

Other Reference Materials

A Reference Manual isn't the only kind of reference material an analyst might ever need. The main other category is technical documentation. This applies mostly to software: a reference to the SQL dialect of a database management system, the application program interfaces of a middleware package, or the commands of a data mining language. Some hardware with significant built-in functionality, such as networking gear, has this sort of reference material too. Such materials are still often produced on paper in 2013, though CD-ROMs are used as well—or, for software, online help that's available when the program is running, supplemented by a small installation guide.

It's not necessary to send this sort of information out proactively. Just make sure analysts know how to get it, or at least how to find out what exists so they can decide if they want it. You should also "grease the skids" with whoever stocks it, to get it to analysts as quickly as possible when they ask.

What different types of analysts need in reference materials

Research Agenda-Driven	Excellent background for in-depth reports. They must include this type of background information on the firms they cover.
Event-Driven	Useful if announcement kits, briefings and so on turn out at the last minute to lack some vital detail.
Calendar-Driven	Helps understand where your products or services fit and therefore how to classify them.
Client-Driven	Important starting point for many client engagements.

7.12. Product Demonstrations for Analysts

BEST PRACTICE

Use demos sparingly. Know in each case why you chose to demonstrate something and exactly what you want the demo to show.

Demonstrations are central to many analyst presentations. Whether it's a briefing on a new product, an analyst day or an analyst visit to headquarters, it's a rare meeting that does not involve showing what a provider's products or services do and that they really work.

Showing off accomplishments is a human trait. (Stop anyone carrying a baby if you need proof.) However, human inclinations do not always lead to the best marketing results. Before showing a product to industry analysts:

1. Figure out the specific points you want to convey by a demo.
2. Understand clearly why a demo is the best way to convey them.
3. Plan a demo to convey those points without spending unnecessary time on others.
4. Tell analysts what those are before the demo.

What analysts think of demos varies with what's demonstrated. Some think "watching another box with blinking lights" is a waste of time. Analysts who follow technologies where there's not much to see when everything works are usually in this group. The same is true of those who follow services—again, you can't tell much by watching. On the other hand, unique interface features or other visual capabilities can be worth showing. A verbal description of Windows 8, even one accompanied by screen shots, wouldn't have the same impact as seeing it in action.

Analysts value the ability to interact with a demo system and engage in meaningful discussions with the people presenting it. A canned demo, a prepared script with no variation, is of less value (unless something goes wrong, which you hope won't happen).

Some technically-oriented analysts like to be able to run a system, or at least to ask that specific features be shown. UNIX analysts, for example, pride themselves on being able to tell something about a system by issuing OS commands. Whether or not they really can doesn't matter. They think they can. Perception is everything. Let them.

What different types of analysts need in demonstrations

Research Agenda-Driven	Usually needed for reports. Even if analysts won't learn anything from the demo, research doesn't seem thorough without one.
Event-Driven	Helpful if a new product differs in a tangible way from earlier ones the analyst knows.
Calendar-Driven	Seldom necessary, but can provide a feel for products they track.
Client-Driven	Depends on client requirements. May make a new product "real."

7.13. Product Launches: An Overview

The previous sections covered many activities that go with announcing a new product or service: analyst tours, press releases and so on. This section pulls them together.

Analysts who follow your firm need to know about your product or service launches far enough in advance to figure out their questions, ask them, and receive answers in time to formulate positions before the press and clients call with questions. They will typically agree to an embargo (short-term non-disclosure) to get pre-briefings. (Analysts with whom you have an existing NDA are already bound by it.)

You can't pre-brief every analyst who might care about your announcement, though you should make sure your list of pre-briefing candidates is as complete as possible. Make sure the rest get the press release and supporting analyst materials by e-mail simultaneously with public announcement. You do *not* want any analyst to respond to a client or press query with "You know as much about it as I do!"

Your launch timeline should include:

- **Advisory group, consulting engagements.** Let a few analysts review your announcement materials early enough to consider their comments in the final version. Analysts can gauge customer and press reactions better than your marketing staff, no matter how competent, possibly can. (Hopefully you used analysts earlier to help set strategy, identify user requirements and market trends, and define functionality. This is just about the pre-launch stage.)

- **Preparation.** Decide who you'll call (and when), who you'll visit (and when), to whom you'll send materials (and when, and how). Then make sure all the necessary people are available, materials are prepared, and your analyst Web site (if you have one) is updated.

- **Pre-Briefings.** Important analysts should learn about your announcement a few days or weeks in advance. The lead time you need depends in part on the complexity of what you announce. Analysts will understand if final materials are not available.

  Notify analysts whom you pre-brief when the actual announcement takes place, and of any slips of more than a day or so. Analysts are too busy to track every announcement. If you don't tell them what's going on, they may make the wrong assumption— in either direction. (Analysts know that plans change and dates slip, so don't worry about their reactions when you tell them. In any case, the sooner they find out about a slip, the better. If you tell them two days before a planned announcement, and they find out that you knew weeks before but didn't tell them, it's not good.)

- **Briefings, Briefing Book.** Analysts who were not pre-briefed must be told of the launch when it happens. Even those who were must be updated with the final information and materials that have now become available. This is a good opportunity to visit major research firms that cover the area of your new product or service. You'll have to line up an appropriate visiting team, train them in speaking to analysts, and prepare a **briefing book** (see Section 11.5) describing who they'll talk to and what these people need. You should also send an e-mail as soon as the announcement is made, with supporting information available on your Web site and/or for download, and have a teleconference for analysts who are not on the tour itinerary.

- **Follow-up.** As you know, analyst recommendations come from relationships built on trust sustained through repeated contact over time. Don't just send out a press release or drop in on analysts as part of a tour, though you should do both of these. Check to make sure the materials were received (if they were sent via e-mail or in hard copy), to see if the analyst has questions, and to encourage the analyst (gently) to use the new information in client newsletters and reports.

- **Sustaining Momentum.** A successful launch will raise your profile with analysts who knew of you and put you on the radar screen of many who did not. This progress is too valuable to waste. Continue with the other activities discussed elsewhere in this book to make sure you obtain maximum value from your investment in launch-related activities.

8 | Attitude factors for analysts

This chapter will cover:

1 Proactivity and responsiveness: two sides of the coin
2 The need for candor and honesty
3 Analysts' overall sense of comfort and ease with you and your firm

Chapter 5 discussed the building blocks of analyst support programs. The third dimension of its cube was the attitude with which you convey the information of Chapter 6 via the channels of Chapter 7. That's this chapter. Read it in the context of those two.

Like those chapters, this one focuses on analysts. Chapter 10, The Consultant Difference, covers how consultants (direct advisors) may differ from analysts in terms of these factors. A few times, where they should be treated the same, this chapter refers to both.

The comment about treating analysts and consultants as extensions of your sales force at the beginning of Chapter 7 applies here. If your attitude toward analysts is one of cooperation because of the benefit they bring to the industry, they will respond by offering you their cooperation. If you come across as antagonistic, their attitudes will reflect that.

The guideline of not starting anything you can't follow through with, also mentioned earlier, is another influence on analyst attitudes. You want to convey credibility to your analyst audience. Reliability and predictability are important in this.

The following three sections will cover three basic analyst attitude measures. They are all important. They are not prioritized in the same way as factors in previous chapters. You and your colleagues should keep all of them in mind, all the time.

8.1. Proactivity

Proactivity keeps analysts aware of you on an on-going basis. Proactivity can use many of the communication channels of Chapter 7. The main ones are:

- Informational communications, including updates and announcement information
- Invitations to teleconferences
- Invitations to analyst events
- Phone calls to keep in touch and find out if the analyst needs anything
- Visits to the analyst firm
- Other communications, including e-mail, etc.

Proactive outreach, telling analysts what's going on, never seems as urgent as handling incoming calls. Urgency, however, is not the same as importance.

Outreach is important despite not being urgent. So what if we don't get the e-mail out today? We'll get it out tomorrow. No harm done. Right?

Right, if we get it out tomorrow. But tomorrow has a nasty habit of being as crisis-driven as today. So tomorrow turns into the day after, which turns into next week, which turns into … Pretty soon the March e-mail goes out in June, or the call you promised to make becomes irrelevant. To harp on a recurring theme, that's the impression the analyst gets: late again, late as usual.

Choosing an Outreach Method

Outreach methods have a hierarchy. Each step up demands more of the analyst's time. Each step up therefore has to be justified by giving more value in proportion to the added time. The **Analyst Communication Value Ladder** shows this:

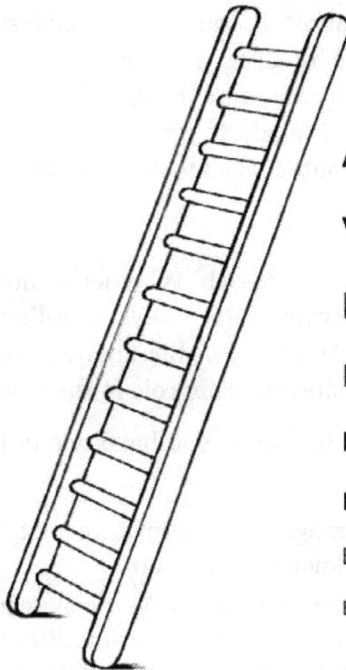

Attending analyst event

Visiting a vendor

Hosting a vendor visit

Participating in a telebriefing

Personal phone call

Paper mail

E-mail with attachments or links

E-mail with content in body

The channels at the top (in larger type) demand the greatest time commitment from the analyst and correspondingly require the greatest justification on your part.

For instance, if you invite an analyst to participate in a telebriefing, you have to justify its time by providing information you couldn't put in an e-mail. You must justify an analyst visiting your facilities by offering something that could not be supplied by your visiting that analyst. (That may be timeliness: perhaps the analyst can meet with your VP next week by coming to you, rather than waiting until the next time the VP is in Chicago.) And so on. You may be able to get an analyst to come to one event on the basis of general interest and wanting to know your firm better, but if you don't come through with solid value, you won't get a second chance.

Before any communication, consider the objectives of the communication and its form in terms of this hierarchy. **Use higher methods only when lower ones won't do.** Send paper only when you have something to say that can't be said, or can't be said as effectively, in e-mail or e-mail plus the Web, and so on.

Informational communications

This is the most important part of your analyst communications. These don't require more effort to reach more analysts, they're not as intrusive on analyst time as a phone call or visit, and they can be customized electronically to each analyst's needs.

Chapter 7 gave suggestions for content, methods, etc. Mailings (including e-mail) are part of the big picture of outbound communication. If you have an analyst newsletter, you may not need as many mailings or as extensive a set. If you call people to ask what they need and then send it, you don't have to put the same material into a bulk mailing (at least not to them; you might want to send it to analysts you didn't call or who didn't ask for it). In other words, plan mailings in the context of all your outreach.

Invitations to teleconferences

The invitation, not the teleconference itself, is the outreach. Whether or not the analyst eventually participates is a separate issue. In terms of the analyst's feeling about your firm, receiving the invitation counts for a lot. That's when the analyst feels you know something about his or her interests and appreciate his or her role in the industry.

Invite analysts to participate in teleconferences whenever you have one in the analyst's area of interest. Two pointers:

1. If your firm has frequent teleconferences on a range of topics, invite analysts only to those ones they care about. That will convey that you know what they do.

    You can also e-mail analysts lists of all your teleconferences if you explain what you're doing. This lets them inform new staff members who may not be on your list yet, accommodates changed job assignments that you may not be aware of yet, and provides an overall view of your firm. Such a catalogue is not a personal invitation.

2. Provide adequate lead time. (See the end of Section 7.7 on this. Insufficient advance notice of teleconferences is a common cause of analyst irritation.)

Invitations to analyst events

The discussion of invitations to teleconferences applies equally to other types of analyst events: from a two-hour briefing in a local hotel room to a three-day get-together at a remote site. Here too, the proactivity is in the invitation.

Expense can be a factor with longer meetings. The incremental cost of one more person can become significant for an event stretching over two or three days. Some locations also have physical limits on how many guests can be accommodated. You may therefore have to limit the number of invitations.

This need not be a major problem. You probably have an idea how many analysts are likely to be interested. On this basis, you can see if your budget will accommodate this number. If it won't, hopefully either the budget or the limit can be changed.

If it's not practical to change either, more people would like to participate in your event than you can handle. This beats lack of interest! One solution is to call the senior manager you deal with at each firm and say "we're scheduling such-and-such an event at such-and-such time and place. We hope you'll be able to participate, but space is tight. Could we ask you to pick the three [or whatever] people for whom it would be most valuable?" Analysts are not unreasonable people. They are not in business to waste providers' money. (If it came to a choice, they'd rather you spend your money on their research services than on hotel rooms and cocktails.) The usual response will be a list of three names—perhaps then and there, perhaps a few days later. Or, it might be "Three is tight; we have these four people, these are their areas of interest, ..." You'll probably reach a compromise that is acceptable to both of you.

Phone calls to keep in touch

Analyst relations, as its name suggests, is a relationship business. It takes effort to maintain any human relationship.

Telephone is a good way to maintain a long-distance relationship. Regular phone calls remind each party that the other exists, give each a chance to update the other, and remind them that the other one will be there if need arises. Therefore, plan to keep in touch with key analysts by telephone.

Analysts vary in how often they want to be contacted, from "stay in my face" to "don't call me, I'll call you." We suggest:

- Ask. They'll tell you. That may mean more or less contact than they'd like from other providers, depending on where you fall in their professional interests.
- If you don't know, don't call just to keep in touch until a minimum of six weeks since your previous contact. Less than this may be annoying. If you hear "I was wondering if you lost my phone number," call sooner next time.

- If an analyst has a research agenda, you can ask "Are you working on or planning any reports that we might give you information for?" This shows you understand how that analyst works and can give you valuable lead time to collect the information.

- If an analyst's business is driven by different factors, however, this question shows that you don't understand how that analyst works. You'll probably hear "I don't know, are you planning any announcements I should cover?" The first time you ask, you'll be forgiven. Ask twice, it shows you weren't paying attention.

- Another important question, which you don't have to ask every time, is "Are you still the right person for us in this area?" Research firms, like providers, reorganize. People change jobs and get promoted. Or, perhaps you were originally contacted by someone for a one-time project outside their primary area, and they were never the right person to keep up to date on the topic at all. A phone call is a good way to check on this.

For an average call frequency of once every two months per analyst, if each call lasts a quarter-hour, you can keep in regular touch with forty analysts in twenty minutes a day (allowing for leaving some voice mail messages).

Visits to the research firm

Visiting analyst firms can be the worst sort of outreach in terms of its demands on your time, and (perhaps surprisingly) also on that of the analyst organization. In total time commitment on the part of a research firm, visits can easily exceed even analyst days, since the visit's duration is multiplied by the number of analysts who participate.

Visits can also be the most effective method to give analysts information and build constructive relationships with them. For this to happen, they must meet analyst needs as outlined in Chapter 7.

Consider visits as an element of your proactive outreach to the most important firms. Much as you'd like to visit everyone, it's not practical. "Most important" doesn't always mean "largest," of course. If a one-man shop in the hills of Carmel, California or Fort William, Scotland has a major impact on your employer's fortunes, head for the hills!

8.2. Responsiveness

Responsiveness is the other side of the proactivity coin. With proactivity, you initiate contact. With responsiveness, the analyst does.

As you've read, an analyst's or consultant's only first-hand basis for judging your firm's responsiveness to its customers is your responsiveness to that person. When you respond quickly, you work for a responsive firm. If you respond slowly, you convey the impression of a sluggish one. It's your choice.

None of us can always be as responsive as we'd like. There are days with more work than time. There are lags in getting answers from colleagues, whose priorities are not necessarily ours. There are phone and e-mail delays. And there are questions whose answers don't exist. (Will Feature X be in Release 3.2? Nobody knows yet.)

To appear responsive despite these, you must keep the analyst aware that a request has been received, what you're doing with it, and when you expect something to happen:

1. Acknowledge everything as soon as possible. An e-mail auto-responder can confirm that your server has received a message. A standard reply, which you can send out with a mouse click, can confirm that you received it in person. A real personal confirmation, by e-mail or voice mail, doesn't take much more effort.

2. If you'll need more information or clarification from the analyst, ask as soon as possible even if you won't be able to get to the request for a while. This sets a tone.

3. If you need something from another person, tell the requester as much as possible about what you're doing, what you're waiting for, and why you have to wait for it. (The reason for the wait may be obvious to you, but not to others.) You may not want to identify who you're waiting for, so the analysts won't contact that person directly.

4. If there will be an extended delay—someone has to return from a trip, a meeting has to take place, etc.—explain this and say when you should have more information.

5. If the delay affects part of a multiple-part question, send partial answers as they become available or ask the analyst if partial answers are helpful (unless it's obvious from the question).

6. If responding takes more than a couple of weeks, update the requester regularly on the progress of the request. Don't make the analyst call you.

Most of these are common sense or normal business courtesy. But they're easy to forget amidst the crises and urgencies of a normal business day. Try to make them a habit.

Always ask "What's your deadline?" That's not an excuse to stall until the day before. It's a way for the two of you to assess how to best meet the need. If the best responder won't be back from Nepal until the week after, you can look for Person B right away.

Support by your firm as a whole

It's a rare inquiry that you'll be able to answer by yourself. Unless you answered the same question in the past 48 hours, or it's something like "What's the dress code for our meeting?," you'll probably have to check. In many cases you'll have to get another member of your organization to communicate directly with an analyst.

When this happens someone else, whose job is not analyst support, has to put down what he or she is doing—which is probably what his or her performance is evaluated for doing. As of that moment, your own understanding of analysts is not enough. The rest of your firm, or at least one piece of it, must also understand them and how to work with them. Analysts' impressions of your firm will also reflect what they do.

This makes it important for you to raise your firm's collective analyst and/or consultant consciousness. There are several ways to do this:

• Discuss their role in the information technology infrastructure as you work with colleagues. You don't have to become a bore. Just make sure they know.

- Get on the agenda of your firm's employee orientation and management training programs. This is especially helpful in orienting salespeople to the role of consultants they'll encounter in their sales campaigns.

- Ditto for other meetings such as sales kickoffs, occasional staff meetings of appropriate groups and whatever other get-togethers your firm has.

- Write and distribute information on analysts to all those who are likely to have any contact. This can take the form of a small handbook.

- Distribute analyst write-ups that mention your firm. It's nice if the mention is favorable, but even a negative one can be useful if it points up a need for change. A monthly compilation of everything that's come out during the month is a good way to do this, if your firm gets enough analyst attention that you get more than one mention most months. If analyst reports are available on line, sending relevant URLs can work.

- Some analyst relations managers have used "brown bag lunches" where everyone interested in analyst relations can gather to discuss the topic. These are an excellent way to build rapport and support among those who are already somewhat supportive, but those who need help most are unlikely to show up.

8.3. Candor and honesty

An analyst asks a question. You, or a member of your firm, answers it. The analyst incorporates the answer into a report, a response to a client inquiry, or a comment in tomorrow's *Wall Street Journal*.

So far, so good. But what happens if the world doesn't turn out as that person said it would? There may be several reasons:

- Someone misread the future. This happens. Admit it, explain if you think that will help, and move on.

- Someone who should have known didn't. A manager thought a problem was fixed because he wrote a memo telling someone to fix it. The fix hadn't been distributed yet, but the manager didn't realize that. To the manager, the problem had been fixed, but to customers it hadn't. Again, admit, explain if appropriate, and move on.

- A project slipped, was canceled, was cut back to meet budget constraints, etc. This happens too. The sin is not in the slip or whatever. Analysts have seen these before, know they'll happen again, and accept them as an inevitable (if not desirable) part of high tech. The sin is not telling them about it.

"Not telling" need not mean a bare-faced lie when asked a direct question. It can also mean knowing, talking to an analyst whom you know cares, and not saying a word. While that may not be dishonest by the dictionary, it isn't candid either.

The worst kind of dishonesty is the out-and-out lie. "It will be ready in the next quarter." "We've tested it with a 50TB database." "We haven't heard that it explodes."

The fact is, as mentioned earlier, that analysts *will* learn bad news. Finding things out is one way they protect clients. They have multiple information sources besides official provider channels. These include users, the Internet, personal contacts inside your organization and your competitors', Roving Rumor Reporters, and enough more to shame the CIA. If you haven't tested it with a 50TB database, they'll get an e-mail from one of your QA engineers within the hour that says you don't have a system with over 10TB anywhere in your company.

Dishonesty, including lack of candor, damages your firm when (not if) analysts find out:

- Their attitude toward your firm will take an instant turn for the worse. That will color everything they write or say, even on subjects unrelated to the dishonesty.

- They won't trust anything you say after that.

Analysts start out wanting to trust a provider. This trust can be lost in an instant. Once it's lost, it takes a long time to rebuild.

If you're new in an analyst relations job, the sins of your predecessors will haunt you. There will be a "honeymoon" during which you'll be given the benefit of the doubt. Still, if there were honesty or candor issues before you took the job, you won't have a totally clean slate. Analysts will feel, with reason, that your arrival didn't change the corporate culture, the executive roster, or the reasons why someone felt that shading the truth was a good idea. A helpful, open analyst may say "I'd like to believe everything you tell me, but after what J. did to me when he said thus-and-such last year, no way am I going to." The less helpful or less open will just think it.

Total candor and honesty are easy when things are rosy. Things are not, unfortunately, always rosy. In addition, corporate policies and concern over competitors learning things sometimes limit what you can say. To proceed in an imperfect world that suffers from such problems, we suggest:

- Never, ever, say anything significant that you know to be untrue.

- Feel free to say "I can't tell you." Be matter-of-fact about it. You won't be the first person who ever said that to this analyst. They may not like it, but they'll accept it. You can blame corporate policy if that's the reason, but *only* if that's the reason. If you say that's the reason and it isn't, you've lied. The analyst will eventually learn that no such policy exists.

- Use non-disclosure agreements. Analysts who need the information for a purpose that would violate such an agreement won't sign one. Once analysts sign NDAs they observe them. They know word of an NDA violation will get around quickly and destroy their ability to get one in the future.

- Explain to your colleagues that dishonesty, while tempting in the short run, never pays off in the long run. The "long run" here is weeks or months, not years. The fallout will occur while most of them are still in their present jobs.

- Think about telling analysts proactively about problems, slippages, etc. This is difficult. Nobody wants to call up an opinion leader and say "Ed, I want you to know that Release 4 will be three months late—and, when it comes out, it won't support SQL Server."

As you've read, analysts *will* find out about this sooner or later. You *cannot* control this. The only thing you have can control is who they find out from (you, or a source you can't control), how it's presented (your way, or by a competitor or unhappy customer) and whether or not you can explain what you're doing about it at the same time. It's better in all of these respects if you tell them first.

The catch: you don't want them to find out any earlier than they have to. If you tell them, you eliminate the possibility that they might not hear for a while. There's no way around that. The benefits of being their information source, in terms of dealing with that specific problem and building long-term trust, outweigh that.

Look at the triangle on page 23 again. Your objective is to optimize messages that go from advisor to client along the bottom link. You control only the left link. The analyst changes your messages rather than just passing them on. Your messages, therefore, must be crafted to as to optimize what the client hears after this filtering takes place. This may mean counter-intuitive messaging. Telling analysts about problems is an example. It isn't something you'd do if you were speaking directly to a customer, but you're not. Its value in improving what analysts tell their clients outweighs the negatives.

8.4. Overall sense of comfort and ease

The relationship between analysts and your firm, between analysts and you, boils down to feeling comfortable with each other. Consider this scenario:

Analyst Lou arrives at his office to find a note from his manager Susan: "Call these six vendors, ask them about X, and e-mail me what you have by the end of today."

Lou will call all six. He has to. However, he might pick up the phone eagerly to call some, because he knows he'll have a pleasant discussion, won't waste time, and will get answers that are as honest as they can be within the bounds of corporate policy. He may put off calling the others in the hope that a later e-mail from Susan will make it unnecessary. Who is in each group?

That, in essence, is the comfort issue. You'd like to be one of the firms Lou calls early. Not because you need the call. Another analyst phone call probably means more work. (If Susan calls off the job later that day, the vendors Lou hasn't called yet get off easy.) But because of the signal it sends.

The signal is that Lou will call you, not a competitor, when he *doesn't* have a list. Suppose the message was from a client saying "Can you suggest two or three vendors we should look at for this application, and who support our environment?" Now Lou gets to pick the vendors. He knows that the same six have this application. He just has to verify that they support the client's environment. Under those circumstances, who is he going to call? Those he feels comfortable with. Who will be on the short list he gives his client? Probably the first three who reply "Yes, we support that environment." If most vendors support that environment, those will be the vendors he feels comfortable with. That's the list you want to be on.

Consistency and authenticity in your relationships with analysts, both from one interaction to the next and with your overall corporate culture, are important. If you tend to be businesslike and to-the-point in your dealings, stay that way. If you tend to be friendly and personal, stay that way. Either works as long as it's really you. Bouncing back and forth from one to the other is confusing and, subconsciously, disturbing.

You can't call an analyst and command "Feel comfortable with me!" It's the result of the other things you do. It's the by-product of intelligent proactivity, responsiveness, and candor, applied consistently from one time to the next and consistently with the rest of what the analyst sees in your company. If you do those things well and with a positive attitude, analysts will feel comfortable with you.

In conclusion...

It's a relationship thing.

9 | The inbound value of analysts to your firm

This chapter will cover:

1 Why you should treat analysts as more than a communication channel

2 Ways analysts can provide value to your firm

3 The role of the analyst liaison in these strategic activities

The last four chapters focused on what analysts need from you, and how to best provide it: the right content, in the right ways, with the right attitude. If that were the whole story, analyst relations would be much like press relations. There would be that bit about analysts sticking their own opinions into what they say, but they'd be just another channel.

As you know, they're not. Your firm should take advantage of their understanding and perspective to further its business. There are a lot of reasons:

1. Analysts know things that matter to your firm. They are more objective about the industry than your colleagues. Using their insight will improve management decisions.

2. As analysts work with your firm they come to appreciate the reasons for its choices, the logic in its products and the capabilities of its people. This can lead to more favorable coverage than it would get if the analyst saw it only from the outside.

3. In working with analysts, you can suggest report topics. You'll suggest, obviously, topics where research and reports can help you. They won't necessarily accept all your ideas, but when they plan their work, your ideas will be in the mix.

4. Analysts appreciate being respected for knowledge and insight, versus being treated as a "mouthpiece." They hold better opinions of firms who show treat them this way.

5. A two-way relationship builds trust. This leads to the analyst trusting what you say in other situations. (Violating it, knowing you'll be believed, may work once. It's not recommended.)

6. In choosing providers (below the top tier, who must be covered in any case) for reports, analysts lean toward firms they know and about which they have or can get information. By working with you they know about you, have information about you, and know how to get more.

7. Finally, while what reputable analysts write (if they write about you) is not influenced by a provider's being a client, not all analysts are reputable in this regard. Analysts are as honorable as members of any other profession, but in any group some people find it hard to resist temptation. With senior people often compensated for business development, temptation arises. Some disreputable analysts are also influential. It is unfortunate that coverage must occasionally be bought, but it would be less than candid to pretend that "pay for play" never happens.

The analyst relations department is uniquely positioned to help with these. It is already in touch with analysts. It knows who they are, what they do. Knowing this, it can suggest firms or analysts for specific situations. It can take analysts' suggestions for where they might be able to help, evaluate them to see if they meet a real need, and take them to the right place. It can bring analysts information about research needs. In short, it can serve as a clearing house for information both ways.

In addition, it can save a firm money. As a focal point for analyst contact, it can monitor contracts to make sure that different divisions don't have overlapping subscriptions, take advantage of corporate purchasing power for quantity discounts, and make inquiry time that might go unused by one division available to others.

Aside from benefits to the firm, involving the analyst relations group in these areas helps position it as a strategic adjunct to business development. This can improve the career prospects of those who work there.

As for disclosing proprietary information to the analyst: you generally needn't worry. Some analysts and firms have policies against consulting to direct competitors at the same time or within a given period. Where this isn't feasible, such as when all providers in a practice area compete with each other, they observe non-disclosure agreements carefully. What an analyst learns in general by working with you will help later with other clients, but what the analyst learned in working with past clients helps you.

The rest of this chapter discusses how analysts and providers can benefit mutually.

9.1. Consulting Engagements

One reason consultants exist is to give people better information than they would have on their own. In high-tech, the people with this information are often analysts.

Companies engage analysts because of their influence on customers, but analysts can be used to drive corporate success in other ways too. In addition to carrying your message to customers and prospects, analysts can provide value by:

- Insight and advice in an important area.
- Feedback on users' opinions, needs and trends.
- Recommendations for new business opportunities.
- Advice on product strategy and development.
- Input on plans, roll-out strategies and distribution channels.
- Assistance with product positioning and message development.
- Competitive assessments.
- Writing white papers or other materials.
- Moving industry trends in the direction of your current and future products.
- Guiding you through difficult situations, being your allies in hard times.

A consulting engagement can also have additional benefits:

- Improved relationship with the analyst. This can justify an occasional "charity engagement." Even in that case, pick a topic where the analyst can make a real contribution, rather than just make-work for the sake of helping the analyst meet a business target.

- Better understanding on the analyst's part of why your firm does things. This often leads to more positive reports, because choices make more sense when the logic is known. Without an engagement in which the analyst spends time with your company, he or she wouldn't sit still long enough to appreciate its thinking.

Your firm is *not* buying the analyst's opinion. No reputable analyst's opinions are for sale. It is buying access, a chance to present its position. It does not guarantee that the analyst will agree with it. However, if you have access, and your competitors don't, your chances of agreement are good. If competitors have access, and you don't …

Analysts who consult to your management on product and strategy issues often have a client base consisting largely of providers. Since they're used to working with firms like yours, they can come up to speed quickly. You still have to confirm that the analyst's orientation—business or technology, tactical or strategic, and so on—is what's needed.

Work that involves understanding users and their needs, though, is often best done by user-facing analysts. Their insight into the user viewpoint, coming from extended exposure to people spending real money to solve real problems, and their ability to reflect that viewpoint to you, is valuable in these situations.

Discussions leading to an engagement can be initiated by:

1. The analyst.
2. The potential client: the manager, engineer or other person the engagement is to benefit.
3. Someone in the analyst relations function.

In any of these cases, analyst and client must ultimately agree on what is to be done, by when, and for what compensation. How they get to that point may depend on whose idea the engagement was.

If the analyst has the idea, he or she may mention it to the client or the analyst relations manager. It is then up to the client and his/her management to decide if the proposed service will be useful, if this analyst is the right person to provide it, and if the price is fair. The analyst relations manager can help by bringing the parties together, perhaps by giving the client information about the analyst and his or her firm, but does not play a major role in the process.

If the client comes up with the idea, the analyst relations manager can perform a strategic function by suggesting analysts who have the required abilities. It's possible that the client didn't think of analysts in the context of the proposed project, perhaps because he or she is only familiar with other types of advisors. The analyst relations manager can raise the client's consciousness vis-à-vis what analysts can contribute.

If the analyst liaison has the idea, he or she probably has an analyst or two in mind. In this case, the client should be sounded out first to see if the idea of using an analyst strikes a chord. Only after "sure, I'll talk to them" should the analyst(s) be contacted. Most analysts will have a preliminary discussion with a potential client at no charge for professional services, though if travel is involved some will ask for expense reimbursement to confirm real interest. Keep your eyes open for opportunities to use analysts in consulting engagements. They can arise in areas such as (far from a complete list):

Functional Area	Typical Opportunities to Use Analyst Insight
R&D	Matching development plans with user needs and industry trends
Marketing	User needs, market sizing, and (within the bounds of proprietary information) competitive strategies and products
Strategic Planning	Candidates for various types of partnering and/or mergers
Business development	New markets that suit the company's existing capabilities

Don't push this to the point that colleagues start to think of you as a shill for analysts, but be alert for legitimate situations where they can be of value.

Once an engagement begins, the analyst relations manager must keep informed to make sure the client is receiving the expected value and is satisfied with the analyst's services. This is vital because the relationship between your company and the research firm can be soured if the engagement is not reasonably successful. If there are problems that can't be resolved by a discussion among client, analyst, analyst relations manager and perhaps the client's management, the AR manager should alert research firm management. They won't risk a long-term relationship with your company for a little billing. If more resources or a different analyst can improve things, they'll take the needed steps.

Analyst relations managers are often responsible for arranging non-disclosure agreements for analysts. They are better positioned to do this than colleagues who work with analysts rarely. They should also already know if the analyst is already under one that could cover a planned engagement.

Other ways of working with analysts may be structured as consulting engagements as well, since that's the administrative mechanism through which one pays for an analyst's time, but their nature is different from that of the typical consulting engagement as outlined above. The next sections describe a few.

9.2. Reviewing Your Materials

When a firm announces anything—product, service, merger, reorganization or anything else—it does so with the hope of making a specific impression on one or more publics. If it's a product or service, the main public is sales prospects and the desired impression is "that's something we could spend money on." If it's a merger, the public may be investors and the desired impression might be "this company has its act together."

Prior to any announcement, materials are reviewed to see if the reviewers think they will have the desired effect. Analysts can be a useful part of this group in several situations:

- If a product or service is being announced, analysts who serve its potential user community are good judges of how it will react. They might, for example, alert your firm to a choice of words that sounds fine within your company, but which, because of unfortunate association with a product of another firm, would be disastrous outside it— or is, perhaps, company jargon that nobody besides your colleagues will recognize.

  You could, of course, go to real users. However, you may not be ready to expose the product or service to them, you may not want to risk a bad first impression on even one or two friendly users, and that would make it harder to keep things quiet.

- If you are preparing materials for analysts—as part of a tour, analyst event or other occasion—analysts are the best possible judges of the reaction. They might say "don't spend time on this, we know it; leave more time for Q&A" or "Any vendor could say that; say how you're different." Your colleagues may be leery of saying this sort of thing to executives. Even if they're willing to, executives may accept it more readily from a respected outside source.

- If the intended audience is distributors, investment analysts, or any other group, analysts who work with that group are in a good position to gauge their likely reactions.

Presentation review engagements are generally carried out at your offices, since they're most effective when the presenters are those who will give them later, and such people probably won't travel for this. Reviewing materials by themselves is possible but not as effective. Materials not meant for presenting, such as press releases or sales brochures, can be reviewed anywhere.

A reviewing engagement will probably last about a day, perhaps less if there are few materials and overnight travel is not required. (Travel often carries a minimum of one day's billing to justify the travel time, over and above travel expenses.) If you have unused inquiry hours on a contract, it allows them to be used in for this, and the research firm has a suitable analyst, this can be a good way to use them.

Expect to have a non-disclosure agreement with an analyst for this type of work, unless the content is already public knowledge in at least its general outlines.

9.3. Analyst Training for Spokespeople

Reviewing presentations and materials is focused on one presentation, one event. You may know of people within your company who will spend a lot of time in front of analysts, perhaps on short notice. It's a good idea to train them in advance for this.

Analyst training for spokespeople is discussed in Section 11.6. Here we note that analysts can be an important part of this training: who knows better what analysts need and how they'll react to something?

Considerations for choosing analysts, compensating them, etc., for helping you with spokesperson training resemble those for reviewing materials (the previous section).

9.4. Advisory Boards

Several high-tech firms have **analyst advisory boards** to advise executives on a regular basis on business, product and/or market strategy, and industry trends. These typically consist of 4–8 analysts from as many firms.

The main benefit of an advisory board is objective advice to management, on a regular basis from people who already know it and the major issues it faces. A potential secondary benefit is that, if some of your executives are negative about analysts, this can (if all goes well!) help improve that attitude.

Analysts who participate in such a review board must:

- ... be experts in the subject matter that the board is to deal with.
- ... be willing to work collegially with analysts from competing firms.
- ... be supportive, not confrontational.
- ... be willing to make, subject to the unexpected, a long-term commitment.
- ... sign a non-disclosure agreement regarding board discussions. (This eliminates any whose corporate or personal policy prevents this. See Section 6.2 on why some analysts may not want, or be able, to sign an NDA.)

Advisory boards typically meet 4–6 times per year for a half-day or day followed by dinner. There is reading, and perhaps a teleconference or two, between meetings. Each meeting's topics are set in advance. Within a general area, discussions are far-ranging.

Participating in an advisory board benefits analysts with a preview of your firm's future and the inside track for consulting. Still, expect to pay for their time, including meeting and preparation time. (You may be able to use a subscription's consulting hours.)

A certain amount of board turnover is desirable to make sure new ideas come in. Normal job turnover on the part of participants will usually create enough vacancies. If it doesn't, it may be necessary to ask one or more board members to leave. Establishing term limits in advance makes this less painful than it would be if someone has to be "fired."

The analyst relations manager's role regarding advisory boards includes:

- If your firm does not yet have one, sounding out one or more executives on the concept and putting the board in place if their reactions are favorable.
- Participating in board meetings as part of his or her role in managing the firm's relationships with analysts. If your management would prefer to limit meetings to board mem-

bers, the analyst relations manager should be made aware of what happened: to follow up on action items and be able to work with its members on an informed basis in the future.

- When turnover happens, recommending replacements for members who leave.
- Handling, or at least keeping informed about, arrangements for analyst compensation to make sure that it is consistent with other analyst activities.
- Providing tokens of appreciation for analysts' participation, typically annually. Office-related gifts such as plaques, clocks and so on are appropriate. So are personal items such as tote bags, though analysts get a lot of those. (Be sure not to violate any gift-value policies of your advisory board members' firms.)
- If a member must be asked to leave the board, working with research firm management to make sure your company's overall relationship with it is not damaged.

9.5. Speaking and writing on your behalf

Analysts often speak and write on the computer industry. As a group, they're good at it. Many of them also know something about your company. Several of these, you hope, hold positive opinions about its products and services. Why not ask them (for a fee) to speak and write on its behalf?

On the plus side, this is a good way to get white papers that have credibility, get speakers who will attract people to prospect seminars or customer meetings, and get quotes to use in advertising or press releases. It also involves an analyst with your firm and thus hopefully improves his or her attitude toward it.

A negative, besides cost, is that some analysts don't want to be seen as favoring a provider. They don't want the "hired gun" reputation that can come from this work. Such analysts usually work for user-facing firms. Perception of provider independence is critical to their reputation. Analysts at provider-facing firms tend to be more flexible about writing for vendors.

A related concern is that analysts from some research firms do this so often that their credibility suffers. This is more of an issue with other analysts than it is with customers and prospects, who generally don't know enough about individual analysts to judge this. You and your colleagues should decide if this might be a problem with your target audience.

Will you get a positive write-up if you engage an analyst to write a white paper? Generally yes, but not because analysts will say anything for pay. An ethical analyst will look at a topic and let you know if he or she feels positive enough about it to create something you'd be happy with. Hence, just about every paid article is positive, but not because analysts write whatever a sponsor asks. It's because negative ones don't get written.

Analysts also make good speakers at consultant seminars. (See Section 10.2.) Consultants appreciate the insight they bring to the industry. Analysts aren't as concerned with speaking to a consultant audience under provider sponsorship as they are with users.

9.6. Your firm's participation in analyst conferences

Besides publishing market research and selling consulting services, analyst firms hold conferences and other events to reach new clients and to add value to existing clients' services. Since many decision-makers and influencers from your customer base and prospect community attend these events, as well as many of the analysts who matter to you, participating in these conferences can be of strategic value to your firm—to say nothing of what you and your colleagues can learn in its discussions and presentations.

These conferences are also a good place to meet analysts from the firm in question. However, analysts need to focus their conference time on their own business priorities. They would rather spend time with clients and prospects than with you. Unless your firm is one of these, expect to introduce yourself, chat very briefly, say you understand the analyst has other things to do at this conference, thank him or her for the time, and indicate that you hope to follow up later when you'll both have more time. If the analyst really wants to talk with you, he or she can then say so, at which point you can set up a time and place. If not, exit politely and follow up afterward. (If the analyst says "I start a two-year trek across Africa next week," at least you learned something.)

A calendar of analyst events will help you be more proactive and strategic in your outreach efforts. Its gives you a longer-term picture of what is occurring in the industry.

Use your calendar to help schedule meetings between analysts and spokespeople, to time your strategic messages and to plan your own events to avoid conflicts.

As this is written there is no master calendar of analyst conferences. However, most research firms put their schedules several months out on their Web sites. Begin creating your calendar with those. You'll need to revisit these sites regularly to keep it up to date. You can keep the task within reason by concentrating on the largest firms and a small number of specialist firms that focus on your products and markets. On some sites, you can register to receive event announcements via e-mail. Finally, many analyst relations consulting firms and PR agencies try to keep current on these conferences. If you use one, they will share their information with you.

An events calendar should be simple. It can be organized by analyst firm, topic, or month—or, with simple data management software, by all three. The organization of the calendar should mirror that of your analyst relations plan so you can spot opportunities for strategic analyst outreach.

Your company's calendar of analyst-sponsored events should include:

- Name of event
- Firm, and division(s)/practice(s)/service(s) if any, holding the event
- Date(s)
- Location

- URL for more information
- Known speakers, both analysts from the sponsoring firm and others
- Brief description: topic areas, how often the event is held, expected audience (size, composition), your company's history with it
- Opportunities for provider sponsorship (yes/no); if yes, cost and other considerations
- Opportunities for one-on-one meetings with analysts

Analyst-sponsored events and forums: attendance and sponsorship

There are at least 500 analyst firms worldwide in 2013. Major ones have at least one flagship conference, plus smaller or regional ones, each year. The cost of attendance and sponsorship vary widely. At the upper end, a company may spend $3,000 per attendee and over $10,000 for sponsorship, exclusive of travel and lodging expenses. Such sums can exhaust analyst relations budgets quickly, so you must assess which events to participate in and on what level.

Sponsoring a conference gets you a certain amount of publicity in pre-conference materials and during the conference, with the opportunity to set up a booth to showcase your firm and its offerings; one or more speaker slots; and additional seats for your firm's attendees, though not as many as you could buy for the sponsorship fee if maximum seats were your objective. Consider it only if the conference will attract your sales prospects.

Sponsorship may not be necessary for your objectives. Providers can speak at research firm conferences without being sponsors—typically if the provider is a client, it hasn't had a speaker at the same firm's conference in the past couple of years, the speaker has something significant to say, and it asks with enough lead time (at least several months).

In determining which events to attend and/or sponsor, revisit your company and program goals and objectives. Prioritize events on the basis of benefits for the company. Consider what your company learns by attending (often for someone other than yourself), influence with users who attend, and influence gained with analysts. These must be weighed against costs of attending, both direct financial costs and the value of what attendees would otherwise do with their time. Factors to consider include:

Category	Factor
Value	Area(s) of coverage relative to what is of value to your firm
	Session tracks, specific topics and speakers
	Opportunity for one-on-one meetings with analysts
	Opportunity to speak with users
	Opportunity for media exposure

Influence with customers and sales prospects	Size of expected audience Nature of expected audience (job level, etc.) Anticipated participation by competitors Area(s) of coverage (again) Opportunity for social interactions with other participants Opportunity to speak at or sponsor the conference
Influence with analysts	Importance of the firm holding the event Number of anticipated analysts in attendance Anticipated participation by competitors Area(s) of coverage (yet again; this is always important) Opportunity for on-one meetings with analysts

Things to do before, during and after a research firm event

Before the event

- Sponsorship:

- Decide: yes or no? (A "yes" may require several months' lead time.)

- Booth: structure, contents, staffing (your marketing department probably has experience and equipment from trade shows)

- Marketing materials

- Participants: Choose as needed in each category: speaker, subject matter expert, booth duty, analyst relations, learning from program. Try to cover multiple objectives with the same person. Plan this in conjunction with potential participants' managers.

- Review presentation materials:

  - Of your company's speaker(s), if any.

  - Of the research firm discussing your company's products and services. (You can usually review these for factual content if you ask, but you'll have to turn them around quickly and will seldom succeed in changing opinions or evaluations.)

- Request analyst meetings if this can be done in advance. Try to meet with as many analysts who cover your field as possible, especially those who have been negative about your firm in the past.

- Plan session attendance using the advance program. (Some conferences request tentative session preferences in advance.) Try to attend sessions in which your competitors are discussed. Someone else can cover sessions about your own company and general industry trends if necessary.

During the event

- Request meetings if you have not done so in advance, or new/different ones based on new information since then (such as learning that a particular analyst will attend even though he or she had not been expected to, or that a new analyst has just started to cover one of your product areas).

- Meet with analysts as scheduled. Invite one or more of your content specialists to these meetings so the analyst can gain a broader appreciation of your company. If you are your company's only participant in this meeting, focus on developing the relationship. Discuss your support for the analyst's work and how you can support him or her better. Unless you can discuss your firm's products or services at an expert level, leave that to others, but offer to set up any meetings the analyst wants on them.

- If you were not able to plan session coverage ahead of time, plan it now.

- Attend planned sessions, with last-minute changes as needed. Take notes on what is said about your company, its competitors, and industry trends that may interest your strategic planners.

- Socialize as much as practical. This is an important part of building a relationship. Keep in mind that some of your company's participants, typically especially those from its R&D organization, may not be as inclined to do this as most analyst relations professionals are.

After the event

Report back internally:

- who from your company attended
- which competitors came
- who comprised the audience in general (size, characteristics)
- which analysts you met with
- points of interest and "red flags" that came up in sessions or meetings
- positive stories (and negative ones, if any; your company needs to know about them too)
- follow-up items
- recommendations for next analyst event
- Follow up as necessary on any action items, such as analyst requests for a teleconference with a product expert.

These are just a few of the ways in which analysts can provide value to your firm, over and above their role in conveying information to your customers and prospects. If you stay alert to opportunities such as these, you will show your management that your business perspective is more than arranging tours and sending out messages. This will benefit both your employer and your career.

10 | The consultant difference

This chapter will cover:

1 How consultants differ from analysts
2 Changes to analyst programs for a consultant focus
3 Ideas for consultants that aren't in analyst relations programs

The last few chapters described the building blocks of an *analyst* support program. Consultants are often an equally important target, at times more so. This chapter will go over all the items of Chapters 6 through 9. It will discuss how direct advisors differ from analysts in each, and how that affects your program. It will also cover a few items that apply specifically to these people.

There is as broad a spectrum of consultants as there is of analysts. (It may be broader, since consultants may also be resellers or systems integrators. If your company has channel programs for them, you'll have to plan how to handle hybrids.) These generalizations are therefore just that. There's no substitute for finding out what each wants.

This is, however, more difficult with consultants. The analyst world is small relative to that of consultants. You can build a database with every analyst your firm cares about. It's impossible to identify every consultant who could at some time recommend for or against your firm. You must rely less on determining individual needs, more on characterizing those who matter and meeting typical needs.

The second key difference between analysts and consultants is that analysts need to know about your firm on an on-going basis. If they cover hotel software, and you sell hotel software, they care about you all the time. Consultants care about you only when they have an engagement with a client that might use your products or services. When they need you, they need you, but before and after that they don't. Therefore:

- You don't know who will care about you next month, but you need to be prepared when that happens. (If it's any consolation, they don't know either.) It's a statistical game. Out of every hundred consultants on your list, ten will matter, but you have to cover all 100 to be sure of reaching those ten. Therefore, a consultant relations program spends more time with people who have general interest but no specific need at the moment.

- When consultants need to know about your firm, they may need more basic educating than if they had kept current with your products and technologies all along.

The main exception is the technology centers of some large consulting firms such as Accenture or IBM Global Services. They function much like a research firm with a product focus. They have just one client—the rest of their firm—but their influence on that client is huge and that client has an equally huge impact on user purchase decisions. In addition, experts at these centers are often quoted in the press much as analysts are. Treat these centers somewhere between the consultants covered in this chapter and the analysts which you read about earlier.

Also, as noted earlier, some analysts also consult. Some research firms employ consultants for this purpose. For instance, a Gartner user client, impressed with the insight in a report, may ask them to apply their expertise to that user's situation. Gartner is then in the consulting business. Recognizing that this will happen, but not wanting to take analysts away from research and report writing, Gartner and others employ people who are good at this work and specialize in it. Most analyst subscription agreements include an allowance for a certain amount of phone consulting. Anything beyond that allowance, or anything that requires a visit to the client, is billed separately.

10.1. Information Types

Just as there's probably nothing about a provider that some analyst, somewhere, sometime, hasn't needed to know, there is also probably nothing that some consultant, somewhere, sometime, hasn't needed to know. Still, there are differences in the usual priorities of the two groups. Here's how they stack up in terms of the eight basic content types:

Information about strategy

Most consultants are not as interested in a firm's strategy as analysts. That's because analysts typically focus on a two-to five-year time frame, but consultants are normally concerned with specific needs right now.

This doesn't mean they don't care at all. It just means that in setting priorities for consultant information, you can move strategy a few notches down from where it sits on the typical analyst's scale.

Information about products

In contrast to strategy, consultants generally care deeply about product information (or services information, if your "product" is a service). You can equate them to the most product-focused analysts in this regard. They are faced with a client need that must be met by a tangible offering. When they recommend a provider, they must usually justify their recommendation with specifics.

Information about pricing

Analysts need to calibrate your prices versus competitors in a general way. Their report will say something such as "X is cheaper," perhaps "...for networks with over 50 nodes," "...if you process 500 transactions per minute," etc. Consultants need to know if X is cheaper for *this* client, in *this* situation. For that, they may need to price specific configurations.

To price configurations for consultants, you must find the core problem. Suppose one asks you to price a network. Its hubs use 4 to 16 ports. Fine—yours support 32, no problem. But why 16? Is that the optimum network design? Or is it because the consultant is used to a different hub, which supports only 16 ports, and subconsciously designed to that limit? If that's why, a closer look might reveal places where 24-port hubs can be used to advantage, reducing the number of hubs and the cost. Using the consultant's design unchanged, your hubs' 32-port capability will exact a cost penalty with no benefit.

Such situations come up in many contexts. Linux-based servers may use more or less RAM than those that use a different OS. A data warehouse using a relational database may need less disk space than the same one using a multi-dimensional structure. A thin client system may need a more powerful server than a fat client solution to the same problem, offsetting savings at the client level. A processor of a given speed may outperform or underperform a processor of the same clock speed but a different architecture— or even of the same architecture, but different cache size or bus speed. Etc.

Your resources are, of course, limited. You can't price every system, network, etc., that a consultant shows you. When you do price one, however, make sure you price out the best solution using *your* offerings, not what might be best if you had someone else's. You may have to justify changing the spec. That, in turn, may mean getting the technical gurus on the phone or keyboard to explain why, in terms of the real need and the way your products work, this is to the consultant's client's (that is, your sales prospect's) advantage.

You might discuss list prices vs. "street" or "deal" prices with analysts. With consultants, this is a total no-no. Pricing is the sales rep's business. *Never* get in the way of that. Even if you know exactly what that sales rep must say, don't say it. Let him or her be the one to reap gratitude for cutting the price or to decide how to tell the customer that it can't be. The rep has to live with the customer. You don't.

Information about shipments

Shipment data are usually of little interest to consultants. If they need to know, they'll get a Dataquest or IDC report. It will put your shipments in their industry context. That's more useful to consultants than just numbers. And, much as we hate to say this, consultants trust those reports more than they trust you—even if the numbers in those reports came from you in the first place!

This being the case, consultant support needn't stress shipment numbers. Mention growth, of course. Growth is good. But you mention it to send the message that your firm is thriving, not because consultants care about the numbers themselves.

Information about the organization

When consultants work with a client, they care about the parts of your organization that their client will deal with: the part of your sales force that serves the client and your support team(s).

To help a client work with your firm, the consultant must understand how these groups work. Is your support divided along pre-sale and post-sale lines, or by product? The latter may provide more continuity in customer relationships and a higher level of product expertise, but less familiarity with how all your products work together and perhaps some finger-pointing when they don't.

Neither structure is right or wrong. However, we all like to deal with the familiar. A consultant who understands which your firm has and how it works will feel better about working with you. This higher comfort level will translate into a preference to recommend you when all other factors are equal or nearly so.

When discussing your organization with consultants, provide more than structure. Explain how it works. What is the process to get different types of support? Which accounts are handled by vertical industry sales teams, which by geographical territories? How are problem calls escalated? What is the background of the VP who supervises the consultant's client's sales representative? Analysts don't care about this sort of information. Give it to consultants, though, as it increases their comfort level.

Conversely, information such as the reporting relationship of a new business unit typically won't interest consultants much. There are some situations where they care, such as if a client might use that division. But these are exceptions. Most of the time, analysts' and consultants' interests in organizational information are worlds apart.

Information about competitive positioning

Consultants are interested in how your firm sees itself versus your competition. This is especially important once a consultant has decided to recommend you. At that point he or she must defend, or at least justify, this recommendation. The competitive information that your sales force uses will come in handy.

Positioning information can also come in handy in your efforts to convince the consultant to recommend your firm. When you use it this way, bear in mind the cautions about using competitive information with analysts. Consultants are just as familiar with providers and products, though they may not have the same technical depth as some analysts. More to the point, they have sat through as many provider pitches and are just as cynical. If you want to provide competitive positioning, make sure it's defensible.

Information about technology

This type of information tends to be more useful to the consulting community than to analysts. The reason is that analysts live with a technology or a market. They become experts on that technology or the technologies in that market. They may know more about it than most of your R&D staff members. (Many have been senior R&D staff members on the provider side themselves. Others could be, if they wanted to.)

Consultants, by contrast, spend more of their time solving client problems. Most of them don't have the time to keep current on every new technology. Since they also don't want to appear ignorant in front of their clients, they read backgrounders and white papers avidly to "get up to speed" on them.

This gives you an opportunity to expose them to the thought processes that went into the design of your products and the logic behind your R&D tradeoffs. Once they buy into your logic they will resist an equally reasonable counterargument from another provider.

That being the case, make as much technology background as possible available to consultants. You probably won't be in a position to get it written if it isn't already written for some other purpose. You can, however, weigh in on the side of getting more written when the subject comes up in a meeting. You can stay on top of what's being written, so you're always aware of what's available. And you can use consultant communications of all types to make sure that your audience knows about it.

Reference accounts

Reference accounts are vital to consultants. They don't know how your product or service will perform for their client, but you're asking them to stake their professional reputation on it. Their best insurance policy is to find out how it performs for others with similar needs.

Hence the need for references. They must often meet precise criteria: a specific industry, a specific product version, a specific computing environment—or whatever applies in your case. The closer the reference account resembles the client, the better. This is psychologically true even when it can't affect whatever the consultant needs to confirm.

Try to work with the sales rep to provide this information. If you don't know who that is, perhaps because you don't know who the prospect is, you can't. In that case, once you find the sales rep, give him or her all the information you previously gave the consultant.

10.2. Information Channels

The second dimension of the consultant/analyst relations cube reflects the channels through which this information is provided. As with information types, there are differences in how you should approach them for consultants vs. analysts.

A central point of contact

You or someone like you is just as important to consultants as to analysts. There is one difference between a central contact's work with analysts and with consultants: consultants can go to the client's sales rep. They don't always do that, because:

- Sometimes the consultant doesn't want to identify the client yet. (Two reasons were mentioned in Section 5.2.)

- Sometimes the consultant isn't near the client and would find it difficult to work with a remote salesperson. The consultant's local sales reps don't want to support an eventual sale in some other region, instead of using that time to go after their own sales.

- Some sales reps, sad to say, view consultants as interlopers who threaten account control. A consultant faced with one of those will try to find an alternative. From your corporate viewpoint, providing a central contact point beats losing a sale. A consultant who has run into one or two such salespeople will turn to a central contact rather than waiting to see if the next one is another.

- Unless the consultant has a narrow geographic and industry focus, each client probably has a different sales rep. Working with you offers a relationship with continuity.

For the last two reasons, consultants may prefer to deal with a central consultant liaison even when they know who the sales rep is.

Local contacts

Local consultant contacts, for part of a large country or at the national level elsewhere, can be an alternative to a central support point or an adjunct to it. Local contacts should never be the sole contact point, though many consultants like the concept. They shouldn't be because:

- Some functions are best done centrally, such as sending out announcement information or making contact with technical experts in your firm's R&D department.

- Some calls will come to headquarters no matter what you do.

- Local consultant support typically works with the local sales force. Clients in other areas have sales reps from a different part of your sales force.

- Some nationwide consulting firms need a central contact.

- Some consultants will feel better if they are handled by the home office.

For small firms, local contacts can make a full-time central consultant relations staff unnecessary. For larger ones, they can improve responsiveness. This job can be a responsibility of local marketing support managers or of a member of the local marketing support staff. Very large firms can have full-time local consultant support staffs.

These people must have a support orientation. It's their job to get consultants what they want. They can ask enough about the request to understand it and how best to meet it, but it is not their job to convince a consultant that a request is stupid. They must know enough about your product line to understand references to a "D-22 Mod B with 64-bit microblat, Version 6." They must have complete, up-to-date product information, with specs, at their fingertips. They must know where to go within your firm to get any they don't have. They must know what information is not to be given out, and how to refuse a request politely or get clearance to provide it. They must be able to keep several balls in the air at the same time without getting rattled. Their telephone and e-mail manners must be impeccable. All in all, a tall order—but an important one to fill if your firm is to achieve the best possible results in the marketplace.

In meeting with consultants, time of day is more important than it is with analysts. Analysts spend much of their day working with vendors, meeting with other analysts in their firm, and sitting by themselves as they write or think about what they will write. Consultants, on the other hand, are far more involved with their clients, often spending full days at client sites. It is harder for them to free up time during the day to meet with you. Your ability to meet after work or over dinner will often make the difference between having a meeting and not having one.

Contact with executives

Since consultants are generally less interested in strategic information than analysts, they generally need less executive contact. There are two reasons to put a senior executive in touch with a consultant:

1. The "stroking" will help the consultant feel good about your company.
2. The executive will be able to assure the consultant about corporate commitment to something the consultant and his/her client care about.

Executives can create an aura of caring that others, no matter how well-intentioned and competent, cannot. Use them for this, but use them sparingly so they know that you won't waste their time unnecessarily. Make sure the executive knows the purpose of each contact and why you need an executive, so he or she can accomplish that purpose with a minimum of wasted time.

By the time executive contact with a consultant is appropriate, a campaign will normally have evolved to the point where you know the sales representative on the account. Executive contact is thus normally with the sales rep's knowledge and approval. It will also often be in the context of a consultant/client visit to your firm, with the sales rep personally involved, or by a phone call, in which case he or she might not be. This differs from analysts, whom executives will frequently go on the road to visit. It is nearly unheard-of for an executive to travel to meet with a consultant, though if an executive visits an important sales prospect, the prospect's consultant may be in the meeting.

Contact with other staff members

In contrast to executives, it can be important to put consultants in touch with staff members about product specifics. Suppose a consultant needs to check if a product can be used in a situation that its descriptions do not address. You could say "Here's a manual, an ftp site for more, and the URL of the support knowledge base. Figure out the answer yourself." However, a short phone call to a developer is more likely to lead to a win.

The hardest part of this is knowing which developer. Fortunately, you're not entirely on your own. Product managers will usually be able to guide you, if not to the right individual, at least to the right first-level R&D manager. That manager can then suggest Kevin, Melinda or Dharmesh. As you work with these people over time, you'll be able to find them on your own.

In order not to overload the developers, urge consultants to work with local sales support before they ask you to go to the R&D team. The specifics of this staff will vary with your corporate organization. In some cases, especially involving new or unreleased products, they may not be of much help. In other situations there may not yet be an identified sales team to use. Sometimes, though, they'll be able to handle the entire problem. It's important for consultants to understand that these people are your first line of defense. Going to the developers is only for when the marketing support teams can't do the job. It shouldn't be hard to convince them to go there first, for two reasons:

1. The consultant wants to develop a relationship with the technical support people. That will enable him or her to contact them later to resolve client problems, thus enhancing his or her perceived value to the client.

2. Consultants, who are for the most part reasonable, understand that developers can't take time to answer every question that comes along. (If they did, nothing could be developed.)

Visits to the consulting firm

These will be rare. Few consulting firms have the clout to justify them. You may call on the corporate headquarters of EDS or Capgemini, but the list of candidates for such visits is very short.

When you call on a consulting firm, it will in all likelihood be on its top management or its top technical specialists. These specialists, as noted earlier, are much like analysts with one large client. Their impact is through telling the firm "if one of our clients needs an X, we think this is the best choice, or these are the best choices." Few staff members will go against this recommendation unless circumstances are unusual. Even then, the staffer usually e-mails the expert to make sure they're really as unusual as they seem.

Plan such visits as you would plan analyst visits, as discussed in Section 7.4.

Visits by the consulting firm to you

When a consultant asks for information from you, he or she *needs* that information. Client satisfaction depends on it. Therefore, the basic reason analysts generally prefer that you visit them—if *you* want to tell *them* something in person, you can get on a plane to do it—doesn't apply. Consultants will, in principle, come to you. This doesn't mean they always will. They must consider time and cost. But it will happen more than once.

In hosting a consultant visit, learn as much as you can about its objectives. Consultants usually want to accomplish them as quickly as possible. This matches your staff's desire to get the consultant out of their hair as quickly as possible.

The usual agenda involves meetings with your technical staff. It may be necessary to work with prototype or pre-release products. Time on these may be precious, especially if hardware is involved, and will have to be arranged in advance. It may also be necessary to prepare an non-disclosure agreement for the consultant. You're the best person to do this, as you're probably the host and few R&D people have much experience with NDAs.

Sometimes a consultant visits with the sales prospect. Such visits follow prospect visit protocols even when a consultant is involved. Unless you are specifically asked to do something, perhaps the consultant asks "while I'm there, could I also ...," you don't have to do anything. You can stop by their conference room to say hello, but that's about it. The consultant is part of the prospect team. The sales rep runs this show.

Consultant expense reimbursement

Be wary of offering reimbursement when a potential purchase is involved. The offer can be misinterpreted as an attempted bribe. If a consultant visits, his or her client engagement should fund the visit. If it doesn't, that's the consultant's problem, not yours.

As host you'll pay for a visitor's lunches, coffee and a muffin from your cafeteria, and probably a dinner or two if the visit lasts more than a day. If you have special rates at a nearby hotel, suggest that the consultant tell its reservation desk that he or she is visiting your firm. (It may be necessary to call the hotel directly. Central reservation offices and Web booking sites don't always know of these arrangements.) That much is normal business hospitality. More is seldom necessary, and may be inappropriate.

Multi-firm briefings

Consultants are an attractive target for local briefings. With rare exceptions, they can't justify personal visits, and they know it. They don't feel analysts' competitiveness about asking questions in front of their competitors, since unique insights aren't their main selling point. And they're often flattered to be invited.

A local consultant briefing or seminar can be hosted by your local sales office, a local distributor or reseller if your firms has them, your corporate consultant relations function, or a combination. Whoever sponsors it, all of those should be involved.

At least one person from the home office should be on the agenda for corporate credibility. If you target technically oriented consultants, choose a programmer, engineer, or manager from your R&D group. This person should have some public speaking ability but need not be a pro. To reach business-oriented consultants, candidates are probably from your marketing organization. They should be a bit more polished than "techies." Whatever speakers you use, make sure they can focus on real issues and avoid the "fluff" that so often characterizes sales presentations.

Outside speakers can be a useful addition. They should be recognized industry experts (analysts, especially with name recognition, qualify) or have something of value to contribute to a consultant audience. You're asking your audience to take half a day to hear what your speakers have to say. This translates into lost billings of at $1,000 or so, or an equally valuable amount of time away from selling. Granted, consultants expect to spend some time keeping up and have factored this into their rates, but you still have to convince them to spend this time with you, at this time, on that topic. A good outside speaker helps do this.

Another way to attract consultants to your seminar is to coordinate it with a product announcement. If your firm is too small to attract consultants to its announcements, put on a joint seminar with other firms whose products relate to yours. If you make graphics adapters, find a manufacturer of high-res monitors and another of graphics software (or action games, which stress a computer's graphics). Put together a program that showcases all three products working together. This program is more attractive than the sum of its parts because it shows consultants how they can assemble a complete system with compatible components, reducing the likelihood of client problems.

Evolution

Smaller firms need not have a seminar program just for consultants. They can invite consultants to customer/prospect seminars, customizing invitations as suggested in Section 7.6. If you have reseller seminars, invite consultants to those, as consultants have more in common with resellers than with end users. Also, if you have seminars for different types of prospects—for instance, in different vertical industries—try to match consultants and prospects. The topics will match their needs better, and they'll appreciate the chance to meet potential clients.

As your firm grows there will be a point at which pure consultant seminars become worthwhile. Consultant attendance at other seminars is a good indicator of this. When they come to prospect seminars in sufficient numbers, it's time to plan separate consultant seminars. You'll often be able to schedule these in conjunction with prospect seminars to take advantage of home office visitors to the field: perhaps a consultant seminar in the morning, a prospect seminar in the same room in the afternoon.

You can also supply speakers to industry meetings which consultants attend. Most professional associations have many consultant members. Many cities have local consultant organizations, such as local chapters of the Institute of Management Consultants in the U.S. All these groups are on the lookout for good speakers about current topics. Your speaker need not be a Nobel prize-winner. Your local or regional office probably has someone who can do a fine job. Different types of consultants, including technically oriented and management-oriented, can be reached effectively through such groups.

Teleconference briefings

Consultants can be briefed efficiently by telephone. This medium works as well for a thousand as it does for an ten, especially if you put materials online.

Specialized telebriefings are a good outreach vehicle for consultants. You can invite a lot, knowing that most will look at the subject matter and say "I don't need to know about that this week" and toss it. Even then, you have reminded them that:

* You care about them.
* Your firm works in the area of the topic.
* They can come to you when they need information about it.

Your database will give you a list of consultants to invite. As regards content, speakers and organization, a consultant telebriefing resembles one for analysts; see Section 7.7.

Online information sources

Consultants will go to your Web site as often as analysts, with similar usage patterns. If your site is analyst-friendly and customer-friendly, it will be consultant-friendly as well. If you have an analyst site, consider making it an analyst-and-consultant site.

Social media

As a generalization with many exceptions, consultants are even more into social media than analysts. Everything in Section 7.9, about using social media with analysts, applies more strongly with consultants. One reason is that they often don't know what they need until they need it. Then they need it right away. As a result, they want to establish as many connections as they can in advance, to be able to call on them in their time of need.

Outbound communications

The biggest difference between analysts and consultants in terms of outbound communications is that there are more consultants. You can't customize materials for each. You must develop a standard package.

Therefore, plan to make maximum use of "broadcast" media that can be distributed widely at small incremental cost: newsletters, standardized mailings, bulk e-mails. (If you use bulk e-mail, be sure you give recipients an easy-to-use way to get off the list. Put it in every message, not just in the "Welcome to Our Consultant E-Mail List" note you send when someone joins it.) RSS feeds are appropriate here.

Customized mailings are more work, even if merging the recipient's name into form is automated. This is a nice touch, but optional.

The content of consultant mailings should be similar to that of analyst mailings, keeping in mind the greater importance of product information, and the correspondingly lesser importance of strategy information to consultants.

Specifics for announcement information

If you send announcement kits to consultants, the discussion of analyst announcement kits in Section 7.9.3 will help you plan them. The most important difference is that consultants don't need pre-briefing. As long as they get your material before their clients read about it, you're OK.

The daily press covers important announcements from large firms. Others must wait for weekly coverage in industry papers. These arrive on Mondays. Most firms make announcements on Tuesday or Wednesday so reporters can meet Friday deadlines. If your material goes out by mail that day, it will reach consultants before the weekly papers so they'll be prepared when their clients call. If they get the information online, they'll be equally well informed. Since both of these happen after the announcement has been made, there is no need for security precautions or NDAs.

Consultants need price information more than analysts. Try to provide as much as you can in your announcement package. This enables consultants to calibrate whether or not your products fall into an acceptable range for their clients. Don't worry about being disqualified if they seem high. For one thing, consultants know that discounts are available. For another, they're just looking for rough estimates at this stage.

What happens if you don't give them pricing? As Section 6.3 said for analysts:

* If your prices have gone down, you'll appear to be at a competitive price disadvantage that doesn't really exist.

* If your prices have gone up, the new prices will be reflected in your bid. A nasty surprise at that point will embarrass the consultant and can't help you. The surprise may cost you a sale that a higher price, if properly conveyed, would not have prevented.

New firms with few products can include a price list in their announcement kit. (This should be done more often than it is.) Firms with more products may find it easier to provide only the prices of the new products and the prices that have changed. If you publish a Consultants' Reference Manual with pricing, send out replacement pages for any pages that have been affected as discussed in Section 7.10.

If you don't send out complete announcement kits, be sure your Web site is up to date with all the necessary information. That's the first place consultants will turn when they learn of about an announcement that interests them.

Detailed reference material

Reference materials are more important to consultants than to most analysts. Some specialized consultants, knowing that they will need specifics about your products regularly, will want to keep a complete set of documentation on hand. Try to provide them if at all possible. Others will need a specific manual in a hurry, but only once in a while.

A consultant may not know which specific manual he or she needs. If your firm has enough documentation for this problem to arise, it probably also has a printed documentation overview or Web page intended to solve it. If it's printed, keep multiple copies on hand, ready to ship. If it's not already there, try to get it on your Web site.

If all your documentation is on your Web site, so much the better—but this does not totally eliminate the need for paper. Sometimes paper is the best medium, such as for a consultant who wants to bone up on a subject during a flight. Therefore, even if your documentation is on line, know how to get paper copies to consultants. If you don't have paper documentation or don't want to send it out, make sure consultants can download PDFs to their laptops, but keep in mind that with 2013 laptop or tablet screens—even of the high-resolution "Retina" variety—it's still easier to read long documents on paper.

The discussion of Consultant's Reference Manuals in Section 7.10 applies, not surprisingly, to consultants as well as to analysts.

Demonstrations

Because consultants don't know they need to know about your product until a specific client need, arranging demos for them ahead of time isn't worth the effort. You may include one in a briefing or announcement road show, but that would be in support of that meeting's primary objective rather than as an end in itself.

Once a consultant has a client with a need, a demo may be in order. There will be specific items to demonstrate, others that don't matter. For example, if you have a business intelligence package, you want to show analysts that it works with all popular databases. A consultant's client, however, doesn't have "all popular databases." That client has one, perhaps two, *specific* and *known* databases. The client, and therefore the client's advisor, only cares if it works with those.

As with visits to you, consultant demonstrations will often include the consultant's client (your firm's sales prospect) as well. The sales rep runs the show here, too.

Newsletters

Due to the wide-but-shallow nature of much consultant relations, consultant newsletters (e-newsletters today, but the old term persists) are often useful even if you don't use them for analysts. A newsletter can be one of your first consultant relations projects.

A consultant newsletter need not be fancy or expensively produced. It should be informative. It should also be literate. Misspellings and poor grammar will destroy your image with consultants as quickly as they would with analysts.

A consultant newsletter should be more product-specific than analysts need. Tips on using your product are a good regular feature. For many consultants, this alone will be a reason to save your newsletters. Analysts, by contrast, couldn't care less about tips. They don't use your product, nor do their clients turn to them for help in using it.

See the Section 7.9.2 for size, frequency, production, etc. Consultant and analyst newsletters are the same in these respects.

Using your newsletter for announcement coverage

If you have a monthly newsletter, it works better for consultant announcement coverage than it would for analysts. The reason: consultants don't have to stay as current on your products. They don't have to send out a client news flash by the day after tomorrow. The press won't call them for quotable comments, so you don't need to get the information to them before the press. Try to provide information that consultants won't see in the press. If they need information before your newsletter arrives, it's on your Web site.

10.3. Attitude descriptors

Attitudes are human, not professional, concerns. One characteristic that analysts and consultants share (despite occasional provider feelings to the contrary!) is being human. Differences in attitude factors are, therefore, smaller than differences in the professional areas that were discussed above. The most important are highlighted below.

Keeping consultants informed

Keeping consultants informed is, as noted earlier in this chapter, less personal than keeping analysts informed. It depends more on broadcast media. The value of keeping them informed, however, is the same.

Promptness in responding

If you're late getting back to an analyst, it will hurt the report. If you're late getting back to a consultant, it may cost a sale.

Consultants draw inferences from responsiveness and lateness just as from anything else your firm does. Late in answering a consultant's call? Your firm will probably be late answering client calls, too. No consultant wants to recommend a provider that responds slowly, since the client will (at least subconsciously) blame the consultant.

The guidelines for promptness in responding to analyst calls apply equally to consultants. Instead of asking about a report deadline, though, the question is "When is your client's next decision milestone, and what is it?"

Candor and honesty

Everything in Section 8.3 about analysts applies to consultants as well.

There is, however, a catch. The consultant is dealing with a sale that your firm will or will not get *right now*. It would very much like to have it. The sales rep's commission, perhaps the sales rep's job, is on the line. If we can keep the consultant from learning the truth until we have a signed contract, we get the sale. If we spill the beans before then, we don't. This can be a more powerful motivation for lack of candor—not to say total dishonesty—than the more distant concept of a better or worse analyst report.

However, consider these facts:

- Telling the truth may not spoil the sale. On the contrary: knowing the downside will often give the consultant reason to recommend you over competitors whose bad news is still unknown. Unless a problem makes your product useless, dealing with it openly can help.

- If a problem really makes your product useless, it would probably be returned with commission charge-back anyhow.

- Unless the contract will be signed within the next fifteen minutes, and both prospect and consultant are kept in a sealed room with no cell signal or Wi-Fi until it is, they could still find out before it's signed. At that point you can be sure that it won't be.

- A consultant who is in a position to recommend you once will probably be again, often in the same sales territory. Once burned in this way, he or she will never, ever endorse your firm. Neither will any other consultant this one talks to, and consultants talk to each other. Unless the sales rep expects to quit next week, which most won't admit even if it's true, it's a bad trade even from that point of view. From your firm's point of view, it's worse.

In short, try to bite the bullet.

Overall sense of comfort and ease

Read Section 8.4 about analysts again.

Lou, in that section, was an analyst. The same concepts apply to his consultant sister Louise. A client left her the same note: "Can you suggest two or three vendors we should look at for this application, and who support our environment?" She also knows of six vendors who support this kind of application. She'll call the ones she feels comfortable with, too.

10.4. The Inbound Value of Consultants

The inbound value of consultants, in terms of using their professional expertise, arises only if your firm happens to need a consultant of that type. If a consultant works in your firm's product area, it's unlikely that you'll need him or her for vendor selection. After all, if your firm has to choose between one of your products and a competitor's for internal use, how hard is it to make that decision?

The major area where you might want to engage a consultant for objective advice is to hear what they say in a focus group or advisory board. Since consultants typically spend more time with users than analysts, their perspective on user-side issues may be deeper. The suggestions of Chapter 9 about using analysts for this apply to consultants as well.

10.5. Sourcing Advisors[4]

With the growth of new and complicated alternatives to the traditional approach of buying a computer and using it, sourcing has become a major strategic concern of user organizations. Sourcing has the three characteristics that lead to the use of external advisors: it's complex, it's changing rapidly, and it matters. Therefore, there has been rapid growth in both analyst services devoted to this area and in consultancies that focus on helping users with this area.

Consultants who advise users on sourcing contracts, especially outsourcing or offshoring contracts, are generally referred to as *sourcing advisors*. They are engaged for any or all steps of the sourcing process: to advise on or design a sourcing strategy, to advise on or manage the supplier selection process, to work with negotiation through contract sign-

---

[4] The author is grateful to Ed Gyurko of Dell for a great deal of help with this section.

ing, and to work with the client on an ongoing basis to ensure that the sourcing supplier meets the service-level agreement or other agreed-upon performance measures.

Sourcing advisors can be viewed as specialized consultants, so most of this chapter applies to them. In working with them, though, it is important to understand their specialized nature. Because they are specialized, they are interested in a far smaller slice of the information technology world than is the typical consultant. Within that slice, they have an ongoing interest in the major providers and a sampling of smaller ones. They resemble analysts more than consultants in that regard: you know they care about you now, not just that they may care if the right client shows up in the future. Working with them has many aspects of analyst relations as discussed in Chapters 6–9. For example, visits to sourcing advisors are not unusual.

The largest sourcing advisory firms as of early 2013 are KPMG, which acquired specialized sourcing advisor Equaterra in 2011; ISG (Information Services Group), which acquired specialized sourcing advisor TPI in 2007; and Alsbridge. There are also numerous smaller firms and independent professionals who focus on this work. The larger firms use proprietary methodologies, and feature these as a selling point to prospective clients. In supporting sourcing advisors who have such proprietary methodologies, it helps to know what their methodology is, which factors it considers (and which it doesn't), and how it weighs those factors into the total. That can help you and your colleagues focus on factors that matter in this particular procurement and not waste time on factors that might matter elsewhere, or plan the right topics to emphasize in a visit.

Firms that provide outsourcing services may call the consultant relations function *Sourcing Advisory Relations*, or, if they are in many segments of information technology, may have a separate function by that name alongside their Consultant Relations department. These groups are usually closely aligned with the sales function: regionally in large firms, worldwide in smaller ones. Wherever they sit on in the organization chart, sales success is usually an important part of how their performance is measured.

10.6. And a few more things...

Since consultants and analysts are not identical, there are some items where we said "this doesn't really matter to consultants, even though it matters to analysts." The converse is also true. Some things are good to do for consultants even though they weren't in the analyst discussion of Chapters 6–9. Here are four.

A consultant directory

This directory isn't information you provide *to* consultants. It's information you provide *to* the public, *about* consultants.

Your consultant directory provides a list of consultants who know about your products so that your customers can find professional help. It tells readers about consultant specialties, practices, and where to find them. Aside from giving consultants in it a copy (they like to see their name in print and can use it as a credential) it should go to your sales and technical support staff to acquaint them with the resource. It should go to your customers, or they should at least be told about it. And you should tell consultants who it went to so they will appreciate the efforts you're making on their behalf. That message is at least as important as any tangible business benefits it brings.

Your Web site is also a good way to provide this information, but it can't substitute for the printed version. A Web page can't match the convenience of a book on a shelf or in a briefcase, or the visual impact of a printed volume in reminding consultants how hard you work for them.

A danger with such a directory is that, to an extent, it puts your corporate reputation on the line. If your firm has a certification program (see later in this section) you can reduce this danger somewhat by including only certified consultants (a bit extreme, since many senior consultants don't do the technical work that most certification programs are designed for) or by including certification information in consultants' listings. Otherwise, state clearly up front that your firm publishes the directory as a service, it hasn't verified the capabilities of consultants in it, it's not responsible for their competence or actions, and that potential clients should check them out carefully before engaging their services. See your corporate lawyers to word this disclaimer, and make it *visible*. Legitimate consultants won't mind it. It may save your hide.

Training

Most firms have training programs for users, or prospective users, of their products. Training consultants is useful as well:

- By making consultants more familiar with your firm and its products, you increase their comfort level with you. This increases the likelihood that they will recommend you over a competitor.
- By teaching consultants how to use your products correctly, you increase the likelihood that their clients will be pleased with the end result. That benefits everyone.

One way to do this is to make sure consultants have copies of your training schedule. If they know you're offering a course in network management, some will show up.

You can make your training available to consultants on a space-available basis. Your training organization probably has an excellent feel for course registration patterns. If they have room for fifteen in a class, and six have signed up a month before it starts, they know if this means it will be oversubscribed or will have five empty seats. They can therefore tell you, well before the course starts, which courses will probably run with seats left over. You can offer these to consultants at no charge or at a greatly reduced charge versus the normal tuition rate.

The benefits here are getting trained consultants and perhaps a little incremental revenue. The downside is that some consultants will take advantage of your offer when they otherwise would have paid full price to take the same course. The number of these will be negligible. Don't worry about it.

Certification

Many firms let technical professionals demonstrate expertise with their products through formal certification. Novell's Certified NetWare Engineer (CNE) program was the first of these to become widely accepted as a credential, though it was not first overall. According to *GoCertify.com*, there are hundreds of IT certification programs in early 2013. Their list is surely incomplete.

Some certification programs focus on completing courses. Others focus don't care how you learned something, if you can show you know it. As with any other type of education, each model has its pros and cons. Each suits the preferences and abilities of some people better.

Consultants are an important public for these programs, as they need to demonstrate their expertise clearly and quickly to people with whom they've had no prior contact. (With permanent employees, certification can be more of a status symbol or a ticket to the next job, though the learning that leads up to certification is undoubtedly valuable there too.) Therefore, you should publicize your certification programs to consultants and offer them opportunities to participate.

Some of these opportunities may be in the form of free or reduced-rate entry to training courses with vacancies, as discussed in the previous section. Another possibility is a reduced rate for certification testing. In addition, consider these:

- Mention consultants' certification in your consultant directory.
- List certified consultants on your Web site.
- Announce newly-certified consultants in your consultant newsletter.
- Provide certified consultants with special certificates and permission to say something like "Certified ABC Consultant" on their promotional materials. If you have a graphic that goes along with certification, make it available to them in electronic form for their printed materials and Web sites.

Advertising

Advertising is a common way to influence an identifiable public of interest. Consultants are an identifiable public of interest which you want to influence. Yet advertising is mentioned here only as an afterthought, not as a basic element of consultant support. Why?

Primarily for a poor reason: many people consider it somewhat undignified, not in keeping with a professional image. Provider consultant liaison personnel, in keeping with this professional concept of consultants, go along. Advertising is seldom part of a consultant relations program. Many people who run CR programs would feel a bit uncomfortable with it. But advertising can be a viable option for firms that are highly dependent on consultants or want to set themselves apart from a large crowd. Ads in media with a high consultant readership, such as *Consulting* magazine in the U.S. (Kennedy Publications, Fitzwilliam, N.H.; *www.consultingmag.com*), or *Conspectus* in the U.K. (*www.conspectus.com*), can be a good idea. Properly worded ads that target consultants won't "turn off" non-consultants who happen to see them.

In addition, it can't hurt to put your consultant support phone number or URL in regular ads. Why make it harder than necessary for consultants to help you sell more?

11 | Internally focused AR activities

This chapter will cover:

1 Technology to help you do your job
2 People to help you do your job
3 Parts of your job that focus within your organization

Chapters 5–10 focused on people *outside* your firm: the analysts and/or consultants whom you target. Some of what you do has an *internal* focus This chapter covers the major items in this category.

Some of these items involve technology. Developing tools to target the right people with compelling, consistent messages and customized information, keeping them up to date, and making them accessible throughout the company will help you leverage their influence and expertise. The key to effective 21st-century analyst/consultant relations is leveraging technology to make personal relationships work better.

None of the technology you need is expensive or, by 2013 standards, complex. Your data can be housed on any desktop or laptop computer. You may need a server to share it, but nearly any server your company already has will do. The space your data will need, and the added load your work will place on network resources, will be negligible. Software, if you don't already have it, will have price tags in three figures—not six. Custom database applications cost more, but if you need them, your company can afford them.

11.1 Databases

Despite the proverb about barefoot shoemaker's children, computer and communications providers can and do use technology to support internal business processes. Analyst/consultant relations is no exception. Its first uses are databases and repositories.

Databases and repositories are both information collections that you can share. A *database* is a structured collection of information organized into files and fields (individual data elements). (Computer scientists have a different definition, but we're not computer scientists.) Databases are generally searchable by the content of any field, or combination of fields, and can generate a variety of reports. A *repository* is a collection of documents in their own formats, such as Microsoft Word or PowerPoint, generally identified by title and perhaps a few key words. These are used via their own applications. Expect people to use these terms, and perhaps others, interchangeably.

Your *databases* should include at least these:

Analyst/Consultant Profile Database

Profiles help you build relationships and target your activities. The information in this database has additional uses as well. Some of these are discussed in Section 12.4.

You should have a profile or "crib sheet" for each analyst who covers your space and each consultant you learn about who's interested in it. Keep profiles updated, since both influencer fields are dynamic: people are promoted, change specializations, move within firms and from firm to firm. Profiles for targeted people will enable you and your company to engage them on the right level with the right content. In addition, they bestow respect and credibility on those who have taken the interest and time to understand the analyst's or consultant's business including areas of coverage, specialization, and "hot buttons."

Profiles should be accessible to anyone in your firm who works with analysts or consultants, anywhere. They should be on your intranet or otherwise available for shared internal use. They are also a key information source for *briefing books* (see Section 11.5).

Content of this database:

Include this information in each profile:

1. Contact information: Name, title, firm, mailing address (it has a postal code or postcode outside the U.S., not a ZIP code; don't limit it to five digits), phone numbers (direct, main company number, fax, mobile, home if you have it), e-mail address(es).

   In a well-designed database information about each office is entered once, no matter how many people work there. Analyst data records are then linked to office data rather than entering it anew for each person at a location. Aside from reducing the likelihood of errors, only one record must be changed if a firm moves or gets a new phone number. (Telephone numbering prefix schemes change from time to time, even if what one thinks of as a phone number doesn't.)

2. Area(s) of coverage and specialization. This is especially important if your firm has multiple lines of business. Nobody wants to be flooded with information about all of them! (Exceptions: some firms' central libraries, and an occasional incurable packrat.) Even if your product line is narrow, you'll get inquiries from generalists and from people whose major professional interests lie elsewhere.

   This information will help you plan mailings and seminars, prune your database over time, and perhaps structure outbound communications automatically. If you have regular or sporadic special-interest mailings, you can use it to decide who gets them. If you don't have specialization information for everyone in your list, send survey e-mails or cards to those for whom you don't. Asking will make your firm look good.

3. Stance on your company and its products/services, including what this person thinks of their strengths and weaknesses

4. Stance on major competitors and their products/services, again including strengths and weaknesses

5. Relationship with the media, including quotes, publications, and the names of reporters who have used the quotes

6. Published research list, emphasizing recent publications

7. Upcoming research agenda, if applicable

8. Past and/or planned company engagements with the analyst, if any

9. "Hot buttons" or soap-box issues

10. Sales campaigns the person has been involved in, with comments on his/her stance and influence if known

11. Information from sales force on customer feedback, if any

12. If this person gets your newsletter, if you have one, and which version, if you have several. (Include this for later flexibility even if you just have one version now.)

13. If you have an analyst/consultants reference manual, whether or not this person has a copy and how current it is. If you charge for the manual, the date at which this subscription expires.

14. An A-B classification. The "A-list" gets full announcement kits, invitations to meetings, and similar special treatment. The B list is the remaining 90%. You may treat your whole audience the same way at first, but set up a classification system now anyhow because you may want it later. You can extend this to three categories if you wish, but more than A-B-C isn't needed.

    Your initial reaction to classification may be that it insults the "small fry." Don't worry. For one thing, you're not going to publicize this designation. It's purely for internal purposes. Second, if they find out, they're intelligent enough to realize you can't afford a red carpet for everybody. Junior analysts and small consultants have few illusions about their status. Finally, since they can get anything they need by asking, they have no real reason to gripe.

15. Information as to where you got the name, when it was entered into the database, and when it was most recently updated or confirmed. (Database software can tell when a record was changed, but it can't tell the difference between fixing a typo and confirming or updating essential information. This needs a separate field, entered by a human being.)

You can expand this content in several directions. A useful one is inquiry tracking. This will indicate who uses your support the most, which products generate the most interest. Heavy usage is a valid indicator of interest, but light usage may not mean lack of interest. Analysts and consultants may have contacts elsewhere in your company. Calls to those people, or hits on the product page of your Web site, won't be in your records.

A computer with any popular file management package, such as Access or FileMaker Pro, can track this information for thousands or analysts or consultants. With such a system you'll be able to select any portion of your database: networking analysts in northern California, consultants whom you haven't heard from in a year, database gurus in the Dallas-Fort Worth area, all Forrester analysts, and so on. You'll also be able to print labels or create personalized e-mails for the entire list or any subset.

If you don't want to build a system, packaged solutions exist. ARinsights' ARchitect (*www.arinsights.com/ARchitect/products.aspx*) suits large firms. SSage Circle offers smaller firms use of the same software via its ARchitect Express (*www.sagecircle.com/index.php?option=com_content&view=article&id=743&Itemid=144*). Small firms should also check out AR Intranet (*www.influencerrelations.com*). If your firm uses SAP, look at its analyst relations module. Your firm might also have an existing CRM system or database that could meet the need with a little customization.

Getting Names for your Analyst/Consultant Database

You can get names in many ways. The major sources are listed below. Most apply to both consultants and analysts. The last few apply solely or primarily to consultants.

- **An initial list** of key reference services, market research firms, opinion leaders, and executives or managing partners of large firms. See Chapter 2 for categories.

  One way to find analysts who cover your field is via press quotes. When you read articles about your firm or others in its market, see which analysts and research firms are quoted. Anyone quoted in two articles, especially by different reporters, should be on your "A" list. Any firm that supplies two or more quoted analysts should likewise be there. Your PR agency may have some of this information.

- **Inquiries** from people who identify themselves as analysts or consultants. These can come to your analyst/consultant support channels or to anyone in your field organization. Urge your sales force to pass these names to your analyst/consultant relations staff even if they have already dealt with the need.

- **Lists of people known to your sales offices.** They will usually have become known through involvement in one or more sales campaigns. Ask your sales offices for these names, with whatever information they have on these people.

- **Product inquiries** such as Web requests for materials, magazine "bingo cards," ad coupons, direct mail and telemarketing responses, and inquiry letters, where the inquiry lets you identify the inquirers as consultants or analysts. Make sure the people who handle these responses in your firm know you want these people identified, and their names passed along to you, for this purpose. (If your Web inquiry page has a "job function" pull-down list, make sure it includes analysts and consultants.)

- **Requests** to be added to your program.

- **Responses to publicity** about your analyst/consultant support programs. You can put your phone number and e-mail address in your firm's ads when they appear where these groups will see them. Any mention of your program in periodicals that reach this audience will also draw requests.

- **Mailings to rented lists.** You can send information about your program to lists of consultants: the membership of the Society of Telecommunications Consultants, for example, or the consultant subset of an industry publication's subscriber list. (Many publications only rent their lists through brokers, but an inquiry to their circulation department will tell you all you need to know to decide if you want the list and who to contact for rental.) You can't simply add names from rented lists to your database, since most lists are rented for a single use. They include dummy names, which go to the list broker, to catch violations. You can, however, use the lists to invite people to join your program. Those who respond go into to your database.

- **Mailings to other lists.** You can get lists of consultants in directories such as those listed in the next chapter for purposes of reality checking. Use the subject index of these volumes to identify consultants you want to reach. Treat these names much as you do names from rented lists, by sending a card inviting the recipient to join your program. Here, of course, there are no limits on how often you can use the names.

  Good general sources of analyst names in the U.S. are AnalystProfiles and Bacon's, though they have weak coverage of the rest of the world. In Europe, PMC's Apollo database contains similar data. (These focus on PR needs, therefore on analysts with high media profiles. These may not be those who have the highest impact on your firm.) In Asia/Pacific, Intelligen (Sydney, Australia) maintains a good regional list. Analyst relations consultancies can also help you identify analysts. In addition, analyst relations database applications such as ARchitect and the Lighthouse AR intranet, mentioned earlier, come pre-populated with analyst lists.

- **Ads inviting consultants to participate in your program.** AT&T ran effective two-page ads for their Consultant Liaison Program in computer and communication industry media. One opened "How do you propose to become a better consultant?" The ad beneath showed a consultant, with his or her name, and discussed how he or she worked with AT&T.

  Advertising must be done carefully lest it smack of desperation. For a company as large and as dependent on consultants as AT&T was when it ran these, they can work. For most other firms, ads directed specifically at inviting people to sign up for your program probably go too far—though, as mentioned before, ads directed at consultants are fine and ads that mention the program are certainly acceptable as well.

Learning more about analysts/consultants in your database

You can flesh your profiles in several ways. This list overlaps the preceding one:

- **People in your company.** Encourage anyone with analyst or consultant exposure to contribute to these profiles, through you or by inputting data directly. (*Wiki* software makes updating online profiles easy.)

- **Firms' Web sites.** Many research firms, and some consulting firms, post professional biographies and contact information of their staff on the Web.

  Some firms restrict analyst information on their Web sites to customers, but you can often find out a lot about those firms too. For example, they may put rotating samples of research on their site, often highlighted on their home page. Their writers' bios are often shown as well. If you return every few weeks, you'll soon have a lot of information. Of course, if your company is a client of that research firm, just log in and read up.

  Use a site's Search function to see who writes on topics of interest. Even if you don't buy reports, you can find analyst areas of coverage by reading report titles. Web searches on analyst or consultant names often lead to bios, too—perhaps in a conference program, or with an article they wrote. (If you find a bio this way, check its date. Four-year-old conference programs, with speaker bios, are still online. A lot can change in four years.)

  Check out the Events section of the Web site to get an idea of the events the firm puts on, which analysts will speak, and which providers will sponsor the event, if any.

Push communications such as online newsletters are becoming popular among analyst firms. Sign up for these as another way to gather information about your target analysts. Many firms or analysts are also blogging. Reading those blogs is a good way to get a handle on their professional positions.

Lastly, visit press room or public relations sections. Firms often highlight important announcements and compelling research tidbits here. The information you find is good background for understanding the firm's focus and direction.

- **Other online resources.** Web searches will turn up a wealth of information. Sites such as LinkedIn are also useful sources.

- **Quotations.** Monitoring what analysts say to the press, and where, will tell you their stance on your company and its products, which journalists they talk to, and often their "hot buttons." (There's more on this in the quotation tracking section below.)

- **Published research.** The best way to determine an analyst's stance is to read his or her work. This also gives insight into analysts' methodologies, which helps you understand how they arrived at their conclusions. (This may not be free.)

- **Account managers/salespeople.** If your company is a research firm client, you probably have an account manager there. Use this person to help you develop profiles and keep them current. Inquire about your targeted analysts' research agendas, too.

- **Analysts themselves.** Once you know which analysts have an impact on your company, ask them about their research. Most will welcome the opportunity to educate a provider about their work, preferences, and needs. (Tell them what you already know, and how.) You can also ask them for names of potentially interested colleagues.

- **Analyst relations consulting firms** track this information and maintain analyst databases. They can leverage those here, offering you economies of scale.

- **Win-Loss tracking.** You can get customer feedback on analysts and consultants via your sales force if it has a win-loss tracking program. More on this below, too.

Some companies use analyst profiles to select press releases and other materials to send to analysts. Many let analysts define their own profiles. If your company's offerings cover a broad range, consider this. If they're focused, don't bother: if an analyst cares about you at all, anything you do will be in his or her area of interest—or close enough that you won't be resented for sending it.

Internal contacts

People are an analyst relations program's most valuable resource. An effective analyst relations manager builds a network within the company to help champion, direct and support the program. Be strategic in who you choose and what role they will play.

Try to have two or three executives aligned with your program for their position and power in the company, but you need a balance between people with power and hands-on people who get things done on a daily basis. You can also create your own internal contacts database for keeping track of your extended team and their roles.

To begin building your network you need a current organization chart with names, titles and responsibilities. It will help direct you in your selection process and will be invaluable when you need to navigate the company in a hurry or escalate issues.

A *subject matter expert map* is also very useful. Ahead of the need, prepare a directory of SMEs within your company to use for planning, fact-checking research and responding to analyst inquiries and surveys. This map can be as simple as a text document, or as elaborate as a dedicated database which you can search by product area or topic. Include this information for each SME:

- Name
- Job title
- Division/department; name, title, and contact information of immediate supervisor
- Contact information: e-mail, phone number/extension, building/location
- Product area(s) of expertise with keywords for searching
- Brief summary of experience, starting before joining your firm if relevant
- Brief description of suitable situations for analyst interaction
- Current AR activities and history of analyst interactions, if any
- Published papers or other recognized technical credentials
- AR content spokesperson training completed, if any

Reference account contact information

As discussed in Section 6.8, the best way to back up your claims is to connect analysts with happy users. Before you do, prepare the customer by going over topics and issues the analyst wants to discuss. This will maximize the value of your customer's time with the analyst, as well as minimize surprises when the customer and analyst talk.

Your reference account database should include:

1. Contact name, title, company, mailing address, phone/fax numbers, e-mail
2. Whether or not the customer has granted permission to be a reference
3. Conditions for contact, such as preferred methods or maximum frequency
4. Internal contact name, phone number and e-mail address (usually the sales rep)
5. Products and services the customer uses, including other firms' if known
6. Overall satisfaction level with your company, its products and services
7. Issues or complaints with your company and its products and services, with description and date of any follow-up action
8. Customer compliments and comments on strengths of your company, its products and services
9. Mentions of this customer in the press, case studies, etc.
10. Date the information in this record was last updated or verified as correct
11. Additional notes, such as unique or differentiating examples of how this customer has

been successful with your products and/or services

Sales, division or line of business managers, PR and marketing managers can all contribute to this list.

Before referring an analyst to a customer, make a last-minute check to ensure that the reference is still suitable—through the sales rep or, if that's impossible, his/her management. Situations change, often quickly. Problems arise without notice. Supporters leave, perhaps replaced by a competitor's ex-employee. Unless you're absolutely, totally certain that your information is up to the minute, check again.

Quotation tracking

One way to learn what analysts think, as mentioned earlier, is by what they say in the press. This isn't a perfect measure—they may adapt what they say to what they think a reporter wants, and reporters may select quotes they agree with—but it's still of value.

The value of quotation tracking is greater if you track comments about competitors too. This is partly because any data is more useful in context than in isolation. Also, comparisons cancel built-in bias. For example, some analysts try to avoid negative comments. If you look only at what they say about one provider, it looks favorable. Comparing comments on two providers cancels this out because it affects both equally, so the conclusions from that comparison are more meaningful.

You can be as systematic as you want in collecting quotations for tracking. Your PR or media relations department is probably already active along these lines. Their objectives differ from yours, but they overlap. You can also find press quotations:

- On many research firm Web sites. Analysts are proud that a reporter thinks enough of them to print what they say.
- Through publication Web sites. You or your PR department know what publications cover your firm. A search with your company's or competitors' names and the keyword "analyst" will turn up many comments, though it will also turn up some articles that mention your firm and happen to quote a systems analyst in an unrelated way. More complex searches use names of major research firms, since an article may read "Gartner research director Sue Sioux says ...," never using any form of the word analyst.
- Via online information retrieval sites that carry multiple publications, such as Lexis-Nexis or Factiva. The comments on searching apply here too.

A quotation database should include this information about each quote:

- The name and firm of the analyst.
- Enough bibliographic information to find the article online or in a library.
- The name of the reporter who quoted the analyst.
- A list of providers the analyst mentioned, noting if the comment was positive, neutral or negative with respect to each. You can use a five-point scale: highly or somewhat positive, neutral, somewhat or highly negative. A finer scale won't add value.

- Optionally, a summary of what the article said, with keywords to assist in retrieval.

- Also optionally, a summary of what the quote said, or its text in full. (An analyst comment is usually a small enough part of an article that including it in full in this database doesn't raise copyright issues, but check with legal counsel if this is a concern.)

A simple database can tabulate this information, using a spreadsheet or a database package such as Access or FileMaker Pro. With a database you can put analyst information in one place, then link each quote to that analyst rather than re-entering it each time the analyst shows up. That also has the advantage that, if an analyst is promoted or changes jobs, you only have to change one entry. If you go this route, this analyst file can also serve as your analyst profile.

A database can also produce reports. You can find out which analysts are quoted about you most often, though those may not have the greatest impact or be the most significant thought leaders. You can find out which firms tend to be more positive or negative about your firm, which can help you put together account plans. You can learn of new analysts in your space sooner than you might have found out about them otherwise. You can compare the favorability of analyst comments about your firm with those about competitors. After a few months, you'll be able to see the trends in the data.

11.2. Repositories

Your *repositories* should include at least these. All should be kept up to date and made available throughout the company, usually on your company intranet.

Message library

Contains your company's corporate messages, based on its strategies. All communications, including presentations, should reflect these to reduce inconsistencies.

The executive team is responsible for these messages. It may rely on analysts, outside marketing and public relations firms, and other industry experts to help shape them.

Presentation library

Contains all presentations made to the analysts. These can be reused by different departments, not just analyst relations. Having a central presentation repository saves preparation time and reduces inconsistent messaging.

The analyst relations department should alert the company to this tool and make it available for regular use. Strategic marketing, communications, advertising, public relations, and sales departments should be trained to use it.

Responses to frequently asked questions (FAQs)

Being prepared for common questions builds credibility. Analysts and consultants will perceive you as knowledgeable and appreciative of their many time constraints if you have a response ready when they ask (though you don't want to rattle it off so quickly that it seems you didn't listen to the whole question). Having these in your repository will also help ensure consistent messages within your department and company-wide.

Most FAQs reflect the end user's or customer's point of view. Responses to these typical questions, some of which overlap each other, should be on your intranet:

1. What customer problems does a new initiative solve? (Show that it's not a "solution in search of a problem.")

2. How does your new initiative impact the customer's business? (Justify a client's spending money on it.)

3. Why should prospects choose your company specifically? (How will you compete?)

4. What's your strategy, at the corporate level and regarding a new initiative?

5. How will you support the strategy? Why should analysts believe that you will achieve your goals in the face of competition? (This is especially important if you hope to pass other firms that are now ahead of you in market share, who work as hard as you do to improve their own products and services.)

6. What will the new initiative contribute over time? (Analysts want to gauge your corporate commitment to the new product or service. If won't contribute much, it will be easy to drop if it's not an instant hit.)

7. How does this complement other areas? (If it ties into other key areas at your firm, your company may be committed even if its direct revenue contribution is small.)

8. What are your sales channels, how does this initiative impact their businesses?

9. What is your roadmap, how do you see this evolving in the future? (A full reply may require an NDA, but you should be able to discuss general outlines.)

And this author's favorite, from his days as an analyst:

10. What is the #1 thing your customers want that you don't have, and what are you doing about it?

The analyst relations manager is in charge of making sure responses are ready for these and similar questions, and that all spokespeople are aware that they exist. He or she should work with other departments and divisions to develop them. Consultant questions are less predictable, but, you can track those that you get. If the same question shows up three times, put it in the Consultant FAQ section of this repository.

Market Research (see also Section 3.2)

A company's analyst relations and market research departments must work together. AR is its voice to the analysts; MR, its ears. The two are often combined in the same people or under one manager. Even if they're not, they must maintain close contact.

Market research that you purchase should be available, license permitting, on your intranet to leverage it for people in separate locations. This is also an effective way to position analysts as more than a communication channel, and thereby position the analyst relations department as more than just a way to send messages.

For reports that include inaccurate or negative coverage, include an item-by-item response. This will provide everyone in your company who interfaces with analysts and the public a consistent factual response to the coverage. (If facts in a report are objectively wrong, and were when it was written, tell the research firm too.)

If your license agreements do not permit placing the research on your intranet, post a list of available reports with instructions on how to obtain them. Your corporate library, public and investor relations, marketing, sales, as well as analyst relations can all contribute to this list.

In addition to the value to your company of having access to analyst information, reading their reports has these benefits:

- Reading analyst research helps you know your own audience. What do they say about you? About your competitors? What are the trends in these over time? What do they have right, where (if anywhere) are they in error? This is vital to your reality check.
- Knowing what analysts write about your firm lets you reflect this knowledge in your interactions with them. It helps you correct errors and rebut competitive arguments.

Analyst subscriptions often include a number of analyst hours for inquiries, broadly defined. These may go unused. This is bad from everyone's point of view: not only is your company not getting the full value it paid for, but analysts value the interactions that come from these hours. If you know that inquiry hours won't be used, you can tell others in the company about them, or use them yourself to expose analysts to your firm and its products in more depth than they'd be exposed to otherwise.

11.3. Contact management

When Oog, in the cave, promised to make a new spear for Uk, he didn't write anything down. If Uk didn't see progress, he'd poke Oog on his way to the cave door and grunt the Neanderthal equivalent of "How're you coming on that action item?"

Our business lives today are more complex. We deal with many issues, not just spears. We have many customers, not just cavemates. Meeting most needs takes a team effort.

It is therefore necessary to keep track of companies you work with, individuals at those companies, activities that involve those individuals (showing who was involved with what) and plans, promises and schedules for each. Colleagues must be able to see and augment this information. This usually means keeping data on a central server, with appropriate software on that server or on users' computers to access it.

Contact management software meets this need. It is, in essence, a shared database with files for companies, people, activities, and schedules. You (or your firm's database specialists, or someone else) can construct a reasonable system in a short time using any database management package. It won't have all the features of purchased contact management software, but will be optimized for your needs and will perhaps cost enough less than purchased software to offset the development effort. Or, you can buy a standard package and customize it. The market leaders in this area, as of this writing, are Goldmine and ACT!, but market leadership may not imply suitability for a given user. Analyst relations packages, mentioned in Section 11.1 above, also include contact management features. The important thing here is to have something: nearly anything is better than nothing.

You can work up from a simple contact management program to a full CRM (Customer Relationship Management) system. That's almost certainly more than you need, but if your company is already using a CRM package you might as well join them.

The biggest issue with any of this software is getting everyone to use it. Suppose Analyst Q. Snidely pumps Harry about your next release and is politely told to go soak his head. Sally, whom Snidely calls next, will only know this if Harry enters it right away. The human side of CRM is usually a bigger problem than the technical.

11.4. Internal reporting and updates

Reports have a fixed format and outline, and are done on a regular basis—often monthly, perhaps with quarterly and/or annual summaries. Updates are as needed.

The best way to keep your management properly informed is to establish a formal reporting process. Your reports should be:

- Strategic and high-level: discuss **why**, not just **what.**
- Brief, 2–3 total pages, unless your management requests a different length. Try to get key points on the first page, backed up by further detail as appropriate.
- E-mailed broadly to managers, executives, and field/sales people, unless your management requests otherwise—in which case you can send a different report to a broader audience.
- Posted on your company's intranet.
- Requesting feedback, since this is a good way to find out more about the analysts that your company works with or that other people in your company encounter.

The Analyst Relations Report is your primary vehicle for enlisting support, educating your company about analyst initiatives, and raising early warning signs. A useful ARR is *not* just an activity list. It should lead to *action*. Make program recommendations and assign ownership of these tasks, as well as reporting on "completed by" dates.

Your analyst relations report should cover the following topics. Each is discussed after the list:

1. Analysis and recommendations
2. Key achievements
3. Planned activity for next month

4.   Relevant analyst research, analyst quotes in the media, share of voice

It should also include a contact name and e-mail address with a request for feedback.

1. Analysis and Recommendations

Discuss your program at a high level. Raise issues that need to be on management's radar screen and offer practical solutions. Recommend who should own the solution and how you and/or your team will follow up to make sure the action items were completed.

Examples:

Sustained Product Momentum: Analysts from Research Firms A and B were briefed on customer usage and satisfaction. Feedback is that momentum has "fizzled." Analysts feel we have a problem sustaining marketing momentum around the product. AR will work with product team to create an outreach plan targeted at key analysts. Progress will be reported in 90 days.

Competitive Announcement: Competitor X is will announce a new release of Y three weeks before our launch. Analyst press quotes on their announcement are positive, but no mention of our launch. We need to create buzz around it. AR recommends pre-briefing five of our most-quoted analysts in this space. Next month AR will provide PR and IR with a list of pre-briefed analysts for press referrals.

Other topics to cover in this section of your report:

- Executive and key analyst changes at research firms
- Negative or positive reviews or reports: a brief mention, more detail in Section 4

2. Key Achievements

This isn't a laundry list of all you did. List achievements that tie in to your program's overall goals and objectives. Map these to corporate objectives. Quantify where possible. Examples:

- Held three strategy-themed analyst roundtables with key analysts from firms X, Y and Z. Analysts from all firms rated the session at least a 4.5 (1–5; 5 is best).
- Ongoing proactive conference calls with shipment data for research firm X resulted in accurate market share reporting for Q2 and Q3.
- The number of divisions holding "buddy calls" with analysts increased this month, leading to more educated analysts and more favorable mentions in the press.

3. Planned Activity for Next Month

In this section, alert readers to key analyst/consultant relations activities coming up in the next 30 days. List the person(s) or group responsible for managing each activity, with dates. This will help facilitate coordination of analyst outreach efforts across the company. Organize these by analyst firm, product/service division or theme.

Examples:

Research Firm A

NDA briefing on newest release of X. (Owner)

Review and comment on draft research report on our new strategy. (Owner)

Quarterly executive buddy call. (Owner)

Research Firm B

Contract negotiations for market research renewal. (Owner)

Facilitate and manage meeting between analyst and reference account X. (Owner)

4. Relevant Research

List new research that supports the issues and/or achievements you pointed out in Sections 1 and 2, or that mentions your firm in sufficient detail for others to want to know about it. (Even if a report is negative, knowing about it ahead of time is better than finding out after a lost sale.) For each report you list, indicate the analysts' stances relative to your company. If the research is available on your intranet, put in a link so readers can go right to the document. Otherwise, put in a link that lets readers request it.

Example:

Broadband Internet Access

Gartner: North American Broadband QOS: DSL vs. Cable, July 14, 2012

Abstract: Cable modems and xDSL are last-mile broadband technologies that compete for dominance in the high-speed Internet access market.

Analyst: Miles Standish

Stance on our firm: positive

Access: Contact Market Research, ext. 2302, marketresearch@ourco.com

Tracking research also allows you to develop some simple measurements. By comparing the changing frequency with which analysts mention you and your competitors in the media and in research, you will get a top-level idea of progress.

11.5. Briefing Books

Those who meet with analysts need information about the people at the meeting and its objectives. A *briefing book* is a good way to do this. Such a book provides condensed information to enable a person with little time to prepare to act appropriately at a meeting. While no book can replace a planning meeting, it can provide more depth, serve as a reminder after the meeting, and fill some of the gap for those who can't attend.

A briefing book is for a specific meeting. It reflects that meeting's topic and participants. However, once you've done one book, you can re-use material that's still current to make later ones easier.

A briefing book is for internal use only. It should say so, in big type, on its cover. It's not meant for analysts. However, they have been known to fall into analysts' hands. Unless you can guarantee yours will be kept confidential by everyone who'll ever see it, including people yet to be hired whose personal friendships you can't possibly guess, and that nobody will ever press a wrong key or click a wrong tool in e-mailing it, don't include anything you wouldn't want analysts to read about themselves. (It's happened. Results have ranged from humorous to disastrous.)

The scope of a briefing book depends on what it's for. The briefing book for the annual analyst summit of a multi-billion-dollar firm, with a hundred analysts in attendance for three days, will be larger than the briefing book for a getting-to-know-you meeting between two of your colleagues from Engineering and a Gartner technical expert. Keeping this in mind, a briefing book can contain:

- Title (of the book)
- Big, prominent statement that it is proprietary and confidential to your company, and is not to be reproduced or distributed further without appropriate permission
- Logistics/itinerary: date(s)/time(s)/place(s), teleconference/travel arrangements as applicable, with directions and map to each location. (People may have to find places on their own, even if the original plan was to travel as a group.)
- Internal contacts
- Purpose of the briefing and key messages/points to support it
- Analyst firm profile(s)
- Participant profiles, including what they've written or said about your firm
- Copies of all presentation materials to be used
- Customer references and case studies that have been cleared for use in this briefing
- Recent company news releases (analysts may have read them, speakers should know what your company is telling the public)
- Frequently Asked Questions about analysts in general

A closer look at some of these:

Title

Give your briefing book a title that reflects the meeting(s) it is for. This will help keep your content spokespeople focused and make it easier for you to file and retrieve this book in your electronic repository.

Confidentiality statement

Your company probably already has one. Make it *impossible* to miss.

Internal Contacts

Names, titles and contact information for everyone from your company and/or agency involved with the briefing. This will help to keep your team organized and make sure questions go to the right contact. These include:

*   Analyst Relations Director, Manager(s), etc.
*   Agency support staff
*   Company spokespeople (executives and others)
*   Technical support
*   Others

Purpose

State what you aim to accomplish with this briefing. What is the desired outcome? Read what the analyst and/or the firm have written about you (if they have; one reason to meet is because they haven't and you'd like them to). If your key messages aren't getting out, stress what analysts are missing.

This section should state the messages you hope to get across to participating analysts. If, for example, the message is that your firm is a technology leader, and you have points in support of that message, it may help your colleagues say the right thing or bring up the right information when they reply to questions.

Analyst Firm Profile(s)

Your briefing book should contain a concise description of each research firm you'll meet with, including general contact information. Include relevant information from your Analyst Firm Profile, such as number and types of clients, research specialty (or, for large firms, a statement that they cover all areas of technology), its relationship with the media, and your company's spending with this firm.

The purpose of this information is not to make your colleagues experts on the firm. Give them enough so they can respond to a question with, for example, "Since you have a lot of clients in the financial industry, you've probably seen ..." when appropriate, but not say it if most of the firm's clients are in health care. So, keep it short and focused.

Include these items for each firm to be briefed:

*   Firm Name
*   HQ location, phone no. for reference if needed in travel
*   Profile Summary (should include these items plus descriptive text; having a standard format with these items tabulated in a standard way can help regular readers)
*   Number of analysts (very approximately, to give a sense of the firm)
*   Number of clients (again, approximately, to give a sense of the firm)
*   Types of clients (users, providers, other)

- Specialty (retail applications, network hardware, ...) or other information that helps categorize what the company does and how it works

- Relationship with the media (frequently quoted or not; if so, where)

- Company spending with firm: subscriptions, reports, consulting, other (what?)

- What they wrote about you, in general and the analysts to be at the meeting

- Brief summary of your analyst relations account plan for them, if any

Participating Analyst Profiles

This section of the book should come from profiles in your analyst database. Edit them to make them as concise as possible and to remove information that might cause unpleasantness if an analyst happens to see his or her own briefing book page. (Murphy's Law: the analyst who does will be the one you least want to.)

11.6. Analyst Relations Training

The analyst relations manager and everyone supporting the analyst relations function should be trained on how to best perform their role. Focused analyst training will bring everyone to a high level of awareness and strategic thinking about analysts.

It's tempting to lump analysts in with press and media, not taking into account the differences between analysts and these other publics. This is an error. PR training isn't for analysts. It says some things that don't apply to them, and leaves gaps.

Analysts differ from other influencer audiences in expertise level, time horizon, ability to filter and analyze, client awareness, specialization and motivations. Therefore, strategies and tactics for successful analyst interaction differ from those for other audiences. Since analysts are an important public with which your company deals, analyst training for executives and spokespeople is as important as the other types of training.

The most important analyst training concerns are *honesty and candor* and *avoiding hype*. You've read about both. To recap briefly:

Honesty and candor: It's analysts' job to learn about your company's problems. (Every company has had them, or will.) They do this job well. They *will* find out. If they don't find out from you, where you control how they are presented and can explain what you're doing about them, they'll find out from a competitor or an unhappy customer.

Hype: Analysts aren't sales prospects. They've heard it all, most of it many times. They see through hype and find it an annoying waste of time. Get to the point—fast—and stay objective.

Several types of analyst relations training are possible. The following table lists them in order of importance, with guidance on who should participate in each. An experienced analyst/consultant relations professional can conduct much of this training himself or herself, or you can engage a specialized firm for it. Some analyst relations consulting firms, or public relations firms with a focused analyst relations practice, offer public training. If such a session fits your needs and timing, it can be both effective and cost-effective. While some people are initially concerned about discussing analyst/consultant relations in front of competitors, this wears off quickly. Everyone soon realizes that the cross-fertilization that comes from having many viewpoints in the same room is of value, and nobody gives away any real company secrets.

Type	Priority	Who Should Attend
Analyst relations training	Top	Analyst relations staff, top to bottom; executives, sales force, staff of outside agencies supporting AR
Content spokes-person training	Top	Analyst relations managers, subject matter experts (SMEs), executives
Competitive intelligence	Top	Analyst relations managers, SMEs, members of the competitive intelligence or information research team
Research methodologies	2nd	Analyst relations managers, SMEs, members of the competitive intelligence or information research team
Business writing, strategic communications	2nd	Analyst relations staff including manager(s) or director, staff of outside agencies supporting AR

11.7. Presentation Reviews

People who haven't had much experience with analysts are often called upon to present a topic. It's important to review their materials carefully before they "go live."

Ideally, you (and/or someone else—per Section 9.2, analysts can help here) will review each analyst presentation, given by the person who will later present it to analysts. This review will let you hear the words that will go along with the slides. After all, if a presenter doesn't add value to the slides, why have one? If he or she does add value, how can one find out what it is from a copy of the materials? (In a pinch, reviewing a copy of the slides is better than nothing, especially if the visuals have been augmented with speaker's notes.)

In reviewing an analyst presentation, look at items such as:

- Are **messages** consistent with the corporate analyst messages?
- Are **strategy statements** brought down to earth, rather than just being goals or hopes? Do they say "how" with a convincing level of detail?
- Is the **subject** put in perspective relative to other products or initiatives?
- Is the **content**, insofar as you can tell without being an expert on it yourself, consistent with what other speakers have said or will say on related topics?

- Are **superlatives** such as "best," "fastest," "most advanced" and so on, or statements about your competition, backed up by specific, objective facts? (If not, take them out or make sure the speaker justifies them.)

- Are **discussions** of a new product, if it's not your firm's first product in its area, related to earlier ones?

- Do the materials (and does the speaker, if you're reviewing a rehearsal) respect analysts' existing knowledge and general expertise? (If there's much "Marketing 101," take it out.)

- Is the amount of material consistent with the speaker's time slot? (If you're not reviewing a live rehearsal, figure two minutes per slide on technical topics.)

- Are there any typos or grammar errors? (If you're not a professional-level proofreader and copy editor, give this part of the job to someone who is.)

If you try to do the analyst or consultant relations job without the technical and human help discussed here, you will have problems. Fortunately, everything in this chapter is well within your grasp.

12 | Putting your program in place

This chapter will cover:

1 Steps in developing an analyst/consultant relations plan
2 Steps in getting your program up and running
3 Measuring and auditing your program

In Chapter 2 we saw the different types of advisors. When you read it, you identified the influencer (analyst and consultant) categories that matter to your organization.

In Section 4.1 we identified what each type of influencer needs. You applied their needs to the categories that you identified in Chapter 2.

Chapters 6 through 10 described the building blocks of an influencer relations program. As you read over each, you identified characteristics of that element of your program. Now it's time to combine these: take the needs of the influencers who matter, combine these with the building blocks, size the blocks to your company, and put the result to work.

Your corporate influencer relations plan is your vehicle for setting and communicating the strategy to the company. The strategies in it dictate tactics, to be achieved via activities in order to reach the program objectives. The plan reflects enough of the tactics to "flesh it out" and bring it from the stratosphere down to a reality that can be used to guide specific activities.

There is a systematic five-step procedure to accomplish this efficiently and effectively. This chapter covers it, one section per step. Chapter 13 gives a timetable.

An effective influencer relations program includes **strategy**, **tactics** to support the strategy, and **activities** to carry out the tactics. Activities require **time** and **resources**, and should always have **measures**. These are the elements of a plan.

The first step in planning is to figure out your strategy. That, in turn, depends on Your goals: what you need to accomplish.

12.1. Determine your analyst/consultant relations needs

This is part of the Identify stage of the IDEAL framework (page 25). In terms of the AR Compass framework (p. 5), everything you do here must flow from your firm's business strategies.

If you haven't done it already, go back to Chapter 2 and write down the major characteristics of the analysts and consultants you want to reach. There may be several types. In that case, you may end up with several programs or at least several variations on one program. (The alternative, treating everyone the same, will not be as successful.)

Then revisit Section 4.1 and write down what these influencers want in general. The examples there are not all-inclusive. Add to them with your knowledge of your firm's major markets and of the types of influencers who operate in them.

Now you're ready for a *reality check*. This is critical. It's easy to jump into developing a plan without first stepping back to assess how analysts view your company. The danger is developing the wrong plan based on what you think your situation is. Below are the steps to complete during the reality check. Each step has a set of questions to help you complete this phase.

Be honest with yourself here. There is nothing to be gained and much to be lost, in wasted or even damaging effort, by pretending your firm needs one type of program when it really needs a different type. The elements of your plan will depend on this check.

Step	Questions to Answer
1. Internal and external inputs	What are the strengths and weaknesses of our company and its offerings? What do analysts, press and others in the industry say about them? What do our customers tell analysts about our company? What is our company's history with analyst relations?
2. Uncover competitive assumptions	What are the strengths and weaknesses of our competitors and their offerings? What do analysts, press and others in the industry say about them? How do customers—ours and theirs—view them? What do our competitors say about us? How does this compare with what objective third parties say? What is our competitors' history with analyst relations?
3. How analysts form opinions	Where do analysts get information about our competitors and us? What do the other parts of our company say about us to the public? What is the relationship between analysts and other influencers? What preconceived notions—positive, negative or neutral; correct or incorrect—do analysts hold about us and our competitors?
4. Where we need to go	Do we need to build awareness? Do we need to correct a problem? Do we need to gain or maintain positive opinions? Do we need to build trusted advisory relationships?
5. Realistic expectations	What is achievable? How long will it take to achieve this? Is this a short-term fix or a long-term solution? What resources are needed? Are they available?

Analyst opinion assessment

Your reality check is an assessment of what analysts think about your company today. You can't develop a realistic plan to move their opinions without a solid understanding of where they must be moved *from*.

There are several clues to analyst opinions of your firm and its products:

- **Read their research.** Do they understand what your offering is about? Do they understand your business model, your sales and distribution strategies? Do they see these the same way you do? If not, they need education.

  If they are sufficiently educated, do they assess your vision, strategy, and product strengths and weaknesses fairly? Does their assessment of appropriate users of your offerings line up with your market targets? Where do they position you in the competitive picture of your industry segment?

- **Read their comments in the press.** Evaluate them similarly, keeping in mind that industry analysts' press comments tend to be positive.

- **Talk to your customers** or obtain their input from your sales force. Your customers use analysts, and know what they say about you—in face-to-face discussions as well as research publications. They may not volunteer this information, but they'll tell you if you ask.

- **Ask the analysts.** Your firm probably subscribes to one or more services. Use some of your inquiry time to go beyond the written reports and find out what issues analysts have with your firm, what frustrations they have in working with it.

If your firm doesn't subscribe to the services of some firms whose opinions you want to assess, you can arrange a short consulting engagement with one of their analysts—or, if they want to cultivate you as a potential client, perhaps a free meeting. (If you don't expect a long-term relationship, don't mislead them into thinking you're a potential client just to save the cost of their time. They'll remember that you scammed them to save a few dollars, pounds, or euros. Better to pay for what you need.)

You can find a list of research firms (not individual analysts) at Barbara French's directory (*analystdirectory.barbarafrench.net*). French headed analyst relations consultancy Tekrati, until 2011, when she took a full-time AR position with a major networking vendor. You can search it for firms that focus on your area(s) of interest, though topic searches may miss generalist firms such as Gartner. More PR-oriented resources such as Cision's Media Database (*us.cision.com/media-database/media-database-influencer-list.asp*) include some analysts, but tend to focus on journalists.

To target consultants, a good resource is the *Consultants and Consulting Organizations Directory* from Cengage (*www.gale.cengage.com*). It's geographic, cross-indexed alphabetically and by specialty. As of this writing it's in its 37th edition, published February 2012, US$1,392.

(Others you may have heard of, such as Kennedy Publications' *Directory of Management Consultants* and Dun's *Consultants Directory*, are no longer published.)

In the UK, Blue Boomerang (*blueboomerang.com*) is the main source of consultant information. It publishes the *MT Black Book* (MT stands for the magazine *Management Today*) in association with the Management Consultancies Association. Its Web site has a search feature for consultants in any given area.

Most industry publications will sell or rent the list of subscribers who indicated "consultant" as their occupation when they subscribed. Commercial lists of management consultants are available, though they list consultants on pollution control and warehouse layout along with the ones you want. Membership lists of groups such as the Society of Telecommunication Consultants (*www.stcconsultants.org*) can be rented. Two directories of professional associations, including those that consist solely or largely of consultants, are as of this writing, are:

- Cengage (listed above) also publishes the *Encyclopedia of Associations*, including associations that consist largely of consultants: 52nd ed., April 2013, US$1,037.
- In the U.S., Columbia Books' National Trade and Professional Associations Directory (*www.columbiabooks.com/National-Trade-and-Professional-Associations-Directory*), November 2012, US$299.

12.2. Plan your initial program elements

This is part of the Drive and Align stages of the IDEAL framework (page 25). In terms of the SOSM framework (p. 5), each element of your program should relate to at least one point of the compass, ideally to two, three or all four.

You should have been thinking about your firm's needs all along. Now it's time to get specific. This plan is the document you will use to tell your management what you will do, how long it will take, and what people, money, etc. you will need to do it. These are the three basic elements of any plan: *activities*, *time* and *resources*.

Your plan is driven by the information you gathered in the reality check, by your overall company goals and by key corporate initiatives and announcements. It typically covers a year, with brief mention of what is expected to happen in the year or two after that.

Involve management early in this plan to ensure buy-in and to solicit advice. The plan should be accessible to anyone in the company working with analysts, even indirectly. Use it as an educational tool to raise analyst awareness throughout your company.

Use the worksheets at the end of this chapter to be sure you cover all elements of the communication channels you plan to use.

The table that follows is one possible outline. Modify it for your situation. Other program plans in marketing, business development or strategic planning can show you how your company writes them. Colleagues who have written plans before can also help. If your company has a standard planning process you must follow it, but try to cover these topics even if the standard plan structure doesn't have specific headings for them.

If you're not planning this program by yourself, you may want to ask the whole team to write down first cuts of this plan, then meet to develop the final plan as a group.

Section	Description
Overall Goals	Your analyst relations program is part of how your company hopes to achieve its overall goals. It is therefore important to know those. List relevant ones here.
Key Corporate Initiatives	Key corporate initiatives such as product/service launches, mergers and acquisitions, etc., will drive some program activities. Think about these strategically. For instance, you could want to position your company with certain influential analysts before a key announcement, or to sustain momentum after a launch.

This section should be both operational and strategic. This is where you list the strategies for achieving your goals. Take key corporate initiatives (above) into account. List and describe activities and events you plan to support each of these goals, with their objectives. These can be stated as desired outcomes. |
| Team | List the people or groups responsible for the activities in your plan. If you will be part of the team, include yourself where appropriate. |
| Activities and Dates | The is where the plan says what you will do. Break activities down to whatever level makes sense to you. For each, state who is responsible for (a) doing it and (b) supervising or coordinating it.

Activities should have target dates. These help your team stay on track and let your management monitor progress. For ongoing activities without specific completion dates, and those which last more than a few months, set intermediate checkpoints to make sure they're on track even if they're not complete. Dates can be adjusted over time. |
| Timeline | A summary timeline provides a "big picture" view of your plan to help you and your team manage the program as a whole. Cross-reference timeline items to the previous section. |
| Metrics | Measurement and evaluation: Describe how you will measure your program's effectiveness within your department, across the company and with analysts. In addition to measuring activities against objectives and completion dates, try to measure it against broader strategic objectives. |

Consider these tasks or activities in your plan:

Internal Activities

- Analyst targeting and segmentation
- Analyst research assessment
- Internal reporting and updates
- Performance measurements

- Briefing books

Analyst outreach and communications activities:

- Strategic analyst communications
- Product or service launches (important for scheduling your activities)
- Company-sponsored analyst events and forums
- Paid consulting engagements with analysts
- Analyst sponsored events and forums
- Analyst tours
- Buddy programs, executive counsel boards

These were discussed in earlier chapters, with the exception of analyst research assessments which were in Section 12.1 under the "Reality Check" heading.

Frequency

Each of the activities in your plan must be used properly, but that's not the whole job. They must be used often enough—but not too often. If you don't use them often enough, you won't achieve your outreach objectives. Use them too often, and you'll annoy analysts without more real communication.

Your objective is to maintain mindshare. To do this, you must (a) maintain a frequency of at least six meaningful touches per year, and (b) keep contact frequently enough that competitors don't push you out of analysts' minds in the intervening interval.

The analyst's objective is to maintain enough knowledge about your firm to be knowledgeable to clients, to be able to get more information as required, and to spend as little time as possible in the process. If an analyst serves provider clients, and especially if he or she has personal business development goals, another may be to enhance the business relationship with your firm.

These objectives must be reconciled. There is a third complicating factor: every person's needs are different from every other's, but the realities of running a program make it impossible to customize your communication to each individual.

Here are a few rules of thumb to serve as a starting point. Adjust them to match your firm's situation.

- **E-mail:** Weekly to monthly as a starting point, plus "extras" when you have breaking news that shouldn't wait until the next scheduled one. You may want to offer two frequency options. In the other direction, offer analysts the ability to sign up for all your press releases as well.

- **Visits to analysts:** Once a year is plenty for a small company. Larger ones should do more, perhaps along lines of business. The reason for the difference is analyst expectations.

A visit takes about the same resources for any size visiting firm. This is smaller, proportionately, for a larger firm, so larger firms can afford to visit more.

If the number of visits you can make to a given firm within a year is limited by their policy to fewer than you would otherwise make, use a top-down approach. Have an executive and product or LOB managers discuss strategies and products/services within their areas at a high level. Analysts can then ask for more detail if they want it. That creates a reason for additional contact. Since it will be at the analysts' request, research firm policies limiting briefings per provider won't apply.

- **Telebriefings:** When something happens, or when you sense enough interest in a specific topic to justify one. This will also be more often at larger firms.

- **Hosting visits by analysts:** Whenever an analyst asks for one with a reasonable justification. You can't schedule these. Just make sure analysts know your welcome mat is out and the light is on for them.

- **Analyst events:** Small firms don't have to do these, though a one-day event is nice.

Medium-sized ones should do one per year. Large ones should have more than one per year, ideally on both North American coasts and in Europe. Each such event can have a different line-of-business focus.

Other types of contact also have a desirable frequency:

- **Phone calls to keep in touch:** once every month to six weeks per analyst.

- **Tweets**: Once a day to once a week.

- **Relationship meetings:** one-on-one personal contact between analyst relations manager and analyst. These should happen at least once a year for key analysts. They can take place at the analyst's office, at your office, at a conference or at a trade show, wherever both will be at the same place at the same time. The purpose of this meeting is to build on an existing relationship or start one if either you or the analyst is new to the job. You can discuss the analyst's support needs, support activity to date, his or her research plans and schedule, speaking engagements ...

- **Executive "buddy system" phone calls:** one to three months. Adding a call from an analyst relations manager can be too much. If one of your executives calls an analyst regularly, you don't have to. In that case, a call from you every three to six months to make sure the analyst is getting what he or she needs is enough.

- **Holiday cards:** always good. Try to add a personal note, even if it's just a few words such as "it was nice to see you at our analyst event" or conversely "hope you can make it to next year's event." The appropriate frequency for these is once a year, whenever it's appropriate in your locale. (This is one type of communication where electronic media haven't yet replaced hard copy in business etiquette.)

- **Attending or participating in the research firm's conference:** as often as possible for all research firms, limited by your budget and time.

- **Referrals**, suggesting resources topics or potential business contacts to analysts: as the occasion arises. Although this is not your main focus and may be infrequent, any interaction that adds value to the analyst makes your personal stock with that analyst rise.

- **Social contacts**, such as taking an analyst to lunch/dinner, sports events, concerts: when convenient. Your intuition is the best guide here.

Timing of these elements should not be random. Consider analysts' business cycles. If an analyst has a known research agenda, such as Gartner's annual Magic Quadrant calendar, plan your activities to meets its needs wherever practical.

12.3. Determine your initial program targets

This is part of the Identify stage of the IDEAL framework (page 25). In terms of the SOSM framework (p. 5), each analyst should be chosen for value along at least one of the three arrows of the figure.

You must now choose your initial analyst program targets. You will want to start with a smaller number of analysts than those whom you will eventually hope to work with.

Ultimately, you hope to target the most influential analysts in your sphere of business. However, influence is not the only consideration in choosing your initial targets. Other factors in this decision include:

- **Existing relationship.** You don't want to drop people who worked with you prior to your new program.
- **Attitude.** If possible, start with analysts who are already favorably disposed to your firm. They'll be more willing to overlook a new program's inevitable rough spots.
- **Location.** All else being equal, start with analysts in your home region of the world.

How do you decide which analysts are influential? There are several indicators:

- **Practice leaders at major firms** are influential. They are listed as authors of reports, usually first of multiple authors. The reports may be restricted to subscribers or purchasers, but their existence and their authors' names are usually public information.
- **Heads of smaller specialist firms** that focus on your marketplace are also influential.
- **Press quotations are an indicator.** There are many reasons analysts are quoted, not all of which indicate high influence (responsiveness to press needs and the coming up with provocative comments on short notice are important), but this is an indicator.
- **Win-loss analysis** or sales impact analysis activities often produce names of analysts who influenced a procurement. People who show up more than once are influential.
- **Customers and prospects** can tell you which research firms are important to them, though sometimes not the names of specific individuals there.

12.4. Develop your analyst/consultant database

This is in the Identify and Execute stages of the IDEAL framework (p. 25).

Uses of this database

Your analyst/consultant database (Section 11.1) is the list of influencers with whom you work. It is your "mailing list" (using that term in its generic sense, to include e-mail and other media), of course. But it's more. It serves these functions:

Outgoing contact: Mailing list; basis for customizing mailings to individual members of your audience; basis for readership surveys and for determining likely areas of interest for newsletter articles, case studies, backgrounders, meeting presentations, etc.

Announcement materials: Mailing list; categorization in terms of materials to be sent, whether they should be sent before or at the time of the announcement, need for personal contact, need for any other special treatment; people in the same firm at the same location who should share any physical materials.

Seminars and other briefings: Invitation list based on postal/ZIP code; basis for determining geographic and professional areas of interest for seminars.

Consultants' Reference Manual, if you have one: Subscriber list; basis for reader surveys; other people in the same location who may use it.

Retrieving information about analysts and consultants who call or write: Which of your divisions or products do they care about? Have they asked for information before? Have their colleagues? About what, how often, how recently? What are their areas of interest? Do they receive your mailings and announcement materials, or do others in their firm at their location? Do they have your Consultants' Reference Manual, if you have one, or do others in their firm at their location? Have they registered for your Web site? Have they visited your firm or participated in one of your programs? If so, which executives and staff members were they exposed to?

Preparing for visits, in either direction: what does the expected audience care about? What is their history with your firm? Share this information with everyone who will participate in the visit.

12.5. Run your program

This is the Execute stage of the IDEAL framework (p. 25).

The big day has arrived. You're ready to start! Here's what you do now:

Tell your colleagues

Make sure the field sales force, the people who answer your main telephone number, those who get "info@..." e-mails, and everyone else who is a potential analyst or consultant contact point know about your program and how to find you:

- Make sure the field knows how important analysts and consultants are to your overall sales and what to do, should these inquiries come into a local sales office.

- If you aren't in the same group as your PR organization, make sure they know to send analyst/consultant queries in your direction. (Most will be grateful for the relief.)

- If you sell via distributors, VARs or any other indirect channel, tell them too.

- Write a small brochure about analysts, consultants and your support programs for them, or have one written, and send a copy to everyone in your firm's field organization.

- Get a half hour or an hour in your firm's sales training program to tell new hires about the importance of analysts/consultants and about your program.

- Put an article in your company newspaper or post one on its intranet.

Notifying the sales force is one of the most important parts of publicizing an analyst/consultant support program. Your sales force brochure should be more than an afterthought. It should define the types of analysts and consultants you want to reach and say why they matter. It should include names of large industry analysis and consulting firms that your sales reps should expect to encounter. It should explain how salespeople should work with analysts and consultants. It should describe your support programs for them and your corporate resources that are available to them. And it should give contact names and information wherever appropriate.

Tell the world

Send releases to the industry press about your new analyst/consultant relations program. Specialized consultant newspapers and newsletters are sure to print the information. Media in your market segment are 98% sure to print it. If you sell networking software, *Network World* will pick it up but *PC Week* will (probably) not. With general industry publications your chances are lower but still substantial. *Computerworld*, for example, prides itself on complete coverage and will likely run your release if your firm has anything to do with computers. *InformationWeek* is more selective, less likely. Don't forget local or regional business publications. You can't handle all of these centrally, so give your field sales offices a standard press release and ask them to send it to business publications in their areas.

Advertising may come into play here as well. As you read in Chapter 10, it may not be appropriate to trumpet "Come sign up for our new program!" But it is appropriate to run ads containing information that is primarily of interest to analysts and/or consultants, to mention in those ads that your program exists, and to tell these people how they can become part of it. Different firms will feel comfortable with different approaches here. Consider it before rejecting it out of hand.

Tell consultants and analysts

Your initial database has a number of names on it, with the most important names plus a sampling of everyday Joes and Janes. Send e-mails or letters welcoming them to your new program. (A paper letter has more presence and gives you the opportunity to enclose materials that don't have the same impact on a screen.) As you get more names, send them letters welcoming them to your (no longer new) program as well. This personalized attention is rare, despite not being hard, and is remembered.

A good example of a welcome letter from a regional contact follows. It was written just after Sperry and Burroughs had merged to form Unisys, before new stationery had made its way to the field. It's old, that's its original date, but the concept is timeless.

Burroughs Corporation

November 20, 1986

Dr. Efrem G. Mallach
[address]

Dear Dr. Mallach:

We appreciate your interest in our consultant liaison program. You have been added to our consultant database to insure continued mailings.

I am the consultant liaison for New England and upstate New York. The program allows bi-directional communication and opportunities. We understand your strengths and can recommend your success to our users. You have a better opportunity to understand our products and capabilities and can recommend them. We need to take the first step by getting together.

I'm sure you are aware of our name change from Sperry and/or Burroughs to UNISYS. I've enclosed a brochure to provide information on strategic direction for our new company.

Please call me to arrange a meeting time convenient for you. I'm looking forward to our mutually beneficial future.

Sincerely,

Yvonne Price
Manager, Consultant Relations
Northeast Region

Another vehicle for telling analysts about your program is your blog (Section 7.9).

Do it!

Each building block of your program is an on-going program or service. None is a one-shot effort to be done once and forgotten. A steady effort is required to make sure deadlines are not missed, announcement kits not delayed, and Web site updates not postponed for "higher priorities." Higher priorities will always interfere if you let them. The hallmark of a successful analyst or consultant relations program is consistency. Consistency builds trust.

Doing all of these takes people and a budget. The process of getting these varies from company to company. Chapter 15 is devoted to estimating these resource requirements. Since getting them also take time, this is reflected in the schedule in Chapter 16.

12.6. Monitor and measure the results

This is the Leverage stage of the IDEAL framework (page 25).

The world changes. Influencers change. Technology changes. Your firm changes. Your program must change with them. You must keep on top of this through audits and measurements.

Measurements determine the results of what you're doing. Audits ask whether what you're doing is still the right way to obtain the results you desire. These are related—how can you tell if you're doing the right thing to achieve the results you want, if you don't know what results you're getting?—but separate.

Audits

Audit your program at least once a year, every six months if possible. Ask:

Are the targets still appropriate? Perhaps your product line has evolved in a direction that calls for a shift in emphasis. New research services and opinion leaders may have emerged to target.

Is the emphasis still appropriate? Your firm may have obtained enough recognition to move from a Building to a Sustaining program. Your actions may permit you to move from Corrective to Sustaining. Or a situation beyond your control may require a Corrective program now, where Building or a Sustaining was called for earlier.

Is the scope still appropriate? Most firms, especially new ones, go through a stage of rapid growth. Program expansion is necessary and feasible. Older, more stable firms may want to change the emphasis of this part of their marketing mix.

Are the components still appropriate? You may want to rearrange your announcement kits, approach to briefings, or other program elements in response to analyst reactions or your own feelings. You may want to try new types of seminars, send a product manager on tour, or shift the emphasis between central and divisional support.

Is participation what you expected? If you're not getting as much participation as you had expected, perhaps more publicity is in order. If you're getting too much, and some of it appears frivolous, you might want to cut down. If you're getting more than expected, and it's all serious—don't complain! You should be delighted. The positive impact of your program on your sales figures will be even larger than you had expected.

A list of specific topics to cover in an audit follows. It's long. Some of it probably doesn't apply to your program, but read through it anyhow to make sure your audit covers all that it should:

1. MESSAGING
Corporate objectives, strategies, resulting messages
Sales objectives, strategies, resulting messages
Division/department/LOB objectives, strategies, resulting messages
Analyst Relations objectives, strategies, resulting messages

2. ANALYST RELATIONS PLAN
Review history of analyst contact before program began (successes, issues)
Strategy (relate to corporate, and LOB if applicable, strategy)
Objectives (measurable? how?)
Major initiatives and milestones, with key internal and external dates
Perceptions (analysts, customers, sales, channels; original, desired)
Clearly identified roles and responsibilities

3. BUDGET AND STAFFING REQUIREMENTS
Staffing (Analyst Relations)
Direct program costs (travel, events)
Launch activities involving analysts
Externally sourced materials/training (manuals, videos, brochures, case studies, ...)
Web site development/maintenance
Tools/technology (costs; see Section 5 below for functionality)
Intra-departmental expenses (salaries, travel)

4. ANALYST RELATIONS PROGRAM
Organization structure
Review of targeted analysts; analyst account plans
Review of subscription services (if AR responsibility, otherwise in #7 below)
Analyst profiles (database content; the database system is in #5 below)
Accessibility of AR Contacts
Analyst events
Consulting/speaking opportunities for analysts
"Buddy" and other executive contact programs
Analyst advisory council
Analyst conference attendance/participation/sponsorship
Communications Tools (analyst newsletter, relationship meetings, etc.)
Other, as applicable

5. TOOLS Analyst database Intranet content
Internal contact database Analyst Relations Web site
Corporate Web site
Tracking Systems for:
Activity and effectiveness
Research content evaluation

Press quote tracking
Briefing and event effectiveness
Project Management (timelines, Gantt charts, software packages used ...)
Competitive Analysis Database

6. PROCESSES AND PROCEDURES (Documented and accessible, for:)
Analyst Visits (tours)
Events (Analyst Days, lab tours, customer site tours)
Announcements (launches, updates, partner/acquisition)
Inbound inquires (briefing requests, questionnaires, surveys)
Outreach (speaking opportunities, consulting, Buddy program, round tables, ...)
Issue Resolution (negative press, not on radar screen, negative internal perceptions)

7. INTERDEPARTMENTAL RELATIONSHIPS
Sales
Marketing
Competitive Intelligence/Market Research (including subscription services)
Product Management
R&D (including subject matter experts) Executives
Corporate Communications (including Public Relations, Investor Relations)
Agency Support if applicable (including PR, external AR consultancies)

8. TRAINING (Completed, ongoing, planned)
Analyst Relations Managers
Spokespeople
Executives
Competitive Intelligence, Market Research, Librarians
Sales
Marketing
Corporate Communications (again including Public Relations, Investor Relations)

9. MEASUREMENTS AND REPORTING
Program Effectiveness
Competitive Benchmarking
Analyst Quotation Tracking
Influence
Win/Loss Analysis
Research Content Evaluation
Analyst Inbound Inquiry Tracking
Analyst Outreach Tracking
Management Reporting (Weekly, Monthly, etc.)
Briefing and Event Effectiveness (Surveys)

To carry out an audit:

- Assemble a team of people who know about analyst/consultant relations and AR programs. Include marketing management (including the manager to whom the program reports), field representatives, and possibly one or two analysts or consultants in whom your firm can confide. Try to get analyst relations professionals. If your company's AR professionals all work in the program that is being audited, you'll need outside resources. In large firms, other divisions can help.

- Give them copies of your reality check, plans and reports. Be available to answer any questions they may have on these. (Many things that are obvious to you, and are therefore not stated in your documents, aren't obvious to outside members.)

- Schedule a one-day meeting where you and your team explain your plans and choices. The world will have changed since you made them. Some may no longer be appropriate. One reason for an audit is to identify these changes and examine their implications. Cover each aspect of the program, reach conclusions, and record them.

- During the meeting, expect a frank discussion of what you've done, what worked (and how well), what didn't (and why) and what you'd do differently now.

- The audit leader will write up the team's report for you and/or your management. It will probably contain praise for jobs well done, criticism where due, and suggestions for changes based on events since your plans were first drawn up.

- Your management will ask you for a response indicating what parts of the audit report you agree with, what parts you take issue with, and how you plan to deal with each change the audit raised.

- The next revision of your analyst relations plan will reflect these changes.

Measurements

Any firm that devotes money, time, and resources to an analyst or consultant relations program should measure the effectiveness of that program and use the lessons learned to improve it. Measurement methods were discussed in Chapter 3. Here we'll look at what you should do with them.

First, you should have a measurement plan that states *what* you will measure and *when*, backed up with more detail that says *how*. This plan must be approved by your management because measurements involve resources. Also, you want your management to see that you take a serious, professional approach to your job.

Use mail, individual interviews, and group interviews. Obtain information about your materials, about your programs, about consultant opinions of your firm, about their needs. Compare this with what you found in previous surveys. The difference between one survey and the next will not be significant, since many random factors can influence the results, but long-term trends are meaningful and will soon be visible. The schedule on which you can expect to see results is discussed in Section 13.2.

In your measurement analysis, tie data to program objectives. Note increases or decreases. Include them in your monthly report.

As part of your ongoing monitoring activity, keep your database pruned. E-mail bounce-backs are one way to do this. However, don't delete a name just because an e-mail update can't be delivered. After you check the spelling (not necessary if this person's e-mail has gone through for a while), put him or her in a suspension category. Most analysts and consultants who disappear from one firm show up at another soon after. Chances are their professional field won't change much, so if they followed you previously, they still will. Keep their record ready to reactivate, perhaps with a "welcome back at your new location" e-mail ready to go out with a mouse click.

Even if e-mails don't bounce, ask people from time to time if they're still interested. Do this with care. Reply cards in newsletters, reply forms on its back page, or e-mail "un-subscribe" links are easy to ignore. Send these e-mails or cards by themselves if at all possible. Individually addressed envelopes are often forwarded when newsletters would not be. (This reflects corporate mailroom attitudes as much as post office policies.) Make the card easy to fill out. Pre-print the participant's name on the card, so that if the information is correct the respondent need only initial a line or check a box. In an e-mail, set up the reply to identify the respondent automatically. If you include the revalidation form with another mailing, such as a newsletter, call attention to it as vividly as possible—and not just on the envelope, since support staff may discard envelopes after placing their contents in a principal's in-tray. Allow several chances to respond. Don't drop a name after one or two e-mails go unanswered or cards don't come back. These precautions may keep a useless name on your list longer than absolutely necessary, but minimize the chances of dropping a still-interested, but busy, person.

Are you getting the results you wanted? An analyst/consultant program is not an exercise in spending corporate cash. It is a business development activity whose purpose is to increase your sales and achieve other goals. It does this via increasing your share of consultant recommendations, improving your positive visibility in analyst reports and making strategic use of these people's brains.

Section 4.1 began "Any communication activity in business should start by asking and answering this question: *What behavior change do you want to see, and in whom?*" Therefore, you should see if the behavior changes you hope for are happening. Use your firm's win-loss analysis program, if it has one, to see if consultants' and/or analysts' impact on campaign outcomes has changed. Monitor analyst reports and their comments in the press to find out what has happened to what they are writing about you. Try to relate these changes to your program and to other events that have taken place in your marketplace. (If a competitor makes a breakthrough that obsoletes your entire product line, the best analyst and consultant relations in the world won't help.)

The reason is that you must strive to stay ahead of the game. Your competitors want good analyst relations too. What you're doing isn't a secret. It can't be. If you've figured out how to support analysts better than they've been supported before, they'll tell your competitors what you're doing because they want the same level of support from everyone. Your competitors will then copy what you innovated. Since their programs will still have their own strengths as well, they'll end up—thanks to *your* intelligence, creativity and hard work—with a better program than you have!

This isn't unique to analyst relations. Every section of your company has it. But knowing you're not the only one with this problem doesn't make it easier to deal with.

The only solution is to keep innovating, keep improving. You have to run as fast as you can to stay in the same place. That's part of what keeps analyst relations challenging!

As you consider your program in the light of audit and measurement results, remember: *nothing is sacred.* "We've always done it that way" doesn't mean you have to, or even should, keep doing it that way. Not many years ago printed newsletters were a staple of analyst and consultant relations programs, but few remain in today's world of HTML-based e-mail. The same goes for multi-volume analyst/consultant reference manuals and instant fax-back services, all obsolete in the Web age.

As the analyst industry changes, its needs change. As the available tools change, the best way to address analysts' needs changes. You must be flexible to meet all these changes. The only constant is that analyst relations remains, at bottom, a *relationship* business.

The following pages contain worksheets to help you plan your analyst or consultant relations program. The purchaser of this book is authorized to reproduce these worksheets for internal use at his or her company for purposes of program planning and review.

1. EXECUTIVE ACCESS WORKSHEET

How will you use executives to support consultants/analysts?

___ To champion your program within your company
___ To speak at your analyst meetings
___ As part of a visiting team
___ As part of a hosting team
___ To speak at research firms' conferences
___ To participate in telebriefings
___ To sign letters/invitations as appropriate
___ In buddy or round-robin call program
___ Available to take important telephone calls

Which do you expect to be most helpful/available?

_____

_____

Have you contacted them to make sure they are available?
___ Yes
___ No (When/how will you? _____

2. STAFF ACCESS WORKSHEET

How will you use other staff members to support analysts/ consultants?

___ To speak at your analyst meetings
___ As part of a visiting team
___ As part of a hosting team
___ To speak at research firms' conferences
___ To participate in telebriefings
___ Available to take appropriate telephone calls
___ To write white papers and other support materials
___ To research consultant/analyst questions
___ To review drafts of consultant/analyst materials

Who do you expect to be most helpful/available?

_____

_____

Have you contacted them to make sure they are available?
___ Yes
___ No (When/how will you? _____

How will you publicize your program to staff in general?

_____

_____

3. CENTRAL CONTACT WORKSHEET

At headquarters:

___ New position, created for this purpose only
___ New position, other duties: _____
___ Add to duties of existing person_____

Points to remember:

___ Voice mail setup
___ E-mail address

Divisional contacts:
___ Not applicable
___ Dedicated divisional analyst/consultant relations staff
___ Responsibilities added to existing staff (who?) _____
___ Division offices asked to refer calls to HQ
___ Other: _____

Regional contacts:
___ Not applicable
___ Dedicated regional analyst/consultant relations staff
___ Responsibilities added to existing staff (who?) _____
___ Regional offices asked to refer calls to HQ
___ Other: _____

4. VISITS TO ANALYSTS/CONSULTANTS WORKSHEET

No. of expected trips/year: _____ Total no. of firms visited per year: ___
Types of firms to be visited: _____

Reason for visits (estimate how many in each category):
___ Initiating contact
___ Keeping in touch, periodic update
___ Announcement briefing
___ Request by analyst/consultant firm
___ Other – what?_____

About how many people will go along on a visit? _____

5. HOSTING ANALYST/CONSULTANT VISITS WORKSHEET

Number of visits expected per year: _____

The following items are for rough sizing of the level of effort. Individual visits will vary widely based on visitors' needs.

Duration of typical visit: _____ hours/day(s)

Typical visit will include:
___ Executive welcome
___ Other executive participation
___ Technical presentation(s)
___ Technical discussion(s)
___ Marketing presentation(s)
___ Marketing discussion(s)
___ Product demonstration(s)
___ Hands-on product usage (beyond demo interaction)
___ Meal(s)
___ Other: what?_____

6. ANALYST/CONSULTANT WEB SITE WORKSHEET

Do you need a special analyst and/or consultant Web site?
___ Yes
___ No (skip the rest of this worksheet)

Types of resources to be made available:
___ Standard Web site
___ ftp site
___ Discussion group
___ Other: what? _____

If you will have a Web site for analysts/consultants:
Password required? ___ Yes   ___ No
Approx. number of new pages needed: _____
To be designed by (name): _____
To be created by (name): _____
To be maintained by (name): _____
To be hosted on (server): _____
Approx. space required: _____GB
Home page URL: _____

7. ANALYST/CONSULTANT MEETING WORKSHEET

Do you need separate seminars/briefings for analysts and/or consultants?

___ Yes

___ No (skip the rest of this worksheet)

Audience(s): _____

Location:

___ Corporate headquarters

_ Regional offices: how many cities? _____

_ With industry/association meetings: which? _____

Approximate number per year, total: _____

Typical duration of each seminar (some may vary):

___ Half day, a.m.

___ Half day, p.m.

___ Evening

___ Full day

___ Multiple days: how many? _____

___ Other: what?_____

Parallel tracks:

___ No

_ Yes: how many/which: _____

Typical approximate time allocation to topics (hr:min):

_____:___ Introduction

_____:___ Outside speaker

_____:___ Corporate executive speaker

_____:___ HQ marketing presentation

_____:___ Regional sales/marketing speaker

_____:___ Standard slide show/videotape

_____:___ Technical session 1: _____

_____:___ Technical session 2: _____

_____:___ Technical session 3: _____

_____:___ Demonstration(s)

_____:___ Questions and answers

_____:___ Breaks

_____:___ Meals

_____:___ Other: _____

8. ANALYST/CONSULTANT TELEBRIEFING WORKSHEET Estimated

Number of telebriefings per year: _____

Teleconferencing facilities:

___ Company-owned
___ Standard package/commercial service: _____
___ Rented for the occasion: from _____

Participants informed/invited by (check all that apply):

___ Information included in other (e-)mailing
___ Special (e-)mailing for this telebriefing
___ Fax (not usually recommended)
___ Phone call
___ Other: what? _____

Visuals made available in advance:

___ Hard copy, mailed
___ Hard copy, sent by courier service
___ Hard copy, faxed (recommended only if analyst specifically requests faxing)
___ Made available on the Web
    ___ On our analyst/consultant site
    ___ Elsewhere on company site, password required
    ___ Elsewhere on company site, password not required
___ E-mailed on request: formats _____

9. MAILING WORKSHEET

Frequency (check all that apply):

___ Every _____ months
___ At announcement time
___ Other: when? _____ How sent (check all

that apply):

    ___ E-mail
    ___ Postal service
    ___ Fax (recommended only if analyst specifically requests this()
    ___ Courier service (is new account needed for internal accounting reasons?)

Content (check all that apply):

___ Letter from Analyst Relations manager or next management level up
___ Letter from executive: who? _____
___ Press releases (___ list only; ___ full content)
___ List of other available documents: _____
___ Product briefs
___ Technology backgrounders/white papers
___ Customer case studies
___ Other: what? _____

10. ANNOUNCEMENT MATERIAL WORKSHEET

Announcement kits are a variation on mailings. Use this section instead of the previous one for them.

Check each item that will be sent to everyone on your list. If an item is only going to some of the names in your data-base, indicate who will receive it instead of checking the line.

___ Press release
    ___ Edited/customized
    ___ As sent to press
___ Background info. on technology, markets, etc.
___ Copies of executive speeches
___ Product specification sheets
___ Product briefs/brochures
___ Product photographs
___ Price lists
___ Suggestions for updating recipient's reference file (what to discard, etc.)
___ Consultant Reference Manual update material
___ Competitive analysis information
___ other: _____
___ other: _____
___ other: _____
___ other: _____

11. REFERENCE MATERIAL WORKSHEET

Are there any types of reference manuals, etc., which you will not give to analysts or consultants, even on request?

_____

_____

Are any types of reference manuals, etc., for which you plan to charge?

_____

_____

Are there any types of reference manuals, etc., which you plan to send to all analysts or consultants in certain categories without a specific request?

_____

_____

(Use additional space as required for the above items.)

12. CONSULTANTS' REFERENCE MANUAL WORKSHEET

Do you need a Consultants' Reference Manual?

___ Yes

___ No (skip the rest of this worksheet)

Est. pages that are:

Section:	New	Reused	Modified
Corporate Overview	_____	_____	_____
Annual Report	_____	_____	_____
Product info.: product line 1	_____	_____	_____
Product info.: product line 2	_____	_____	_____
Product info.: product line 3	_____	_____	_____
Training	_____	_____	_____
Support	_____	_____	_____
Special services	_____	_____	_____
Prices	_____	_____	_____
Other: _____	_____	_____	_____
Other: _____	_____	_____	_____
Other: _____	_____	_____	_____

Filing aids:

___ Custom binders with printed tabs

___ Plain binders, slip-in front/spine inserts, tabs

___ No binders, inserts for reader's binder, tabs

___ No binders or inserts, tabs for reader's binder

___ Suggestions for how user can organize materials

___ None

Updates:

___ With announcement materials

___ Regularly every _____ months

___ Other: _____

13 | AR or CR within your organization

This chapter will cover:

1 Where analyst/consultant relations belongs on the organization chart
2 How the people in the function do and where they should report
3 Working with other parts of your company
4. Working with outside agencies and resources

There are (at least) four issues to consider regarding the organization of analyst or consultant relations: where to put it, how to structure it, synergy with the rest of the firm, and internal analyst/consultant relations tasks. This chapter covers them in that order.

13.1. Where should analyst/consultant relations fit?

Every corporation has a structure. Within it, every employee has at least one manager. The position of one's manager(s) affects that employee's credibility in the firm and his or her claim on its resources. Therefore, in planning analyst/consultant relations work, it's important to put it in the right place.

Responsibility for analyst relations usually falls within the marketing organization. Most chief marketing officers consider it part of their responsibility.

Chances are it won't report directly to the CMO. Most of them group functions to keep direct reports down to a workable number. Analyst relations often goes into marketing communications, public relations, or a similar function. All these can work.

Traditionally, it falls within media and public relations. This works as long as there is a clear distinction between the strategies and tactics used for industry analysts and consultants versus those used for other audiences, and a clear understanding by management of why they must be different. Managers must realize that these are distinct publics, and that their needs differ from those of other publics they probably know better.

Companies that take a more strategic view of analyst relations, especially of how working with analysts can contribute to their own strategies and actions, may prefer Strategic Planning, Business Development or another function that takes a longer view than Marketing usually does, has a broader perspective, and is "plugged in" at higher levels.

Another option is to combine AR and Competitive Analysis, which is usually a primary user of analyst reports and therefore often knows who's who in that world. One problem here is that competitive analysts are usually more inwardly focused, in job and personality, than analyst relations calls for. It's OK to put the function in the same department, but it may have to be done by different people. Another concern is that putting purchasing analyst services in the same place as the folks who try to get analysts' attention can create pressure to link them inappropriately. You can't stop analysts from asking you to buy their services, but it's nice to be able to reply "Sorry, someone else does that."

If your firm's analyst relations function is decentralized to LOBs (see next section), this applies at the LOB level. Your company may require firm-wide consistency in its reporting relationship within the LOB, especially if it has a centralized corporate culture.

Other reporting relationships are possible. Consultant relations (as opposed to AR) can be in Sales, as long as there's some support at headquarters. This is especially appropriate if your firm will have regional consultant relations people, since the sales organization already has a regional structure with staff and offices in all the necessary places. It recognizes that the major function of consultant relations is supporting consultants who advise sales prospects or who could advise sales prospects in the future. Having Consultant Relations in the sales organization can help align its actions with sales objectives.

13.2. How should the analyst relations function be organized?

Analyst relations is a team sport. The size and organizational structure of your company will dictate its roles and responsibilities to some degree. So will its culture. A company with a centralized culture, in which most functions are kept as close to the core as possible, should have a different analyst relations structure than a company that prides itself on the independence of its divisions. This is true even if all visible factors—size of company, number of locations, breadth of product line, marketing channels—are identical.

This question won't arise when your firm first identifies analyst/consultant relations as a function, because in a small firm it will involve just one person. As any firm grows, all its functions also grow. Influencer relations follow this rule.

Centralized Analyst Relations

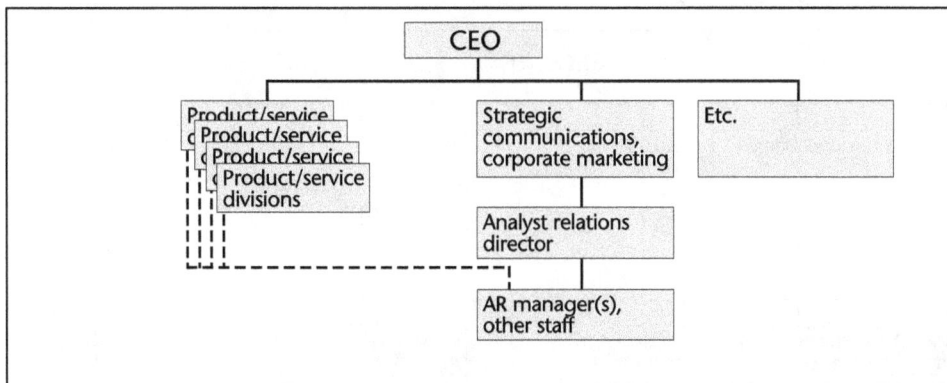

In a centralized model, AR is part of the corporate staff. Ideally, its director or manager is part of the team that sets overall company goals and objectives and develops messages.

The figure shows the function in the strategic communications/corporate marketing area, but other places (as discussed in the previous section) can work well too.

Navigating within product or business divisions to get things done is a challenge with the centralized model. Members of the analyst relations staff therefore need to be closely aligned with, often having a dotted-line reporting structure into, these divisions.

Decentralized Analyst Relations

In the decentralized model, the analyst relations function is divided among the divisions or other organizational elements of a company.

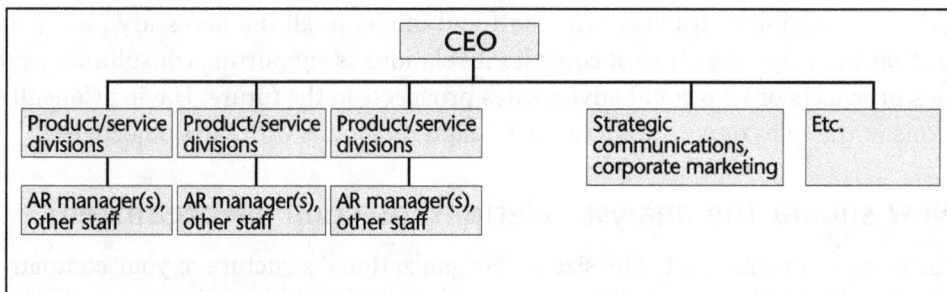

A risk of a decentralized structure is that each unit may set its own direction, creating the impression of a company whose parts are not coordinated. (Analyst practices seldom follow the lines of your organization. Besides, analysts covering different parts of your firm talk to each other. Therefore, analysts will pick up quickly on any lack of coordination.) This structure therefore requires, in all but the most unusual situations, coordination by a program *owner*. The owner can be the head of strategic communications or another high-level manager. He or she is ultimately responsible for setting analyst relations program goals and ensuring its success.

Hybrid Analyst Relations

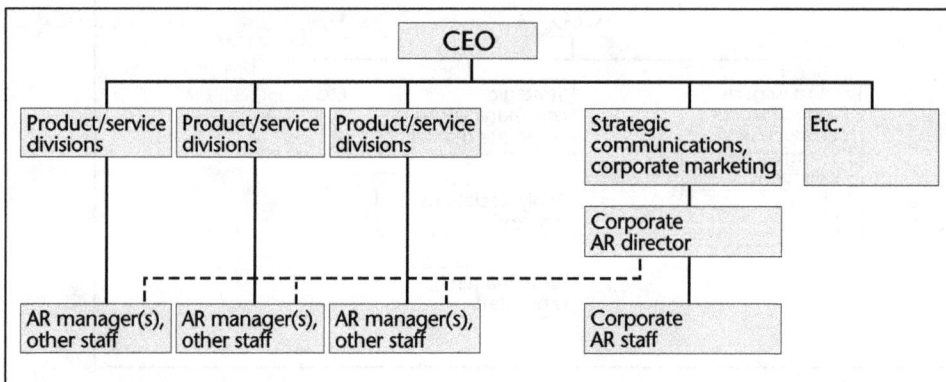

In the hybrid model each division has its own analyst relations staff, but there is also a central corporate group to coordinate divisional efforts, provide central services and support analysts in areas related to corporate topics (such as arranging high-level strategy briefings).

This seems to provide the best of both worlds. Its risk is wasting resources through duplication, and a need to spend more time and effort on coordination than in the others.

Once more than one person handles analyst/consultant relations at your firm, there are several ways to structure their relationships to each other. The following models, each from a different real company, run the gamut:

1. One firm's six analyst liaison professionals, four of them located in product divisions distant from its California headquarters, all report to the head of world-wide AR. She manages them directly. She, in turn, is a member of the central corporate staff.

2. This firm's analyst liaison function is largely in the central corporate staff, with specialists in each major area as members of the central group. They have identified individuals in each group to handle the few questions that are best dealt with locally. The corporate director of analyst relations manages the central group personally and has dotted-line supervisory responsibility for divisional staff for this part of their jobs.

3. A third company's analyst relations activity consists largely of people in each division, with a central staff providing corporate co-ordination and handling functions, such as analyst e-mail updates, that would be wasteful to duplicate. The corporate head of AR has advisory responsibility for the divisional personnel and chairs a regular meeting (monthly by phone, quarterly at rotating divisions) in which all participate.

4. A fourth firm's seven analyst liaison professionals report into three different lines of business. There is no central manager, no corporate staff or anything else. Coordination is handled by meetings, informal contact, and a general awareness on the part of the seven people that their firm must present a unified face to the outside world.

All these work for the companies that use them. An organizational structure is, after all, only a way to accomplish objectives through people. People differ. The ways in which they work best together differ. It's natural for the best organizational structure to differ from one firm to another.

The fourth approach is too extreme for most firms. It works there because six of the people are in the same complex (four in the same building), the firm is stable with little turnover, the divisions sprang from a single organization so they share a culture, and the people get along. If the firm were more geographically dispersed, had grown via merger and acquisition rather than internal growth, were in a business or geographic area with more turn-over, or the personalities were different, their approach would be less successful. Whether it will still work in a few years, when some turnover will have taken place and everyone will be used to being in separate divisions, is an open question.

Leaving that option aside, what is the best structure for your company? Whatever works. Your company, culture, and people are unlike any other. What's right for Company X is almost certain to be wrong for you, even if X is a market and technology leader in your industry segment. Don't fall into "they do it this way, so we should."

To get an idea of what works for your company, look at its other functions. How is, say, Purchasing organized? Is there a corporate Director of Purchasing, supervising purchasing managers in each division? Or, does each division's Purchasing Manager report to that division's director of operations? In the field, does each region have its own technical support function, or is there a one technical support group with its own regional management structure?

You'll probably find a range of answers, some with "dotted-line" secondary reporting relationships. A pattern will emerge: centralized, decentralized or in between. A company with a centralized culture, with most functions close to its corporate core, should have a different analyst relations structure than a company that prides itself on the independence of its operating divisions. Follow your company's pattern for analyst/consultant relations unless you see a good reason not to.

13.3. Positions in the Analyst Relations Function

The size and organizational structure of your company will to some degree dictate the analyst relations roles and responsibilities within the company. So will its culture. This section gives a high-level overview of the types of people that need to be involved, their roles and responsibilities.

13.3.1. Analyst Relations Director

This is the overall head of a firm's analyst relations program. In a small company this may be the only person formally charged with analyst relations, and the title may be less exalted. However, the roles of the position, other than supervision, are the same.

Companies of typical complexity in typical markets assign a full-time analyst relations person by the time they reach about $100 million in annual sales. This figure has stayed about the same for several years. It dropped in real terms, as more and more companies recognize the strategic value of analysts and understand that variations in their needs makes it difficult to cover them all with a single, uniform approach. However, currency inflation has offset this to keep the number steady.

This person's role is both strategic and tactical. The strategic aspect produces the most important results. The AR director drives strategic analyst outreach, is the central point of contact for the analyst community (or manages multiple points of contact, each with their own areas of responsibility), and analysts' advocate within the company.

The analyst relations director's job is to:

- Develop the corporate AR plan (see previous chapter). This top-level plan describes your firm's overall analyst relations activities and their reasons. It is written, at least in part, for an executive audience and should reflect their strategic perspective.

- Create and proactively drive a structured program that involves various groups across the company to engage the right analysts at the right level with the right content.

- Ensure consistency and synergy with related groups such as Corporate Communications, Media and Investor Relations, and Market Intelligence/Competitive Analysis.

- Identify appropriate external communication opportunities with analysts.

- Drive the development and communication of corporate umbrella messages, division objectives and product roadmaps to analysts.

- Develop relationships with executives of major research firms and key analysts.

- Manage and leverage resources (people, tools and budget) to achieve results.

- Measure and report effectiveness of the analyst relations program.

13.3.2. Analyst Relations Manager(s)

As companies grow to and beyond about $250 million in annual revenue, they usually expand their analyst relations staff. The exact point at which a second person is brought on board, and the number of people in this role in larger firms, depend on the size of a company; its complexity in terms of product lines, markets, and channels; analyst impact on its business; and its use of outside resources to supplement in-house staff. These people are typically called analyst relations managers or analyst liaisons. If both titles are used, "analyst liaison" usually designates less seniority.

When there is more than one person in the analyst relations group, it is important to keep responsibilities clear. Responsibilities can be based on geography, division or product.

An analyst relations manager may be physically located with the region or division whose analyst relations he or she manages. That's in the next subsection. This one is about analyst relations managers who share the central (headquarters) workload.

The job of the analyst relations manager typically includes the following. Most reflect a subsetting of the analyst relations director's job. (In a small company where one person handles the entire analyst relations task, that person is responsible for the tasks of this section as well as those of the previous one.)

- Develop analyst relations plans within assigned area(s) of responsibility. These flesh out the corporate plan in specific program areas, providing operational detail where the corporate plan provided strategy and perhaps some tactics. For example, if you will have a series of analyst tours in which you present your firm and its products/services to analysts at their offices, the analyst relations manager would develop a plan for them or perhaps a plan for each. This plan, or these plans, would provide more detail than the high-level corporate plan.

- Develop individual account plans for a firm and/or analyst. These explain why this firm or analyst is important, why a specific plan to work with it/him/her is necessary, what this activity is expected to accomplish (objectives/benefits), what is to be done and when, and what resources (people, money, other) will be required.

- Develop detailed plans to communicate company messages to the analyst community; drive the development and communication of these messages and related content.

- Ensure consistency and synergy of divisional and/or product messages with related constituencies such as Corporate Communications, Media Relations, Investor Relations, and Market Intelligence/Competitive Analysis.
- Identify opportunities to use analysts strategically within assigned area(s).
- Develop and foster relationships with analysts within assigned area(s).
- Measure success within the appropriate area(s).

13.3.3. Divisional, departmental and regional analyst relations managers

Once a company's analyst relations organization gets beyond a handful of people, some are usually located in divisions or geographic regions. In a decentralized or hybrid organization they report to these groups' managers, perhaps with a "dotted-line" reporting relationship to the corporate analyst relations director as well.

Someone in a smaller department or location can have other responsibilities as well as being the analyst contact for that component. Such a person's role is a composite of this section and the roles of "Other spokespeople" later in this chapter.

The exact job here depends on the culture of the organization. Who generally initiates programs? Do they go bottom-up, coming from remote corners and moving up as needed for approval, or top-down, where headquarters sets guidelines and others fill in the details? The degree to which the divisional analyst relations program initiates on its own versus supporting the central group will depend on the degree to which the organization overall does one or the other. The tasks below should be understood with this in mind.

Responsibilities of divisional and/or geographic analyst relations managers include:

- Develop the divisional and/or geographic analyst relations plan. It mirrors the corporate plan at the divisional, regional or line of business level, going into more detail as needed. For example, if you will have divisional analyst tours, the divisional analyst relations manager plans them.
- Serve as internal analyst relations contact for the product line or division.
- Support the corporate analyst relations function.
- Act as subject matter expert (SME), depending on ability and other responsibilities.
- Drive the development and communication of divisional, departmental or geographic messages and roadmaps to analysts.
- Identify analysts who become visible in specialized professional communities, adding them to the central database as applicable.
- Engage specialist analysts in specific technology and product areas.
- Review research for accuracy, with support from the division as needed.
- Pass on information obtained from analysts, including competitive information.
- Coordinate tasks and activities with other parts of the company.
- Provide customer references for division products.

13.4. Analyst/consultant relations corporate synergy

No analyst or consultant relations program operates in a vacuum. No program can possibly have its own experts in every area an analyst or consultant might have to know about. An effective program must draw on the resources of the firm. This section discusses the areas that must be prepared to support your program. If suitable support is not available, analyst relations staff or external resources will have to do comparable work. This may raise costs or hurt effectiveness. In some cases, replacement may not be practical at all.

Corporate Executives

Executives are the top level of corporate management. Their direct and indirect support is critical to analyst relations success. Their involvement with the program sends a top-down message that analyst relations is a cross-corporate initiative. The level of executive involvement depends on a company's size.

At best practices companies, executives are personally involved in analyst relations and (see Section 7.2) with analyst interactions. Industry analysts continually give highest marks for analyst outreach to providers whose top managers are visible and accessible.

The responsibilities listed below apply to many or all executives at your company. Within this group you should have an executive "champion" or "sponsor" for your program. This person talks up the value of analysts, and hence of analyst relations, in the company; sets the tone that your company cares about analysts; supports analyst relations for resources in top-level meetings; and serves as an escalation point for critical analyst issues. This person can also help defuse any conflicts that come about with executive-level colleagues who don't fully appreciate the value of working with analysts.

Corporate executives should:

- Set the tone for corporate analyst relations efforts.
- Set an example for others in working with analysts.
- Set and communicate the company's overall goals and objectives.
- Initiate and approve corporate umbrella messages.
- Allocate resources for marketing programs, including analyst relations.
- Engage key influential analysts on company direction, strategy and vision.
- Represent the company in analyst meetings.
- Be the executive contact for a small number of suitable analysts in a "buddy system."

In terms of content, there is little a top corporate executive can say that can't be said equally well or better by somebody else. (Exception: corporate strategies, which they often perceive best.) Most executives would agree with this in private.

Yet there are times when only a corporate executive can make a desired impression. When Ken Olsen, then CEO of Digital Equipment Corporation, announced that his firm didn't like the then-proposed Manufacturing Automation Protocol, the world took notice. (This example is ancient, as is the next, but human nature hasn't changed much in four thousand years.) Had a software developer deep in Digital's software group said the same, he or she would have been ignored. Anybody who noticed the comment would have attributed it to momentary pique over an elusive bug. Things executives say carry weight. If you want a statement to carry weight, ask an executive to say it.

This translates directly to analyst and consultant relations. A receptionist and a CEO can both say "We're glad you came to see us today." The content is identical. But the CEO's statement means "talking with you is the most important thing I can do right now." The same principle applies to other executives. If an engineer says "we looked at options and chose to support 16 cores," an analyst will infer that a few colleagues chatted about it over coffee. If the engineering VP says the same thing, listeners infer a serious study.

This inference is probably wrong. Whatever study there was can't be affected after the fact by the title of whoever says this. But people like to hear things said by top executives. They ascribe great wisdom to people they respect. (Check out the idiocies mouthed by Henry Ford and Charles Lindbergh in areas outside their expertise—and the credibility those once received.) Your firm will be considered wiser, its plans better laid, its products better planned, and its markets better understood, if executives speak to analysts and consultants. If you keep your requests to a reasonable level, don't waste the CEO's time on every freelance programmer who stops by, explain the reason for each meeting, don't ask them to give detailed presentations that are better given by someone else, and spread the load around, you will probably be able to satisfy your needs in this department.

An example of effective executive participation: On July 20, 1987, Wang Laboratories hosted a consultant seminar at their headquarters. This was also the day on which Wang announced their financial results for their fourth fiscal quarter and fiscal 1987, which ended on June 30. Results were up dramatically from the beginning of the fiscal year. They represented the success (temporary, in hindsight) of moves that new president Fred Wang had put in place about six months earlier. With all the demands on their time from the press and the financial community that day, Mr. Wang and five of his top lieutenants spent an hour at that seminar answering consultant questions. This said more about the importance of consultants to Wang Labs than anything else could have.

Finally, executives can help by lending their names. A good example is the letter on the next page. This is an actual letter I received, edited to remove anything that identifies the sender.

Computer Company, Inc.

May 18, 2011

Dr. Efrem G. Mallach
[address]

Dear Dr. Mallach:

    I wanted to follow up your invitation to attend the press and analyst reception at *CCI In Concert* on June 2 with a detailed agenda of the three-day event.

    Please consider attending other *CCI In Concert* activities because it's an excellent demonstration of our commitment to working "in concert" with our customers to provide the best solutions for their computing requirements.

    As a reminder, the reception for the press and the analyst community will be held at the Marriott Marquis Hotel, 1535 Broadway at 45th St., in the West Side North Ballroom on Tuesday, June 2 at 10:30 AM prior to the official opening of *CCI In Concert*.

    The reception will include announcement and demonstration of new networking products and a talk on our communication strategies. A buffet luncheon will be served after the presentations.

    Please notify us by e-mail to AR@cci.com or by calling 800 xxx-xxxx if you wish to attend any of the seminars or portions of the event other than the press and analyst briefing. Please RSVP to the same e-mail address, or to Mary Lastname at 978 555-xxx, if you'll attend the press and analyst briefing on June 2.

Sincerely,

(name)
President, Computer Company, Inc.

I'm not so naïve as to think that the president of "CCI" singled me out for personal attention. I'm fairly sure he didn't write the letter himself. But the message is clear: he cares enough about analysts to lend his name. This message—"CCI, from the top down, cares about you"—is important. It relates to resource availability. CCI's analyst relations manager could have invited me, but her letter could not convey that message.

There is no substitute for executives when they are needed. You can't hire an actor in an expensive suit to play Executive Vice-President for a day. (Maybe you could, but we don't recommend it.) A few large firms have had people with fancy titles but few other responsibilities for such appearances. This was more common in an era when it was hard to terminate senior people who had outlived their usefulness. Today, it's rare. Companies know that keeping high-paid greeters around is transparent and wastes money. When you want an executive, you'll need a *real* one.

Other spokespeople in general

While executives are your company's best representatives on high-level strategy or when a statement must be made with authority, there are many subjects on which they are not the best informed. If an analyst needs to know why your product runs clockwise rather than counter-clockwise, how your sales break down in five European countries, or who uses your latest release in an acute care hospital with 200–500 beds, there is (in all but the smallest start-ups) a better source for the answer.

You should identify spokespeople from the R&D, product management and marketing organizations who can address areas that analysts and consultants need to know about. Doing this in advance gives them a chance to prepare for analyst interactions. It also saves you the need to rush around looking for someone when an analyst or consultant calls, since you'll already know who can answer. Even if the usual spokesperson can't handle a question, his or her contacts within the organization will usually help find someone who can answer it more quickly and easily than you could yourself. You can then enter their names into a database as discussed in Section 11.1.

Being an analyst/consultant spokesperson should not be a volunteer activity, though they should of course be willing to do it. It should be considered part of their jobs and reflected in their performance reviews. Your executive sponsor may help you make management connections for this purpose.

The responsibilities of non-executive spokespeople include:

- Be available to answer analyst and consultant questions and make presentations within area(s) of expertise.
- Represent a product or market area at analyst meetings.
- Review analyst reports with quick turnaround, or identify someone else who can.
- Be able to identify colleagues who can answer questions outside his or her expertise.
- Write "white papers" for analysts and consultants, or identify those who can.
- Pass information obtained from analysts, including competitive information, to others as appropriate.

The major categories of non-executive spokespeople are covered in the next subsections.

Marketing Communications

These are the people who prepare marketing literature for customers and prospects: product brochures, spec sheets, price sheets, ads, and everything else your firm puts out. They may also manage your Web site. (Analyst/consultant relations may be part of Marketing Communications on the org chart, but we're discussing the other "marcom" functions here.)

Many materials produced by Marketing Communications can be used, as they are or with minor editing, for analysts and consultants. Product literature should be included in announcement kits and available on request or for distribution in meetings. Much of a customer update can, with modifications, be used in an analyst or consultant update. Anything else produced by this department should be evaluated for potential use also.

The second element of synergy with Marketing Communications is that its professional skills are of value to analyst/consultant relations. Even if existing materials aren't suitable for consultants, the people who created them know how to create materials of that type. They can write, edit, design, lay out, and produce. You need these capabilities for your materials too. If you can't use in-house resources, your options are:

- To do an amateurish job. A "geeks in T-shirts" start-up may be able to get away with this, but it is best avoided there and is unacceptable anywhere else.

- To hire your own editing and design staff. This can be justified only for the largest firms with the heaviest analyst/consultant writing load. Smaller programs won't be able to keep these people busy with suitable work.

- To go outside for specialized help. This is usually the best alternative. It yields professional results, costs less than full-time editors you don't need, and avoids trying to keep writers busy with other work that isn't what they signed on for and for which they're not qualified. The downside is that these people don't know your firm.

A third area where this function may be vital to a consultant relations program is advertising. The ad department often falls under Marketing Communications. If you want to advertise to consultants, orient some of your advertising to consultants, put some of your firm's advertising in media that reach consultants, or mention your consultant relations program in your firm's ads, you have to work with these folks. There is usually no practical alternative, as most firms don't allow anyone else to place ads.

Public Relations

These are the people who deal with the press and other media. They work with management to define how the company wants to be seen by these constituencies and thus by their audiences. They create materials, such as press releases, to support that visibility. And they work with the press to ensure that the correct impressions are made.

That's how most corporate PR sees itself. The P stands for *press*, not *public*, even if they won't admit it. This is unfortunate because, as you know, there are other influential publics besides the press. (Analysts and consultants, to name two.) Firms therefore create analyst, consultant, investor, etc., relations groups to work with those, but often leave the term "public relations" in place for those who deal with the press. These other groups, with their specialized functions, may report to PR or be separate. Here we focus on the press relations task and how it can work with analyst/consultant relations.

The activities performed by Public Relations vis-à-vis the press resemble those performed by Analyst and Consultant Relations vis-à-vis those groups. They include sending written information, answering questions as they arise, making contact with other elements of the firm when necessary, some "hand-holding" and relationship-building.

As a result, there is a wealth of material and expertise in Public Relations that can be used to advantage by Analyst/Consultant Relations. Press releases and backgrounders are probably suitable for consultants after some editing. (See Section 7.9.3, under the subhead "Customizing Your Press Release.") Just as with Marketing Communications, anything done or produced by the Public Relations function should be evaluated for potential use with analysts or consultants.

Another connection between Public Relations and analyst support arises from the overlap between some analysts and the press. Specialized newsletters and Web sites have aspects of both. Analysts who write them often complain that providers don't know how to treat them. Unfortunately, for everyone who complains of being treated like the press rather than an analyst, there's another who's upset about being forced into AR when he or she would prefer to be seen as press. No single approach can keep everyone happy.

So, coordinate contacts to make sure you deal with these hybrids via the most appropriate channel. One way of choosing this channel is to ask. Some will prefer to be treated as press, some as analysts, and some will want to be on both lists and to be able to contact either group with requests. If you allow this—you might as well, it costs little and keeps influential people happy—be sure that all contact with either group is relayed immediately to the other. This helps your firm appear coordinated. More importantly, journalists and analysts have been known to ask the same question of several people in hopes of turning up something interesting. If all those who are asked know what's going on, they can direct the caller to the same source, return consistent answers, or (in extreme cases, with a smile) confront the caller with a request to "cut it out."

Using Agencies for Analyst/Consultant Relations

Many firms contract out some or all of their press relations to outside agencies. Analyst relations can do the same. Agencies offer this service to earn additional revenue, to offer varied work to staff members, and to strengthen their relationships with their clients (you). There are also specialized analyst relations agencies you can turn to.

There are, unfortunately, a few negatives to using agencies:

- Reporters are used to working with agencies, but analysts and consultants are less used to it—or perhaps, because they are used to client deference, more arrogant. When they ask to talk to someone in the company, they mean someone *in the company*.

- Analysts/consultant relationships are more personal than those with reporters. If an agency "owns" these, a firm may be less able to change agencies or go in-house when that would otherwise be in its best interest.

- Analyst relations (more than consultant relations) is not just an outbound communication channel. It is, or should be, a strategic business development function too. Agency people are less likely to be tuned into this area than your firm's staff and less likely to have the relationships with your top management to make it happen. As a result, even the best agencies tend to focus on the outbound side. They may be able to advise you on strategic issues, but they can't do that part of your job.

There are also reasons in favor of using an agency for analyst/consultant relations:

- Agency staff may be more qualified than in-house staff. (Don't take this personally. It's a statistical generalization.) Some people like to work where their job is the reason for the firm's existence, not a support task. If they're in PR, that's an agency. An agency also offers income and promotional opportunities that a computer firm can't offer these people.

- You get resources as you need them, without having to hire extra people or scrounge for help for peak loads. Agencies have specialists, such as editors or Web designers, which you couldn't justify on the departmental payroll. If a particular one doesn't, it has a network of free-lancers it can call on transparently to its clients.

- If the agency has a focused analyst/consultant relations practice, its staff sees lots of analyst/consultant relations programs. They can give you the benefit of this experience. They can also function as members of your strategic team if you want them to.

The better PR firms (in this regard) can handle much of the analyst/consultant relations task with skill, especially the less strategic "arms and legs" parts of the job. If you use an agency:

- Allow them to handle tactical and operational aspects of analyst and consultant relations, but keep control of the strategic side. Listen to the agency's advice, especially if they have a dedicated analyst/consultant relations practice staffed by people with that specific experience, but your firm has to make the decisions.

- Have an analyst/consultant relations contact point at headquarters for people or situations where, for any reason, the agency isn't the right answer.

- Avoid having the agency simply relay queries to someone in your company whom the analyst or consultant could have called directly. This adds delays and misunderstandings. Instead, plug the agency into your organization so that they can call the same person you would, or at least call an identified person in each part of your company.

- Make sure analysts and consultants know who to contact, especially if the agency doesn't do all the work. (One firm handled large research firms in house, but used an agency for small ones. This created confusion when analysts changed firms. Some who left big firms to set up shop on their own resented what they perceived as being "shunted aside" to the agency, though their personal influence may have increased.)

- Make sure the agency isn't motivated to act against your interests. For example, an agency may agree to set up a certain number of analyst briefings. If it's "under quota," even for a reason (perhaps you moved a fall announcement to January, so analysts want to be briefed next year) it is motivated to pressure analysts for briefings, though the analysts have no interest in them and you have nothing to gain. The outcome can damage relationships with no offsetting benefit to provider or analyst.

- Obtain independent feedback on how well analysts feel the agency meets their needs and represents your firm to them.

- While there may be synergy if one agency handles both press and analyst/consultant relations, consider splitting the two. That makes it easier to replace one agency with another or bring one function in-house, if that's the right thing to do in the future, without impacting the other area.

- As with any other corporate relationship, try not to engage an agency that has personal ties to your firm's management. One well-known U.S. software firm suffered for years from poor analyst relations because of agency ineptitude. Those who understood the problem were powerless to do anything about it because of family ties between one of the agency heads and a top-level executive of the software firm. It is best to have a strong policy against any dealings of this sort.

Product Marketing

These are product specialists who know how your firm's products are supposed to work for users. They provide technical information for Marketing Communications' product literature. They provide speakers for prospect presentations when the subject matter isn't too deep. Depending on the breadth of your firm's product line and the size of this organization, its staff members may specialize in individual products or areas. Because of their product focus, Product Marketing usually has closer contacts with the R&D organization than the rest of the marketing organization.

Product Marketing has several roles in support of analyst/consultant relations:

- The first source of information to your central contact in answering questions. If they don't have the answer, perhaps if a question is too technical, they know who does.

- Speakers for analyst/consultant seminars and briefings, just as for customers.

- Information for custom analyst and consultant materials such as announcement coverage, section overviews in a *Consultants' Reference Manual*, edits to press releases, competitive positioning comparisons and strategy statements.

Your alternative to using your firm's Product Marketing organization for these functions is for your analyst/consultant relations staff to spend time with developers, planners, strategists, and market analysts to obtain the same information. You will then have to spend still more time to translate it into English (or German, or ...), since specialists may lapse into jargon or internal terminology. Fortunately, most Product Marketing professionals will understand your needs and cooperate to the greatest possible extent.

Research and Development

Technically oriented analysts assess product technical nuances and make recommendations on that basis. Consultants consider technical features in client recommendations.

To do this, they may need technical details only your firm's R&D group has. When such a request arises, your alternatives are to provide the information or lose the recommendation to a competitor who will provide it. (If you wonder if the requested information should be divulged, ask: If a potential supplier to *your* firm refused to give your company or its advisor this type of information, would you buy from them anyhow—or look to its competitors for a more cooperative supplier?)

You may need a non-disclosure agreement before you can discuss this type of information with someone outside your firm. Be sure it allows the information to be used for its intended purpose, such as to justify a recommendation to the consultant's client. If this means the client must also sign a non-disclosure agreement, so be it. The consultant will see the logic in this.

Developers can also speak with opinion leaders and at analyst/consultant meetings. These audiences often need background information on development approaches, technology, and product functionality that is not available from any other source. They want the feel for a company that comes from talking with developers. They respond positively to the attention reflected in letting them meet with developers. Your firm should have some R&D managers and senior engineers who can speak coherently to intelligent technical people about your products.

The capabilities your firm's R&D group provides to support analyst and consultant relations can usually not be replaced by any other internal or external resources. You have no alternative to the development group. If you keep your requests to a minimum and can make a convincing case that you have no alternative, most R&D managers will support your needs.

The people you should include in your network and their responsibilities are listed in the following table:

Resource	Analyst Relations role
Executive champion	Show visible commitment to the program, enlist company support Provide strategic direction Secure additional resources if needed Serve as top escalation contact if needed
Executives	Set, communicate corporate goals and objectives
SMEs (subject matter experts)	Engage analysts on product-specific topics on a regular basis Assist analyst/consultant liaison in responding to inquiries, surveys Review analysts' research and event presentations for accuracy Assist in developing responses to negative research reports, press quotes Attend analyst events as speaker and/or technical resource Provide competitive information
Virtual analyst and/or consultant relations team	Bring parts of company together to focus on analyst/consultant relations Act as advisory council Help coordinate outreach efforts, including messages, across firm Offer feedback on program, recommendations for improvement Support measurement initiatives: analyst surveys, win/loss analysis, ...

Sales force contact	Supply customer reference account names and contact information Feed back what analysts/consultants tell customers re company, products Support measurement initiatives such as win/loss analysis Provide competitive information from the field
Corporate library or market research contact	Make market research accessible (e.g., on company intranet) Assist in contract negotiations for market research subscriptions Analyze market research spending and usage, report it regularly Assess company research needs, recommend ways to meet them Provide competitive information
Investor relations contact	Keep AR manager informed of investment analyst outreach efforts Leverage activities by including industry analysts when appropriate Assist AR manager in responding to inquiries and survey requests Supply investment analyst names, contact information for industry analyst referrals
Public relations contact	Keep AR manager informed of press relations outreach efforts Leverage activities by including industry analysts when appropriate Assist AR manager in responding to inquiries and survey requests Refer journalists to analysts screened by AR for press comments
Legal contact	Determine if an announcement is legally material information Provide guidance on timing of material announcements to analysts Review non-disclosure agreements to ensure information protection, regulatory compliance
Admin. contact	Schedule and coordinate event logistics: travel, hotels, food, etc. Schedule/attend virtual team meetings, record/distribute action items Print and package materials for analyst meetings and events

It is impossible to generalize about the best way to mobilize resources in your company. Each has its own culture, its own way of doing things. Small firms tend to have a "we're all in this together" feeling that makes cross-functional requests easier to fulfill. Larger ones may get bogged down in bureaucracies that complicate life, but have other advantages to offset that. A well-reasoned justification should, in virtually every case, obtain the cooperation of the groups and people whose support you need.

14 | The value of your AR/CR program

This chapter will cover:

1 The bottom line value of analyst/consultant impact on your sales

2 Factors that determine that value

3 A process for calculating that value in your company

4. A fully worked-out example and a worksheet for your use

Chapter 1 had a few rough numbers to indicate how important analysts and consultants are to the information technology industry as a whole. Your management cares about how important they are to your firm in particular. This chapter presents a process to help find out, and perhaps help persuade them that improved analyst/consultant relations are worth the cost.

The method given here is not the only way to calculate the value of an analyst/consultant relations program. Its major shortcoming is that it only takes into account advisors' impact on sales. Other ways in which they bring value, especially those discussed in Chapter 9, are not included. Those benefits raise the value of effective analyst/consultant relations above what figures you can calculate this way suggest.

There is an example of the method right after the steps are described. The last page of this chapter is a worksheet to organize your calculations.

(This chapter uses the term *advisor* to avoid writing "analysts and/or consultants, whichever your program is for" over and over again.)

14.1. The method

1	Write down your sales target for twelve months, starting 6–12 months from now (depending on how fast your company moves).	$
2	Write down the percentage of those sales that will come from existing customers upgrading, buying additional copies of your software, or continuing their ongoing relationship however that applies in your case. This may approach 100% in mature markets. New firms with no existing customers should enter zero.	%
3	Multiply your sales target (Row 1) by this percentage (Row 2) to get the revenue that is yours with little effort, based on prior customer experience with your firm. These customers are unlikely to use advisors for provider selection.	$
4	Subtract this from your sales target (Row 1) to figure the revenue you must fight for. For a new firm with no existing customer base, this is the same as the figure in Row 1.	$

5	This step involves judgment. Write down the fraction of your competitive ("new name") prospects who will make up their minds on their own, having seen only your advertising, mailers, sales representatives, Web site, demonstrations, and proposals, and talked to friends and colleagues. If your firm has been in business for at least a short while you may be able to get insight into this figure by sampling your customers. If not, try these numbers: • For a $3 magazine, use 100%. • For a $30 book, use 99%. • For a $300 software package, use 50% to 80%. • For a $30,000 server or software that defines a network infrastructure, try 10% to 20%. • For anything over $1,000,000, use 0%. Nobody spends that much on a truly competitive procurement without outside advice.	%
6	Multiply Row 4 by Row 5 to get the sales volume you have to compete for, but which you can get without advisors' help.	$
7	Subtract Row 6 from Row 4 to get the sales volume that advisors affect.	$
8	Estimate the impact of advisors on these sales. How much of a typical purchase decision is based on advisor inputs of all types, versus other information sources? If you're a recognized market leader, put down 5%. If you're an established firm with a solid reputation, put down 20%. If you have been around for a while, are past the "garage shop" stage, but don't make too many short lists (be honest!) put down 30%, which is also a typical figure for the IT industry overall. If you're a start-up looking for your first customer, or even your tenth, put down 50%. Adjust these figures from your own experience with your customer base.	%
9	Multiply item 7 by item 8. This is the impact of advisors on your sales volume, how much they can give or take away. This volume is yours if the advisor world is always on your side, someone else's if they're all against you.	$
10	The advisor world is never 100% for or against you. Now estimate the difference that a positive analyst/consultant relations program can make. If your product or service is clearly superior to every competitor in all its target markets, put down 10%. Under these conditions, advisors will almost always be with you. If it's pretty good, better than much of its competition for many prospects in most of your markets, try 50% or any other figure you feel comfortable with. At the other end of the spectrum, if your product is well behind its competition, put down 10% again. No support program can do much it that situation. Analysts and consultants aren't that gullible.	%
11	Multiply item 9 by item 10. This is the sales impact of a good analyst/consultant relations program.	$

| 12 | Enter your gross margin as a percentage of sales. (You might call this Contribution to Overhead or something else.) It's what's left of each revenue dollar after subtracting costs incurred just to earn that dollar. In other words, you subtract costs of materials, sales commissions, and similar variable costs, but not the fixed costs of office space or your CFO's salary. Those don't change when you sell another copy of your software. The gross margin of most hardware firms is around 60%. In software, where the incremental cost of one more copy is low, it runs higher. Distributors, who have to buy product for each sale, and services firms, where most of the revenue pays people to do the work, have lower gross margins. (If you don't want to guess, check your firm's last annual report or ask someone in the finance department. You can tell the finance person that you just need a rough estimate, to the nearest five percent or so.) | $ |
| 13 | Finally, multiply item 11, the sales impact of an analyst/ consultant relations program, by item 13, the impact of each sales dollar on the bottom line. | $ |

This is the bottom line value of good analyst/consultant relations in the year you chose for your analysis. If you can put together a solid program for less than this figure, it will have a positive net financial impact on your firm.

If the program you want will cost more than this, it may still be desirable if your firm is new and establishing itself. All of a start-up's expenses are high relative to its current and near future revenue levels. That's why start-ups lose money for a while. This is a normal in starting a business. Analyst/consultant support is no exception to the rule.

14.2. An example

Let's run through an example to see how this works. Suppose we work for a firm that makes Web servers. We're in our first full year of volume production and expect to sell $10 million worth of systems. Next year, the first year in which our analyst relations program will have an effect, our target is $25 million. We calculate as follows:

1.   Our sales target is, as just stated, $25,000,000.

2.   Since many of our customers are resellers, they will continue to buy our systems. Hopefully they will buy more next year than this year. We plan to get 60% of our sales from existing customers. Analysts and consultants won't influence this. If advisors were going to influence these customers they would have done it when the resellers first decided to use our systems, not when they choose to stay with us next year.

3.   60% of $25,000,000 yields $15,000,000 of "minimum effort" sales.

4.   Subtracting this from $25,000,000 means we must compete for $10,000,000.

5.   At most 30% of our new users will buy purely on the basis of what we and our competitors say to them in our ads, in our proposals, and in person. This is a high figure. We use it be-

cause resellers often do their own in-depth technical evaluations. They don't rely on outside advisors as much as end users do.

6. 30% of $10,000,000 or $3,000,000 of potential sales are uninfluenced by advisors of any sort.

7. Advisors therefore influence $10,000,000 – $3,000,000, or $7,000,000, of our sales.

8. People have heard of us and of our product but we are far from a market leader at this point. Assume that the advisor influence on these sales is a typical 30 percent.

9. Advisor impact on our sales is therefore 30% of $7,000,000, or $2,100,000.

10. Our product is competitive, but so are many others. In our business the most recently announced product tends to have the most attractive specs and price-performance. Leadership passes back and forth. Assume a good program can swing analyst and consultant opinions about 30%.

11. The sales impact of such a program would be 30% of $2,100,000 = $630,000.

12. Our planned gross margin before taxes, next year, is 60%.

13. The bottom line impact of improved advisor relations next year will therefore be 60 percent of $630,000, or $378,000.

Since no new analyst/consultant relations program will cost close to $378,000, the numbers justify the concept of a good analyst/consultant relations program.

14.3. Worksheet for calculating the sales-based benefits of an analyst/consultant relations program

1. Twelve months' sales: $_____

2. Fraction from existing customers: _____%

3. Easy sales volume: item 1 times item 2 $_____

4. Hard sales volume: subtract item 3 from item 1 $_____

5. Fraction who will make up their own minds: _____%

6. Advisor-independent volume: item 4 times item 5 $_____

7. Advisor-dependent volume: item 4 minus item 6 $_____

8. Fractional impact of advisors on this volume: _____%

9. Advisor impact on volume: item 7 times item 8 $_____

10. Consultant relations program swing factor: _____%

11. Volume impact of program: item 9 times item 10 $_____

12. Gross margin on sales: _____%

13. Bottom line value of program: item 11 x item 12 $_____

15 | Your program resource requirements

This chapter will cover:

1. The people you need for an analyst/consultant relations program
2. The cost of other elements of an analyst/consultant relations program

The major resource requirements of any analyst or consultant relations program are people, money, and computer facilities.

Computers are easiest. You will need very little in this area. Your main needs will be word processing, perhaps moving up to desktop publishing; Web publishing (or preparing materials, if someone else will put them on the Web); accessing the Internet (including e-mail, obviously) and maintaining your databases. Any desktop or laptop computer will handle all these adequately. The software you'll need is free or inexpensive, too.

If two or more people will need to access your database at the same time, or if someone else might need to access it while you're using your computer for another purpose, it would be nice to have a server for your shared databases and repositories. Once your firm grows to the size where this is a concern, it will have people who understand servers and can make them work.

That leaves people and money. They are discussed in the two sections that follow. These sections are organized in the same sequence as the Information Channel building blocks of Chapter 7. Resource requirements for items that aren't information channels follow at the end. Go through this chapter item by item, adding numbers for the program elements that apply to you as you go.

15.1. People

Analyst/consultant relations tasks can be performed by:

- The staff of a dedicated analyst/consultant relations group.
- People in related functions such as sales support or public relations, part-time.
- People in support functions, such as marketing communications, as needed.
- External resources brought in for any of the above roles.

In this section we are concerned with two questions regarding people needs: how many people you will need, and the best place to get them.

A central point of contact

Much of what an analyst/consultant relations professional does falls under this general category. Answering the phone or e-mail, finding people to deal with an analyst or consultant request, and making sure they get together (in person or otherwise) is the biggest part of this job.

In-house staff is best for this. The position is externally visible. Ease of information flow within an organization makes answers easier to come by if requested by an insider. Most firms need the equivalent of a full-time analyst or consultant support person when they reach a sales volume in the high eight or low nine figures. The need may not be visible since it may be handled by parts of many people, some of whom do the job on an informal basis in local offices (especially for consultants). But it is there.

This workload depends on the number of analysts and consultants you support and on how big a part of their professional life your firm is. For analysts who follow your firm on a regular basis and follow other firms as well, one person should be able to support several dozen. For consultants whose needs are more sporadic, a couple of hundred. People who focus on your firm's products take more time—but if your firm is important enough to justify that sort of attention, it will be able to afford the staff to support them.

Parkinson's Law (work expands to fill the available time) plays a part here. People who aren't completely busy will make more outreach calls, be more interested in sitting in on conversations between managers and analysts, send more e-mail messages on more topics, come up with more ways to refine their database, study their firms' products to be able to answer more questions directly, and generally find things to do. These are useful, but not essential. The workload estimates in this chapter assume that you're concentrating on the basics, not creating unessential work (even if it's useful).

Contact with executives

This is included with other categories, such as the central contact's job, briefings and visits. The actual time spent participating in meetings and phone calls, if that is done (see Section 7.2) should be negligible.

Contact with other staff members

Same as for executive contact—included in other items.

Visits to analyst or consultant firms

Many firms send people on periodic tours of major research firms. (See Section 7.4.) Once this begins, opportunities to expand it are endless. A visit program should be coordinated by an analyst relations manager. It can justify making that a full-time position.

Visits can consume a lot of your time, especially if you focus on analysts (vs. consultants). If you plan to visit each of twenty research firms twice a year, that's forty visits. There is no way you can visit more than four a day. You'll only hit that rate in a few concentrations of analyst activity: Silicon Valley, southern Connecticut, the Boston area, the Thames Valley west of London—and even there, only for short visits with brief updates. Elsewhere, or for visits with more content, two a day are the maximum, often just one.

So, figure twenty working days for these visits. It will take time to arrange each one as well, since you'll have to coordinate with the analyst firm on schedule and agenda, then coordinate with your colleagues, then get back to the first analyst firm because another one can't make it on the 23rd of next month ...

All told, for each research firm, figure three days a year visiting them, traveling to and from those visits, and arranging them. Since there are about 210 productive days in a work year, visiting seventy firms twice a year each is a full-time job in itself.

In doing this calculation:

- There are some economies of scale as the number of firms goes up, but not many.
- Figure this based on of the number of firms, not the number of analysts. The effort of visiting a firm doesn't depend on how many people are in their conference room.

Visits by analyst or consultant firms to you

An analyst or consultant coming to you is not as time-consuming, since the visitor absorbs travel time. (As you know, that's one reason they like you to visit them.) Scheduling is simpler because you're not trying to force multiple visits into a practical schedule. However, arranging them takes extra time:

- Each visit is different. You can't pick one team to visit six firms.
- Because your whole firm is potentially available, it takes more time to identify the right people.
- Because a visit is often for something the visitors can't get in the field, its content and agenda will probably involve more special preparation.
- For the same reason, visitors often meet with people who are not used to working with analysts or consultants. Your firm's participants will need more preparation.
- As host, you must make logistical arrangements (conference rooms, meals, refreshments, parking, etc.) that firms you visit make when you travel.

Figure, then, a day of someone's time to arrange a visit of this type, plus participating in the visit itself to the degree that you wish. (If a database consultant is learning to optimize indices and clusters for data mining, you have better things to do than watch.)

Many of the presenters at these meetings will be marketing and R&D staff. They may be used to talking to customers and prospects. You'll have to brief them on how analysts/ consultants are different, as well as the visit objectives. They may be excellent speakers but can fall into a rut with standard material. If they can't or won't customize their talk for this audience, get different presenters.

How often will these happen? If you have regular tours and events, not often. Assume half the research firms you work with will visit over a year. As for consultants, a lot depends on how well your field organization is set up to provide local support. If it's good, HQ visits will be rare. If it's non-existent, figure one a month for every hundred consultants who are registered for your program. That may be high or low, depending on how familiar the consultants you work with are with your products, but it's a start.

As we mentioned earlier, this doesn't count customer or sales prospect visits that happen to include the customer's or prospect's consultant in the entourage. There will hopefully be many of these, but account reps arrange them.

Multi-firm briefings (analyst or consultant "days")

The big time saving here is handling the equivalent of ten or more visits in one day. As with visits to you, though, it's not a one-sided decision. A multi-firm briefing is more work than arranging a visit by a single firm. The additional work falls into these areas:

- Planning an agenda that meets the general needs of many attendees, rather than one set of focused needs you can discuss with your visitors in advance.
- In many cases, dealing with parallel tracks and/or some type of interest survey as part of the planning process.
- Arranging for and inviting outside speakers.
- Logistics at a hotel or similar facility.
- Invitations, name tags, place cards and similar stationery items.
- A registration desk of some sort (optional for small, informal briefings).
- For a major get-together, cocktail hours, entertainment and leisure-time activities.
- If the meeting is important and will be held at a distant site you've never used before, a check visit on your part. (This may not be entirely a burden.)

All in all, it will probably take two weeks of your time to arrange a medium-sized seminar for analysts or consultants, longer for something like a two-day off-site meeting. If you plan a series of regional consultant seminars, there are economies of scale. Most of this time will be spent at the meeting and in the 2–3 weeks before it, with the rest spread out over the preceding few months.

Teleconference briefings

These are much like visits to analysts, but shorter and without the travel. A day of your time to arrange each should be adequate. Multiply this figure by a rough estimate of the number of teleconferences you expect to have in a year.

Analyst/consultant web site

This is the 21st century. Your firm has a Web site. Someone else set it up.

You can leave things that way. Unless you're willing to take on a big job, we recommend it. Get consultant and analyst feedback, make sure that feedback reaches your Web staff, and encourage them to listen. Then tell your audience about the site and encourage them to visit it. That's enough.

If you reach a point where you want to develop an alternative entry point, an alternative site, or custom pages for analysts or consultants, talk to your Web staff about the tools they use, design standards to follow, and the effort involved in creating it. Use their estimates to plan your resource needs.

Setting up a Web site is not something you'll do yourself. It's a rare analyst/consultant relations program that can justify its own specialist, an even rarer analyst liaison who has the skills or the time. Therefore, expect to use your firm's Web developers or outside staff. The involvement of analyst/consultant relations will consist of:

- Working with Web developers to plan content and organization, access control and other user-visible aspects of the site.

- Testing what they come up with before it goes live.

- Getting analyst/consultant feedback as the next step of the testing process, again before it goes live, and thereafter on an ongoing basis.

- Updating content within the existing design and layout. Procedures for this should be part of what any Web developer hands over to you.

Outbound written communications

You'll spend a good deal of time planning, writing, editing and sending written (mostly electronic) communications. How much a "good deal of time" is depends on:

1. How often will you send something?
2. How much will you send each time?
3. Who will write what you send?

Take into account both regular mailings and announcement mailings. Make an educated guess at how many announcements your firm will have next year.

Taking these in order:

1. Part of the effort involved in sending out a mailing depends on size. If you'll send 120 pages a year, this part of the effort is the same for one big package, monthly packages of 10 pages each, or a page every three days.

   There is also a level of effort associated with sending out each mailing no matter how large or small it is. You have to write a cover letter or e-mail message, deal with reproduction and packaging of anything going out in hard copy, make sure your lists are up to date, figure out which subsets of your lists get which versions of the package, and manage physical and electronic distribution. Once you get good at this it will take a couple of days per mailing, though the first few will be longer. In other words, a monthly mailing is 10 percent of your time before you put anything in the package.

2. Some aspects of mailings get more complex as the mailings get larger. The sheer volume of pages you mail each year will also affect the amount of time that mailings take. Estimate the number of pages you'll send out, all told, and figure half an hour each for this factor alone. This does not include any writing, editing or reviewing you'll have to do—that comes next.

This estimate also doesn't include folding, envelope-stuffing, postage-affixing, etc. If you'll send hard-copy mailings, don't have clerical support for things like this, and will mail more than a few dozen sets, consider hiring a local high-school student to help. Your time is too valuable to do this all yourself. For a smaller number—you might only mail a small number even if your list is long, if most recipients prefer to receive information electronically—it won't take enough time to matter.

3. If you have to write the material yourself, use your personal knowledge of how long it takes you to write a finished page in your planning. Double your initial estimate to allow for management and technical review, followed by time to revise what you have written in the light of the reviewers' comments. If someone else will write the material for another audience and you have to modify it for analysts and/or consultants, cut this estimate in half. (Modifying an announcement press release falls in this category.) If someone else will write it specifically for an analyst/consultant audience, cut it in half again. (If you use something unchanged, such as a spec sheet in an announcement mailing, you don't have to allocate writing time, but you count it in your page count total.)

The size of your list doesn't matter much. Depending on the medium, it takes little or no more effort to send a package to 1,000 people than to ten once the package has been prepared. The effort goes into maintaining the larger database. We'll discuss database maintenance later in this chapter.

Detailed reference material

Finding technical reference materials for analysts and consultants, and sending them out, is part of the central support task we already covered. Don't add more time for it.

A Consultant's Reference Manual, should you want one, is a separate effort and must be estimated separately.

Much of such a manual will have been originally written for other purposes, such as announcement material and product literature. In this case you have little to do beyond preparing the index and cover memo, and getting binders or cover/spine inserts designed. A week of effort will be more than ample for that, including figuring out what to include, designing the indexing scheme, allowing your management to review the cover letter and dealing with their requested changes. (Some managers feel they're not doing their job if they don't suggest changes. If you have a manager like that, you probably know it.)

Once you get to the stage where you need custom-written material for each section you will need resources to write it. Some options:

- This is a good job for marketing communications personnel during slack periods between announcements and other bursts of activity.

- It is also a good task for the analyst or consultant relations staff, since they know what analysts or consultants ask about most often. These people will probably need editing assistance since they are not usually hired for their writing skills.

- Failing either of these, consider an outside writer. An outside resource has the advantage of knowing little about your products and therefore not succumbing to "everybody knows that" or lapsing into your firm's jargon. If you don't use an outside writer, try to get an outside reviewer—ideally, a member of the manual's target audience.

With any writer or writers, first estimate the number of pages you'll need. Then ask them how long it will take them to write that number of pages. Double the estimates to allow for rewrites after reviews. If you're not the writer, add half the original estimate for your own time in reviewing and coordinating.

In other words: say you've estimated twenty pages. Your writer, who is not you, estimates productivity of five pages per day, or four days total. (This is high, especially if the person knows nothing about the subject matter. It's to keep the numbers simple.) Double that estimate and assume the writer will spend eight days on the project before it's wrapped up. Cut it in half and assume that you, or someone else from the analyst/consultant relations function, will spend two days reviewing and coordinating.

Demonstrations

You probably won't spend a lot of time arranging demonstrations of your firm's products. Assume it's included in the appropriate other categories of this section: arranging for consultant visits to you, planning analyst events, and the other situations in which the need for a demo may arise.

Newsletters (electronic or hard copy)

You won't have to do much original writing for your newsletter until your firm gets large. Much of the material that goes into it can come from other sources: customer newsletters, press releases, internal sales support material, articles and papers written by your technical staff, materials written by your customers, letters to the editor. Intelligent "plagiarism" is the key.

Materials originally written for other purposes will need editing before you use them. Editing is a profession. Most marketing professionals can't edit. (Most editors can't write a marketing plan, either.) Newsletter editing can therefore properly be assigned to another resource.

If your firm has a marketing communications function or a similar group, they're ideal. If it doesn't, or they can't take this on, use outside resources. Every city has freelance editors. You can find them through the Yellow Pages, ads in local business publications, Web lists, or word of mouth. Check work samples before you pick one.

In either case, make sure your editor understands the newsletter's audience and objectives. (Buy him or her a copy of this book.)

A newsletter requires a fraction of a person on an ongoing basis. The larger the newsletter, the larger the fraction. A sixteen-page monthly newsletter, or its equivalent in new electronic content, might need a full-time editor with no other responsibilities, assuming that the editor writes some (but not most) of its content. A four-page monthly newsletter is roughly a quarter-time to one-third-time job.

The workload cycle of a monthly newsletter has no significant peaks or valleys. There's something to do every week. A quarterly newsletter gives its staff time to do other things between issues. While workload planning isn't your problem if you use outside resources, this can be a factor in how an internal department handles the job.

Advertising

If you advertise to consultants, or want to include consultant-oriented content in ads that you expect them to read, you'll have to work with your firm's ad department and/or agency. Your consultant relations staff (advertising to analysts isn't usually productive) will have to spend time to plan the consultant-oriented advertising, but this shouldn't be a big drain unless you mount a major campaign directed solely at consultants.

Planning an ad campaign, even with support, is a big project. Don't even think about it until you have a full-time consultant relations staff of three or more. And be sure it will be productive for your program—there is, after all, a reason such campaigns are rare.

Running a small ad or two is less of a project, but still involves time. Expect to spend a week of your time discussing themes, writing copy, reviewing copy, editing copy, discussing placement, etc., etc.

Putting a consultant-oriented tag line into existing ads is mostly a matter of the people in charge of your advertising going along with the idea. This will require a meeting or two, either to convince them or to reach a consensus that it isn't. (It may not be, since everything in an ad that's not related to its primary purpose takes space away from it.)

Database maintenance

There are two aspects to database maintenance:

1. Database administration: maintaining the database structure, formats, and screens; adding and removing authorized users as necessary; keeping it current with new releases of its software package; moving it from platform to platform as necessary, etc.
2. Keeping database content up to date.

An analyst/consultant relations program should try to get professional help for database administration unless it is of the simplest desktop variety. It's not that analyst/consultant liaisons can't learn how to do this. Of course they can. It's that it's not their job. It uses a different skill set. It makes sense to find someone who has that skill set and let that person do what he or she does best.

A well-designed database, though, should not require technical skills to update its content. That—inserting new names and updating data for old ones—is the job of the analyst or consultant relations function.

Unless you're in the initial stages of entering a large number of names, you should be able to keep up with normal changes to a database of a few hundred people in less than an hour a week. That's hardly worth including in your time allocation estimates.

If you plan to send questionnaires to your constituents, you'll probably send them all at once. This means they'll all tend to come back around the same time. For a short time you'll be entering everyone's new telephone area codes and updates to their practice areas. For those few weeks make sure you have clerical help available, bringing in a "temp" if necessary. Then the level of updates will fall back to its normal slow pace.

Administrative support

Any analyst or consultant relations program has paperwork and administrative activity. It's easy to say "send out invitations," but somebody has to pull names from the database, put mailing labels in the printer, watch it print them, stick them on invitation envelopes, rerun the ones that get jammed... Someone has to stuff newsletters in envelopes. Someone has to make sure the server announcement goes to analysts who care about servers, not services. (At least one major firm got this one wrong.) Someone has to enter new names into your analyst database. Someone has to word-process the modified version of a press release even if changes are trivial. Someone has to call the cafeteria to order coffee and pastries sent to the conference room before a consultant visit. Someone has to make travel reservations for the analyst tour. Someone has to... This someone is usually the long-suffering secretary or administrator.

One way to start getting administrative support for analyst/consultant relations is by adding it to the responsibilities of the marketing support or marketing communications administrative staff. Track how much time they devote to this function. When it becomes large enough to keep a person busy, assign it to a single person. That will pay off in continuity and in that person's ability to operate independently. If you don't yet have a professional to manage analyst or consultant relations, this administrator can also be the initial contact. While he or she will have to route queries to other people for answers, they will appreciate having a single contact point.

Periodic reviews

Plan to spend a day each year doing nothing but meeting with colleagues, your manager, and perhaps an outside advisor or two to review your program. It will take you another two days to prepare for this meeting, one more to summarize it and document its recommendations. Total: four days a year. Round it up to a week.

The picture that emerges is one of a steady workload with peaks at times such as announcements, briefings, analyst tours, and database updates. The variety of required skills suggests using supplementing the analyst or consultant relations resources, by specialists in writing, editing, and from time to time other areas such as database management. The availability of specific resources in your firm will influence your decision.

15.2. Money

There is an inverse relationship between the use of in-house resources and the need for money. Any functions you outsource must be paid for. You can obtain quotations for newsletter editing, for example, from any PR agency, possibly from your ad agency, and from freelance editors. External resources may at first glance look expensive, but consider savings in overhead costs (office space, support, supplies, phone) before you decide. Also, you get specialized resources for each task rather than trying to fill the time of a full-time employee who may be good at some, less good at others.

Every aspect of the program also has a direct cost. The major ones are:

Visits to the analyst or consultant firm

These will involve travel and living expenses for the visiting team. If you don't feel up to estimating these, your travel coordinator or agency can.

Newsletter

If your·newsletter will be 100 percent electronic, ignore this section.

Reproduction costs will be a few cents per page, times the number of pages per issue, times the number of copies you print. (Don't print fewer than 500 if you're using photo-offset or any other high-quality reproduction method. The savings are negligible since press set-up is the major cost.) Add any charges for stapling, stuffing envelopes, and affixing labels. Postage, of course, is additional. (Your firm almost certainly has bulk mail procedures in place. Some discounts require sorting by ZIP/postal code. Check with your mailroom.) Multiply by the number of issues per year.

If you plan to produce your own newsletters via desktop publishing and your firm doesn't already have a system, you will need one or the use of someone else's. It's a rare desk that doesn't have suitable hardware. Good desktop publishing software costs in the middle to high three figures. The market leaders as this is written are Quark XPress and Adobe In-Design. Both support both Windows and Macintosh. A low-end package such as Microsoft Publisher (Windows) or Apple Pages (Mac) will get you through the first few issues, but you may bump up against its limitations and have to move to more capable software later. If you see this task going to a pro at that point, the low-end ones are easier to learn.

Commercial typesetting from desktop publishing files typically costs $5 to $10 per page. It's worth it, since the quality difference between typesetting and what most office printers produce is visible. At most typesetting shops the price per page depends on the number of pages you print. Printing one newsletter will put you near the high end of the price range, but if you commit to producing a year's worth at one shop you may be able to negotiate a lower price per page on the basis of your total annual volume. You'll still need the computer, a word processing program, and a page layout program.

Announcement materials

A similar calculation. Include only the cost of incremental copies of materials which are already being produced for other purposes, such as price lists and product briefs. If your list is short, you can probably get all you need by asking. A typical kit with no unusual inserts should cost under $5 per copy in quantity.

Seminars

Invitations, meeting facilities if you don't use your offices, coffee and pastries, lunch if it is served, speaker's fee for any outside speakers if applicable, travel expenses for outside speakers (if they're not local) and for your home-office staff (if the seminar isn't in your headquarters city).

Consultants' Reference Manual

Ten to fifteen dollars each for binders with tabs, reproduction costs for the contents. The real cost here is writing time, which was covered in the previous section.

Support contact

The major cost is the staffing. In 2013 the major components of electronic support, such as voice mail and e-mail, are a given.

Database

Any computer you have will be satisfactory, as analyst/consultant databases consist largely of text and numbers and take up negligible disk space. If you have to buy database management software, it will cost in the low-to-middle three figures.

Advertising

Ads are expensive. Repeat: ads are expensive. A sixteenth of a page in a regional (e.g., southern California) computer paper will cost several hundred dollars. Full pages in major publications begin in the thousands and go up from there. This suggests that most smaller firms, if they want to advertise their programs at all, should think in terms of including consultant-oriented content in other ads rather than a full-scale ad campaign for consultants. Larger firms may find consultant-oriented ads worth the cost. If you add a line or two to ads that are already in your firm's advertising budget, there isn't any incremental cost.

16 | Your program timetable

This chapter will cover:

1. How long it will take to put your program in place
2. How long it will take for your program to have an impact

Things take time. God took six days to create the world. (Then even He needed a day off.) An analyst or consultant relations program may be a smaller project, but it won't happen overnight.

Your analyst/consultant relations program timetable has two aspects:

- The schedule put the program in place. This is under your and your management's control—as much as any project is under control, of course.

- The schedule for it to have an impact. You do not control this, but you can predict it to a degree.

This chapter discusses both, with the major variables that affect them.

16.1 Timetable to put your program in place

This section suggests some guidelines for planning the implementation of your program. However, we can't predict your corporate environment. Some firms take longer to do things than others. Larger ones usually take longer since there are more people to consult with, they are scattered over a wider area, and time-consuming formal procedures tend to go along with growth.

The figure below shows the tasks laid out over time for a conservative but fairly typical firm. Fast-moving companies can reduce the times, but don't expect things to happen instantly. (To avoid cluttering the figure, it doesn't show every topic discussed in this chapter.)

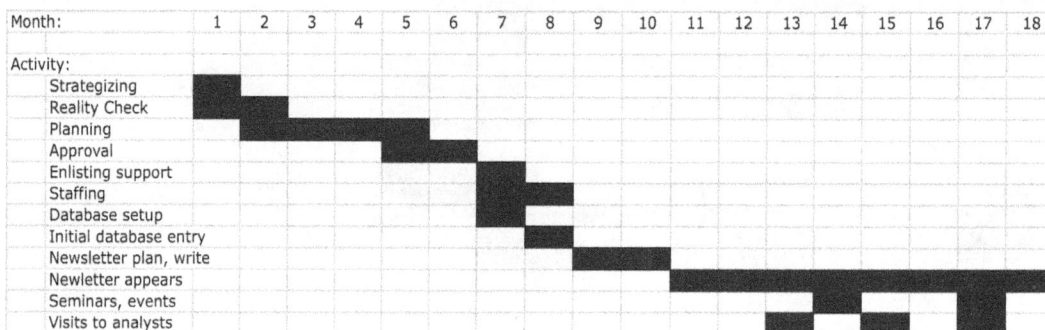

Month:	1	2	3	4	5	6	7	8	9	10	11	12	13	14	15	16	17	18
Activity:																		
Strategizing	██																	
Reality Check		██																
Planning			██	██														
Approval					██													
Enlisting support						██												
Staffing							██											
Database setup								██										
Initial database entry								██	██									
Newsletter plan, write									██	██								
Newletter appears											██	██	██	██	██	██	██	██
Seminars, events														██	██		██	██
Visits to analysts											██	██			██	██	██	██

Strategizing the program

Before you start any project you should know you want to end up. As the Cheshire Cat said to Alice, when she asked which road to take (slightly paraphrased): "If you don't know where you want to go, which road you take doesn't matter."

So, before you think about databases, Web sites and road trips, think about why you're doing this. You know analysts and consultants matter. But which? What do they say or write now? If that's not what you'd like, what would you prefer? What must you convince them of for them to say or write that? What are the best vehicles for doing that?

Your management must buy into these concepts. That is because a successful program is an ongoing effort over time. Start-stop programs don't work. As you know, they're worse than nothing because they convey inconsistency. (If you have no program at all, analysts or consultants may not like it, but they know what to expect.) Long-term commitments can only come from management.

The best way to obtain management's support in most organizations is by discussions. Specifics vary from firm to firm. You know your organization. (If you're new, ask colleagues who have been there for a while, including whoever hired you.) As a by-product of getting buy-in to support the program, executives will become familiar with it and will come to understand why they must be available to analysts and consultants later. In the other direction, you'll get a feel for their personalities and accessibility.

We've allocated a month to this in the timeline. You may need more or less, depending on your corporate culture. Fortunately, other tasks don't have to wait until this is done.

Reality check

In addition to obtaining management buy-in, this is the time to obtain a "reality check," to find out what your analyst and consultant targets think of your firm now.

People can't see themselves objectively. We all like to think we're above-average in intelligence, personality, and other characteristics. We bring this attitude to our business lives: we believe our employer's products, services, etc., are all above the norm.

This attitude is reinforced daily. We work with people who share it. We talk to customers who use our products and services to solve problems and have no way to know if someone else's could solve them better. We talk to people who want to sell us something; they say nice things no matter what they really think. We talk to family and friends who don't want to hurt our feelings.

Analysts and consultants don't suffer from this. Much as we hate to admit it, they're usually pretty objective. Their bias is for their clients, against anyone who makes it hard for them to serve those clients. What they think of providers is usually close to the truth.

Besides, how close to the truth it is doesn't matter. What they think of us is their reality. Their perceptions feed their reports and their recommendations. If we don't know what those are, we can't fix them.

Therefore, it's important to do a thorough reality check before embarking on an analyst/consultant relations program. This is the time to do it. Since it involves people outside the firm, some of whom may be hard to reach, we've given it two months. It can begin while you're strategizing.

Don't do it yourself

Involving outside resources in your planning activity can help. They bring a perspective that a group of people from the same firm often lack. In addition, outside advisors have credibility with your management for many of the same reasons that they have credibility with sales prospects. You and a consultant can say the same words, but they'll believe the consultant before they believe you.

Outside resources can also be helpful in your reality check. The best way to learn what analysts think of your firm is to ask analysts. The best way to find out what consultants think of it is to ask consultants. They'll tell you. You may have to pay them for their time, but it's worth it.

You don't have to ask them yourself. You can use an outside organization to ask, as discussed earlier.

Planning program tactics

Once you have a strategy—a concept of where you want to go—you're ready to work on tactics, frameworks to guide your activities. These are the basis of your program. You read about analyst tactics in Chapters 6–9, with consultant differences in Chapter 10.

Using this book, a marketing professional should be able to lay out a first cut at the specifics of a program and its associated budget in about a week of full-time effort. Allow additional time if the person who develops the plan has other concurrent responsibilities.

Ideally, the final plan won't be an one-person effort. Accordingly, allow at least two more weeks to distribute a draft, hold a review meeting, and reflect the discussions of this meeting in a revised plan. (This review meeting will be at a lower level than the earlier meetings for buy-in and strategizing.) If your corporate culture suggests a limited informal review before the formal review meeting, that's another week or two. If you want external input into the plan (you should, if you can get it) allow two months to plan, schedule, conduct and analyze a focus group or mail survey.

All told, the planning phase should be given three or four months if there are no unusual impediments. The chart shows four, one of which overlaps the end of the reality check.

Time saved at this stage comes off the overall schedule, since nothing else can start until the plan exists. A company with a "let's try it and see what happens" culture might do it in a month but the plan would suffer from the lack of external input. Taking longer than four suggests "paralysis through analysis." As General Patton said, as true today as it was in the 1940s: a good plan today is better than a perfect plan tomorrow!

Getting approval

Corporate approval processes vary. You may have to conform to a calendar, if new initiatives are considered in the context of your firm's budget cycle. In this case the annual or quarterly budgeting process will determine your schedule. If not, you'll probably have to go to a senior manager who can commit funds. Intermediate approvals may be needed before senior management considers budget proposals. There may also be an accounting review to make sure the proposed budget conforms to corporate norms and does not omit important elements.

A month is a minimum for this process in all but the fastest-moving organizations. Two months until final approval is a good basis for planning unless you know that your management can, and wants to, move faster. The chart shows two months. The first of them overlaps the planning stage because when you're that far into the plan you'll have a pretty good idea of what you're asking for and can begin to line up support for the plan among those who will have to approve it.

Enlisting organizational support

You will not establish a self-sufficient consultant or analyst relations organization at first, if ever. You'll use the supporting elements you read about in Section 13.4.

As part of your planning process, you kept these people aware of what was going on and what you'll need from them once the program is under way. Your budget and management review made these clear all the way up the ladder. Now, it's time to get specific. Meet with managers of the supporting organizations and get commitments of people, resources, and time. Work out charge-back procedures, if any. Allow a month for everything to be signed, sealed, and delivered. You should be able to beat this schedule if the groundwork was properly laid. If you can do this in parallel with the budget review and approval process, as shown in the chart, this won't add to the overall schedule.

Staffing your program

Analyst or consultant support is a new function in your formal organization, though people have probably been doing it as part of their other responsibilities for a while. How long does it take your company to assign people to newly created positions?

- If someone (you?) was hired to run the program and is ready to start, this takes no time.
- If analyst/consultant support will be an added responsibility for a person who's already on board, and this person knows it, a day or two after the program is approved.
- If you plan to transfer or promote a person into the position, about two to four weeks until the transition is fully effective, perhaps with part-time involvement sooner.

- If you recruit a new employee, the usual time frame is about two months until a new hire is on board and up to speed, but it can take much longer.

The chart shows two months to allow for recruiting, starting when the plan is approved. You may be able to start sooner or avoid delays by using contract help or your PR group until the internal transfer or new hire arrives.

Developing your database

This is an ongoing process. It need not extend your schedule for two reasons: you don't need much of a database to get started, and you can start it in parallel with planning. The longest lead times will be for setting up the database system and getting names.

Getting a database system set up can take as little as a day if you have a computer, know how to use it, have a suitable data management package, and are (or can use) a competent user of that package. If you're starting from scratch, allow a week to purchase a computer, get it installed, and get its hardware and operating system fully operational. It may take less time if you're lucky or have good computer skills, more if you have to get a purchase order approved. Then allow a week or so for an experienced "power user" to learn a new database package well. If you're a computer novice and want to do it yourself, allow a month and expect to spend much of it in training. The chart allows a month for this stage, but assumes it can be done in parallel with budget approval.

Once your database is set up, you can enter names. Your initial efforts at identifying key people will have given you a short list. You can enter it in hours. If you have a longer list from another source, a good keyboarder can enter a few hundred names per day.

Some lists are available in electronic form, perhaps making some type of electronic data transfer possible. The specifics of this process depend on the computer and the software package you use, the medium of the list, and the data transfer options available to you. Unless you have hundreds of names to enter, or have access to someone who has set up similar transfers before, it will probably take longer to set up electronic transfers than it would take to key in and proofread the data from scratch.

To get names from your field organization you send a request, they respond with names, and you enter those names into your database. Timing factors are your relationship with the field, any field sales management leverage you can obtain (such as having your sales VP sign the memo that asks for help) and the field's opinion of analyst/consultant relations in their personal priority schemes. You'll probably need to send a follow-up memo to most offices. Allow two months for the entire process. By then you'll have 90 percent of the responses you'll ever get. More will come in as your sales force encounters new consultants, but that's part of database maintenance rather than initial construction.

You can also add to your database by sending materials to names on commercial mailing lists. Some sources were in Section 12.1. (As you read there, you can't enter names from rented lists into your database directly.) Allow a month to study available lists, in parallel with database setup and final budget approval. Subsequent to budget OK, allow another week to obtain the lists or directories themselves, unless all your sources will be online. Two weeks for the mailing, a month to get all the responses that will ever arrive, and another two weeks to finish entering them complete the time line in the chart.

Publicizing your program

You can send letters to names in your database as soon as you have a database and a program. E-mail can go out right away. If you're new to the company, you might want to have your manager look at your first few e-mails to make sure they convey the proper tone and don't violate any policies or unwritten behavior norms.

If you go with hard copy allow a week or two to write a letter, have it reproduced, print and stuff envelopes, apply postage, and mail them. Automatic equipment speeds folding, stuffing and stamping if your firm has it. If you don't, going outside for this is probably not worth the set-up time for the size of a new database. Hire a local high school student for a few afternoons. Business instructors can recommend good ones.

For long lists, such as commercial mailing lists, some type of automatic folding, stuffing, and postage application is worthwhile. If your Marketing Communications group doesn't know about these, all commercial printers do.

If your list is short, which would be the case if you plan to work with a small number of selected analysts, plan to call them too. The call can follow an introductory e-mail or letter. (You may not have their e-mail address, but you have their firm's postal address.) It should say that you plan to call and indicate a time frame. It should be self-contained enough to stand on its own without the call. You may not be able to reach an analyst on the phone. When this happens you don't want to leave the analyst wondering about anything of importance or unable to reach you through the medium of his/her choice.

If you want to appeal to a broad cross-section of small consultants, you'll also want to publicize your program via the print media. Don't count on a release appearing in a weekly paper less than three weeks from the date you send it. While news sections of these papers close much later—often on Friday before a Monday issue date—editors like to plan as much of the paper as possible one to two weeks ahead. No matter how important your program is to you, its announcement isn't top priority news.

Monthlies take longer. Anything except late-breaking news which isn't in an editor's hands by mid-May will probably miss the July issue (which appears in June). Editors with strong interest in your announcement can work closer to publication dates, but don't press them. Your PR department or agency can give you specifics, or you can call the publication and ask. It will be on the magazine's Web site much sooner, of course.

Press publicity can go out as soon as you have formal approval for your program. The chart assumes you prepared the press releases during the final month of the approval process so you could send them out immediately. They'll start appearing on Web sites right away, in print about two weeks after you send them, and will continue to appear in monthly media for another two months or so after that.

Advertising takes longer than releases because more people are involved, more different tasks are involved, the creativity issues are more complex, and ads are best planned as part of an on-going program with an overall theme and purpose. Plan on at least a few months, longer if your firm and its ad agency take a formal approach to long-range planning. You can get the specifics here from your advertising manager. (Advertising isn't shown in the timeline figure because few consultant relations programs, and virtually no analyst relations programs, advertise. You can add it if you wish.)

Finally, ask your corporate Webmaster to put a page on your firm's Web site. This page should describe the major benefits of your program and tell analysts and/or consultants how to register for it. It can also have a "Login" button for the password-protected part of your site, if there is one—but that's optional if the major purpose of the page is to publicize your new program to interested parties. You can always add a button later.

Getting the program building blocks running

The lead time here begins when you have a staff available to perform the required tasks. It varies with the program element, as follows. (Personal contact to introduce yourself and your program was covered in the previous section, so it's not in this list.)

Outbound written communications

You should figure out what these will consist of in the planning stage. Preparing each involves writing a cover message and collecting materials from other sources in your organization. Some of these may have to be edited or modified for your audience. Plan on a minimum of two weeks on an ongoing basis to prepare each package, assuming you have a normal workload of other activities but are not traveling.

If you plan a regular e-mail newsletter, two months is a minimum for the first issue if your writers are on the job, four to six months if you have to start recruiting. The chart shows two months from the time your staff is on board, continuous issues after that. (We may think of electronic communication as being instantaneous, but being able to send documents in nanoseconds can't get them written or reviewed in nanoseconds.)

If you'll produce a hard copy newsletter, add a month to the schedule of the first issue and two weeks for each issue after that. If you're unfamiliar with the production process you'll use, practice with trial material so production goes smoothly. If you can't do a test run, add another two weeks to the first issue's schedule.

Announcement kits

Analyst or consultant relations managers have little control over announcement schedules. You'll have enough advance notice of upcoming announcements to decide when to start sending out announcement material. You need less than two weeks' lead time to edit an existing press release for consultants or analysts, to have it printed on special CONSULTANT FLASH! or ANALYST UPDATE paper (it need not take more than two weeks to get this; in a pinch you can run off a few dozen pages on your color printer) and mail it to names in your database. More extensive announcement information kits take longer to prepare, and assemble. (E-mails should go out immediately, but that's part of outbound communications.) The chart assumes you can deal with announcements that take place a month after your program is staffed.

Seminars

Don't plan a seminar for less than three months after your program is running. It takes that long to line up speakers, send out invitations with a month's lead time (add a few days for printing if you send hard copy invitations; they're a nice touch) and publicize the program to its audience, and arrange facilities. You can shrink this to two months, especially if you'll use your own facilities, but seminars aren't usually urgent enough to justify a crash program. For analysts, you should wait longer to gauge potential interest.

Full-day or multiple-day briefings need more lead time because your audience has to clear their calendars for the duration of the meeting plus travel time. You should allow them at least two months' lead time for this. Therefore, the location and approximate schedule must be firm at least that far in advance. This suggests at least four months, probably more, from go-ahead to the event. The chart shows five, then some sort of seminar every three months. Most of these will be small, with one large annual event.

Telebriefings, while often announced on less notice than meetings, should not be. Their impact on participants' schedules is the same as showing up in their offices in person. Try for at least two weeks. There may be situations where you don't have two weeks, but truly unforeseeable events are rare. (If an event was truly unforeseeable, analysts will accept the lack of notice. If you knew about it but didn't plan, they won't.)

"Road shows" and other visits

Private briefings for major analyst or consultant firms, at your facilities or theirs, need less lead time. Logistics aren't an issue, since you or the firm you're visiting has the space. You can invite people on the phone (be sure to follow up in writing or via e-mail), and the date is selected for mutual convenience. The hardest part may be finding an unbroken stretch of time where all the necessary members of your organization, as well as all the firms you want to visit, are available. Fortunately, you'll usually have some flexibility in exactly who participates within each important category of people.

The chart shows two months for this. You can squeeze this if there is a reason to have a tour sooner, such as an announcement planned for soon after your program starts. It then shows a trip every two months.

Consultants' Reference Manual (if you have one)

This is a big job. One person could probably write it in a month or two of uninterrupted effort, but that's not how these are usually written. One person is unlikely to have all the necessary knowledge, to say nothing of the writing ability. (If there is such a paragon in your organization, he or she surely is already doing something else.) Reviewing will be required. Uninterrupted effort is the exception.

Allow four months for an edited, organized, and indexed collection of marketing materials with overviews of each area. This gives you time to pass out writing assignments, have the material written as a background activity, edit the results professionally, have sections reviewed for content, and have the final version professionally produced. Binders take less time and can be done in parallel. A minimal manual, with a binder, tabs, and table of contents, does not require the writing time and can be done in two months.

This isn't shown on the schedule, since a new program is unlikely to have this as one of its initial activities.

Telephone and e-mail support service

This is in business the day somebody says it is. Calls and e-mails will start arriving quickly and will increase in volume as your support becomes better known. It's good that they'll start slow, since it will take you (or whomever) longer to answer the first ones as you work your way through the organization and learn who knows about what.

If you plan to have regional support contacts, it is best not to announce any until all are in place. This need not take more than a week or two if analyst/consultant support is added to the job of existing personnel.

It shouldn't take more than a week to get the word out within your organization that this support is in business, though it may take them longer to get used to the idea. The chart shows a month here. That allows some additional time for a newly hired staff member to become familiar with your firm and its products.

16.2. Timetable for your program to have an impact

A welcoming letter, one announcement kit, one press release, and Issue 1 of something that says it will be a monthly e-mail will have zero impact on analysts and consultants.

Consistency is a must. It takes time to establish consistency.

Whatever your intentions and your management commitment are, no program is consistent when it first appears. The first issue of *The New York Times* looked just like the first issues of other papers that folded in a month. You have to establish credibility and consistency by continued performance over a period of time. It takes about seven exposures over 12–18 months, each reinforcing your basic themes, to obtain an impact.

The other time factor is building your database. As far as a given person concerned, your program starts to exist when he or she becomes aware of it. The consistency timetable and seven exposures start the day that person starts receiving materials. Nothing before then matters.

From the day your program is officially under way, then, three factors determine when it makes a difference:

1. It will take about two months until materials appear and contacts happen. It will take another three to six months before their flow reaches its planned rate. Add staff recruiting delays to this time, unless you offset them by using outside help.

2. It will take 6–12 months beyond that before multiple exposures have made your program accepted as solid and reliable. You will receive inquiries and will have some positive impact before that time.

3. Your database will build steadily over several months, then more slowly forever after. The 6–12 month impact clock starts for each new name as it is entered.

This being the case, there will be little change in analyst or consultant attitudes if you check six months after your program gets a green light. Six months after that, 12 months after you start, you should notice a positive impact. That's why we used a year starting nine to twelve months in the future when we calculated the value of a program in Chapter 14. In another six months, or eighteen months after the start, your program should be well established and contributing to your firm's sales. From that time on its value will grow steadily as its credibility grows, its database grows, its materials are improved, and the steady growth of your company permits you to provide more and more support to the analysts and consultants who help fuel that growth.

As an example of the impact time frame, IBM received very low evaluations in studies of analyst relations effectiveness in the early 1990s. They put changes in place to improve matters. From 1994 to 1996 their evaluations moved from bottom-tier to the top group and remained there for several years after. While not every firm has the resources to effect such a dramatic turnaround in 24 months, not every firm needs to. This is a realistic time frame for an analyst or consultant relations program to show an impact.